TOOLS FOR CULTURAL STUDIES
AN INTRODUCTION

TOOLS FOR CULTURAL STUDIES

AN INTRODUCTION

Tony Thwaites

University of Queensland

Lloyd Davis

University of Queensland

Warwick Mules

University of Central Queensland

First published 1994 by
MACMILLAN EDUCATION AUSTRALIA PTY LTD
107 Moray Street, South Melbourne 3205
Reprinted 1995

Associated companies and representatives
throughout the world.

National Library of Australia
cataloguing in publication data.

Thwaites, Anthony G. (Anthony Guy).
  Tools for cultural studies.

  Bibliography.
  Includes index.
  ISBN 0 7329 1935 5.

  1. Culture. 2. Semiotics. 3. Culture – Terminology.
  4. Semiotics – Terminology. L. Davis, Lloyd (Lloyd
  Benjamin). II. Mules, Warwick. III. Title.

306

Typeset in Optima and Century Old Style
by Typeset Gallery, Malaysia

Printed in Hong Kong

Designed by Anne Stanhope
Cover design by Sergio Fontana

Contents

Acknowledgements

We would like to express our particular gratitude to Bruce Parr, who did all the hard work on copyright permissions; to Peter Debus, Elizabeth Gibson and Diana Giese at Macmillan, for their encouragement and help; and, of course, to our partners, Jennie Day, Julia Duffy and Helen Miller, for the crucially phatic.

The authors and publishers also wish to thank the following for permission to reproduce copyright material:

Figure 1.3: Yves Saint Laurent; Figure 1.6: Kellogs Australia; Figure 2.4: Uncle Ben's of Australia; Figure 3.1: *BBC Good Food*, Redwood Publishing; Figures 3.3, 3.5: Printed with permission, the *Toowoomba Chronicle* and the *Courier-Mail*; Figure 3.6: from Stephen Jay Gould, *The Mismeasure of Man* (Harmondsworth: Penguin) and John S. Haller, Jr, *Outcasts from Evolution: Scientific Attitudes of Racial Inferiority, 1859–1900* (Urbana, Illinois: University of Illinois Press, 1971); Figure 3.8: Andrew Chapman; Figure 4.1: Printed with permission of Rothmans of Pall Mall (Australia) Limited; Figure 4.2: Campbell's Soups, Australia; Figure 4.3: Revlon Manufacturing Ltd; Figure 4.4: Sony; Figure 4.5: Seven Nightly News, Channel 7, Sydney; Figure 5.1: ABC TV News, Brisbane; Figures 5.2, 5.3: Mirror Australian Telegraph Publications; Figure 5.4: 1990 American Express International Inc. All rights reserved. Reprinted with permission; Figures 5.5, 5.6: ABC TV News, Brisbane; Figure 6.1: Potter Warburg Asset Management; Figure 6.2: Simona Pty Ltd; Figure 6.3: Sancella; Figure 7.1: ad for United States Rubber, the *Saturday Evening Post*, 23 April 1960; Figure 7.2: Printed with permission, the *Sunday Mail*, Brisbane; Figure 7.3: Holeproof, *Daily Mirror*/Syndication International; Figures 7.4, 7.5: *Morning Bulletin*, Rockhampton; Figure 7.6: Printed with permission, the *Sunday Mail*; Figure 8.1: Printed with permission, the *Courier-Mail*; Figure 9.2: Sheridan Cotton Man, 1985, Sheridan, 34 Wilson St, South Yarra, Victoria 3141; Figure 9.3: Austral International/Rex Features; Figures 9.6, 9.8: Poem and commentaries cited in I.A. Richards, *Practical Criticism* (London: Routledge and Kegan Paul, 1964), pp 162–64, 174–76.

Reading this book

This book can be read in several ways, depending on the detail you are after.

> **Definitions** of key terms are placed in boxes, like this. Taken together, the boxes provide a glossary of basic terms, and direct you to fuller discussion in the main text.

The main text is unboxed, and in the same typeface you are reading now. It should be read in conjunction with the boxed definitions. Major occurrences of **key concepts** in the main text are indicated by **bold** type. Important subsidiary concepts are often in *italics*.

The whole text is broken up into fairly short sections by descriptive headings and sub-headings, to enable you to locate particular topics as easily as possible. Each chapter is followed by exercises, which can be used for further investigation in the classroom, and an annotated selection of further reading.

Introduction: Tools for cultural studies

Culture

If it is obvious that cultural studies involves studying culture, what may not be nearly so obvious is just what culture is. We are going to approach it in a way common to much (though not all) of cultural studies: as a matter of meanings.

> **Culture** is the ensemble of social processes by which meanings are produced, circulated and exchanged.

Let's take the implications of this a bit at a time.

Culture is that aspect of the social which is concerned with **meanings**. There are, of course, many other aspects of the social, with many other concerns (economic, legal, governmental, educational, etc.), but in some senses culture would seem to be very basic. One can at least imagine what societies might be like without money, exploitation, government or the like—there's an entire branch of fiction, the Utopian romance, which does as much. A society which does not produce and circulate meanings, however, is strictly inconceivable.

In its concerns with the processes of meaning, culture *overlaps* into economic, legal and governmental areas. It is not at all clear where one might end and the other begin. Perhaps, then, rather than take meaning and its processes as a strictly defined area within the social world, we should see it more as an *emphasis*, a point from which to see things. Constructed in this way, cultural studies is a series of questions about what we can say about a variety of areas (governmental, legal, economic, etc.) if we approach them as processes of meaning. If, for example, economics is concerned with the production, circulation and consumption of wealth, some of the things cultural studies will be interested in might include how wealth acts as a meaningful sign, the various meanings it produces, and the ways in which those meanings are circulated and exchanged.

Culture is the site of the **production of meanings**, not the expression of meanings which exist elsewhere. Meanings come about in and through social relations, those among people, groups, classes, institutions, structures and things. And because they are produced, circulate and are exchanged within the social world, these meanings are *never entirely fixed*. Some meanings may be quite stable, of course, but others may be highly and rapidly variable. This means that although meanings always come about in a social context, we must also say that they are *never wholly determined* by the original context. Meanings migrate from one context to another, sometimes ending up very far from where they started—they are always getting displaced, diverted, reworked and exchanged. This is not something which goes wrong in the transmission of meanings. Rather, it is itself the very process of meaning. A document is intelligible even if we don't know its author or the circumstances under which it was written. A photograph makes some sense even if we've never met the people posing for it. This is not to say that meaning is ever *free from context*. All it means is that a knowledge of the author or the sitters provides a *different sort of context*.

Lastly, we should simply add that culture is not a single unified process, but an **ensemble** of processes. These may work together very tightly, but in other cases they may be in considerable conflict with one another. We shall have to keep the disparate nature of cultural processes clearly in mind as we proceed.

Tools

Here we will examine some of the ways in which meanings operate in their social usages. From that we will ask how these processes can best be described in general terms, in a **model**.

Often, especially in older textbooks, you will find meaning described in terms of the **communication** of a message between two points, something like this:

sender ———————————▶ receiver
message

There are quite a few variations on this, and quite a few reasons why we find them all unsatisfactory here. The most obvious one is that this model simply doesn't answer the question we're interested in, of how meanings come to be produced in the social world. It says nothing about the social, simply assuming meaning is already there, rolled up in the message. What's more, it assumes this meaning simply travels intact from one point to another, like a solid projectile.

Neither does it help to modify this model to take into account possible interferences with the projectile:

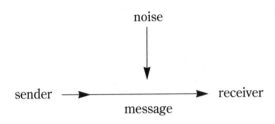

This still doesn't help us understand how meanings come about, and though it nods in the direction of the ways in which meanings alter in circulation and use, it writes all this off as a matter of purely external, accidental interference, which it calls by the catch-all term 'noise'. Even modified, this model is not going to be much use to us in trying to figure out how it is meanings can be so enormously flexible and varied, or how it is these variations may nevertheless have considerable, if complex, regularity.

In short, what we will be interested in here is all the ways in which meaning is a more complex matter than the accurate and efficient transmission of a message.

To investigate this, we will have to look more carefully at some features of cultural sign-activity. From these, we will try to put together some different models of what is happening, in an attempt to account for some of that variety. We will treat these models critically. At each stage, we will want to know not only where they can usefully be called into play, and where they seem to provide some genuine understanding of the processes they model, but also where their *limits* are. What questions do each of the models allow us to ask? Just as important, what questions do they *not* provide for? And how, as we try to ask at the end of each chapter, can we get to ask new questions?

We want to encourage a critical attitude not only to all the disparate phenomena of culture, but also to the models which provide ways of thinking about them. It's necessary to know some of the main conceptual schemas which inform the enormous volume of literature on cultural studies, and also something about how they work, and why. The critical approach we'd like to foster would be one which is also capable of opening up other approaches, raising other questions. Hence the title of this book.[1]

Note

1   We don't, of course, claim this to be the only way of approaching cultural studies. The field is too diverse for that, too full of the hubbub of its multiple, disparate, diverging voices. The way we take here is largely that of an influential **semiotic** stream which developed historically out of linguistics.

Though semiotics is far from uncontested, it is still the basis for most introductory pedagogical material. We see several possible advantages in this, which we hope to take up here. Semiotics opens up a vast amount of critical material to the beginning student; it works well in the classroom, leading quickly to hands-on investigations; and it has generated a varied and valuable body of criticism. For these reasons, our approach here will initially be semiotic, though as the book progresses, we seek to open that out to others, many of which extend beyond the semiotic as originally conceived. We are not trying to advocate a particular theoretical model, which it will then be your job as a student to apply dutifully and accurately to a number of actual situations. We use some classic semiotics to raise questions about what signs do within the social world, and, just as importantly, about how these might be thought through. Other questions include the conceptual tools that might need to be developed, and the limits of their use. What do we want this toolbox to do? What sort of tools will let us? How do we go about making them?

Sources and further reading

Raymond Williams's *Keywords: A Vocabulary of Culture and Society* (London: Fontana, 1976) has a valuable short essay on the many and varied meanings of culture, which Williams suggests (p. 87) is 'one of the two or three most complicated words in the English language'. Williams is generally regarded as one of the founders of cultural studies in its British version. For a brief history of how cultural studies developed in Britain, see Graeme Turner's *British Cultural Studies: An Introduction* (Boston: Unwin Hyman, 1990).

The sender-message-receiver model is generally known as Shannon and Weaver's model. Claude Shannon was an American engineer who in 1948 published a technical paper on the mathematics of telecommunications. This was a highly technical piece, which addressed a very practical problem in the construction of telephone systems: how much information can be sent without distortion down a line of given characteristics? In the following year, Shannon and Weaver published their book, *The Mathematical Theory of Communication*, from which this model comes. Most use of the Shannon and Weaver model in the human sciences is content to take the diagram and ignore the mathematics. You will find the technicalities of Shannon's theories explained in John R. Pierce's *An Introduction to Information Theory: Symbols, Signals and White Noise* (New York: Dover, 1980).

A measure of the sheer diversity of cultural studies is the huge volume edited by Lawrence Grossberg, Cary Nelson and Paula Treichler, and simply named *Cultural Studies* (New York: Routledge, 1992), which came out of the 1990 conference on 'Cultural Studies, Now and in the Future' at the University of Illinois at Urbana-Champaign. The conference drew papers from some of the best-known names in cultural studies in the English-speaking world, some forty-two of which (plus transcripts of discussions) are gathered into this large-format volume of almost 800 pages.

1 Some aspects of signs

An opening move: the sign

In the Introduction, we set a very broad agenda for cultural studies: its object of study is the social production of meanings. Here we had better start with the actual location of meaning:

> A **sign** is anything which produces meanings.

This is a very broad description, but it allows us to keep in mind three points emerging from the Introduction's brief discussion. They might act as guiding principles in our investigation:

1. Signs are not just comments on the world, but are themselves things *in* the world—and specifically, in the *social* world.
2. Signs do not just convey meanings, but *produce* them.
3. Signs produce many *meanings*, not just one meaning per sign.

This chapter will attempt to outline in a very broad way some aspects of the sign which we will investigate. We will use two examples (Figures 1.1 and 1.2) to ask general questions about the ways signs function. These examples are complex, compound signs—**texts** of signs, in fact—but they are also commonplace. It's that banality of meaning we want to examine here.

Content

One of the more obvious things a sign can do is *refer* to something. In different ways and to varying extents, each of the letters in Figure 1.1 and 1.2 is concerned with conveying certain information about certain topics, such the facts and events of Sam's life, from his address to his educational qualifications and professional experience. They refer to things in the world and the relations among these things: they represent, depict, propose as real, make statements, stand for. Whether these are true or false is not the point here: what

Figure 1.1

23 Avenue Road
Graceville
Queensland 4075

25 October 1994

Ms Lauren Hazard
Personnel Manager
Great Big Bank
3142A Queen Street
Brisbane Queensland 4000

Dear Ms Hazard

I wish to apply for the position of Branch Manager Trainee which was advertised in the *Courier Mail* on 4 October.

This year I shall be completing my studies at the University of Queensland, where I've been majoring in economics and English (communications and cultural studies). Because I've been interested in a career in banking, I decided to research the functions of the various banks in my home town of Mackay as a component of my economics major. I wanted to know what services were most used by the customers of these banks and how the banks were working with small businesses to help them expand or improve their facilities. Mackay, like so many smaller Queensland towns during the tourist boom of the early 1980s, has had to revitalise its downtown business area in order to compete with the new malls outside town. Such renewal has been possible because of the co-operation of the banks, the town planning committee, and the business-people. Writing this thesis has shown me how important a part of a community a bank can be when it takes an active interest in the growth of that community.

I've had practical experience in financial affairs as Business Manager of the Student Union newspaper, *Semper*, and in my vacation part-time work as a book-keeper. In fact, doing the books for a small hardware store which wanted to expand gave me a good picture of small business problems. It was this experience that started my thesis research.

I'd especially enjoy working for Great Big Bank because of the innovations in banking you've introduced and because I am looking for a challenging position in a bank that gives the same attention to the small businessperson as to a large corporation.

I have enclosed my résumé, and if my credentials interest you I am available for an interview at your convenience.

Yours faithfully

Samuel West

Samuel West

Figure 1.2

23 Avenue Road
Graceville
Queensland 4075

25 October 1994

Dearest Vivian

Great to arrive home after a hard day in the library and find a breath of Canada waiting for me. *You* might be getting out more and more warm clothes and seeing the trees starting to get that threadbare look, but it goes the other way round here. Summer's started early here, and with a vengeance: it even hit 33 a couple of days ago. And in October! The air conditioning in the library broke down the other day, leaving me sweltering over a stack of company reports. I would have taken them out and sat down under a tree with them all if they'd have let me get them out the door, but no such luck. The jacarandas will be out soon too, and we all know what that means for anybody who goes through the Queensland education system. Sometimes I think the thing I envy you most at the moment is the cool weather. (*And* that you might even get some skiing in before you come back!)

So how does it feel now that you've not only finished and submitted all the work, but have also had a couple of weeks totally free? Enjoy it—you've certainly deserved it! And *don't*, whatever you do, worry about whether it'll get through or not. The bit of the thesis you sent back to me looked terrific. I don't know what Canadian examiners are looking for, but

I'm sure they recognise quality when they see it. Relax and enjoy all the things you've been too busy to enjoy until now. Well, not *too* much: spare the occasional thought for me slogging on here at home. I'm almost finished here, too: two more intensive days in the library should do it, and then there are only the exams to worry about, but they'll be fine.

Just wanted to get a quick letter off to you to say I'd got yours, and how great it was—as always—to hear from you. Once I've got this library work out of the way in a couple of days, I'll sit down and write you a *proper* letter, a long one, get you up to date ('up to date', it's only a *week* since the last one! Do you think I must be in love?) Excuse the rather formal look of the word processing: I've just been doing a job application at the Prentice Centre, and thought I might as well keep going with a quick note to you. More about that later. Watch the mails.

Anyway, take care of yourself, and roll on December! Can't wait.

As always, all my love

Sam

we will call the sign's **referential function** is simply the way in which it proposes something to be the case.

> A sign's **referential** function is its ability to invoke a *content*.

It may be tempting to see the referential function as the principal feature of a sign. It is certainly a very important factor, and one which may be highly valued. The physical sciences are an obvious case in point. Nevertheless, as we shall shortly see, it is hardly the only function, even in the sciences. These texts do various things that cannot be reduced to conveying information: they attempt to persuade, for example, and seek to establish or maintain relationships.

Codes

As you read the two texts, you no doubt very quickly became aware of what *sort* of text they were. They are both letters rather than, say, film reviews, advertisements, transcripts of interviews, limericks or mathematical arguments. In fact, you almost certainly realised that *before* you started reading them, from cues in their layout. You doubtless also realised that they were different kinds of letter. One of them is a job application, and the other a personal communication.

Signs suggest ways in which they may be read: they cue in certain **codes** for interpreting them. The *type* of text it is (its **genre**, as we'll later call it) is a very powerful example of this process. Knowing what sort of text it is sets up a complex set of expectations about what it will say, and how. These need not be adhered to, nor do they have to be consistent: a text may thwart as much as satisfy the expectations it sets up, and this allows for quite complex plays of meanings.

Figure 1.2 is a case in point. Though at first glance it may appear to be one type of letter (business), it turns out to be another sort altogether (personal). The difference between that first impression and its purpose is great enough for this letter to include a passage explaining the discrepancy:

> Once I've got this library work out of the way in a couple of days, I'll sit down and write you a *proper* letter, a long one, get you up to date ... Excuse the rather formal look of the word processing: I've just been doing a job application at the Prentice Centre, and thought I might as well keep going with a quick note to you.

This is an unusually overt example, where the passage is actually suggesting how the text could, or should, be read.

That signs in general include some sort of **metalingual function** like this indicates that a sign's meaning is far from a given fact. Instead, it is something to be actively worked out, or *negotiated*, and is always subject to renegotiation.

A sign's **metalingual** function suggests the *codes* by which the sign might be understood.

The idea of code is quite a crucial one in any study of signs, and we will be elaborating on it throughout the book, particularly in Chapters 2 and 3. In Chapter 5, we will turn to a more detailed examination of genre and the roles it plays.

Format

Before you even started reading Figure 1.1, various aspects of its formal layout probably suggested to you that here was a letter of some sort—features such as the indented address and date, and the opening and closing salutations. Other features—the font, the blocked paragraphs, even the use of the space of the sheet of paper—suggest a business letter in particular. But these are purely *formal* aspects of the document. They depend not on what is said, but on how it's said: how the sign deploys its formal features, including the space and medium in which it exists.

> A sign's **formal** functions involve its *formal structure* and the *format* which it takes.

This example shows how various functions may be linked. The formal function (the layout) also works metalingually, suggesting the type of document. One sort of meaning gets cued in by the formal function, then immediately this gets taken up by the metalingual function.

Address

Another very important set of functions involved in all sign activity is that of their **address**. Signs address.

Consider some of the problems involved in address. Signs may go astray, and be received by other than those for whom they were intended. The letters in our examples are *addressed to* 'Ms Lauren Hazard' and 'Vivian', but their *actual receivers* include the readers of this book, whom they do not address. Nor do signs necessarily come from where they say. Letters may lie, or can be forged. In cases like this, the place they are *addressed from* may differ considerably from their *actual sender*. (These letters are addressed from 'Samuel West', but it's quite possible they were written by the authors of this book.)

For these reasons, we should start off by making an important distinction: between the actual sender and receiver of a communication, on the one hand, and the ways these are represented in the text, on the other.

> The **addresser** of a text is the position it constructs as its source: where it *says* it is from.
>
> The **sender** is its *actual* source.

> The **addressee** of a text is the position it constructs as its destination: where it *says* it is going.
>
> The **receiver** is its *actual* destination.

Sender and receiver are actual people. Addresser and addressee, on the other hand, are purely constructions of signs. They are like fictional characters, in that they have no existence other than in signs, and they may bear very little resemblance to the actual sender and receiver. Nothing either of the letters can do will guarantee they are telling the truth: that Sam really does have some experience in banking, or that he is fondly counting the days until Vivian arrives home. Each of them *constructs* a Sam, and a different Sam in each case: a diligent student and prospective employee on the one hand, and a fond lover on the other. It is these constructed figures of addresser and addressee we react to, and which make the text intelligible even if we do not have access to the real sender and receiver. (Indeed, in this case how could we? For all we know, Sam, Lauren Hazard and Vivian may be entirely fictitious characters.)

The relationships between these two sets of terms, sender and receiver on the one hand, and addresser and addressee on the other, may be quite complex. Different senders may share the same addresser. For instance, the agony column of a magazine may always appear under the same proper name, but the actual writers may vary from week to week. Likewise, different receivers may share the same addressee: think of the thousands of actual readers addressed by a newspaper headline, or the thousands of viewers who hear a television newsreader's 'Good evening'.

On the other hand, the one sender may produce a number of different addressers: we construct ourselves differently in our words, depending on whether we are applying for a job or writing to an absent loved one. And correspondingly, one receiver may be addressed as a number of different addressees: any one person plays a number of different roles (friend, colleague, parent, spouse, daughter/son), each of which brings a different mode of address.

To speak of sender and receiver in all of these cases, then, we would have to know (or guess at) the psychologies of actual people, and this may not be knowledge available to us. When we speak of addresser and addressee, though, we are talking about what happens in texts made up of signs, and how they construct roles or positions to occupy within the text, for both sender and receiver. Sender and receiver are actual people; addresser and addressee exist only in texts. The two sets of terms are logically quite distinct from each other, and belong to two different orders of being.

Though these may seem fine distinctions, they are crucial. They suggest that we may be able to talk about what happens in texts in specifically *textual* ways, without having recourse to hypotheses about what their sender may have intended them to mean, or without having to guess about what their effects on a single given receiver might be. In short, the separation of addresser from sender, and addressee from receiver is what lets us do semiotics rather than psychology.

A sign's **expressive** function is its construction of an *addresser*.

A sign's **conative** function is its construction of an *addressee*.

There is another very important factor to consider here. As well as constructing the positions of addresser and addressee, any sign must also establish a **relationship** between the two.

The classic case of a sign which functions mainly like this is the word 'hello'. It serves to establish the possibility of communication. Depending on the tone of voice with which it's said, it may work to open up or close off an interchange. There are more complex examples in the two letters we've been using. Their salutations each set up a certain relationship: 'Dearest Vivian' is much more informal than 'Dear Ms Hazard' (the metalingual functions indicate that that 'Dear' is not the expression of affection it might be elsewhere, but a purely ritual greeting). Throughout the job application, the syntax and diction function to maintain this respectful, businesslike relationship between addresser (this possibly fictitious 'Sam', the eager, would-be employee) and addressee (the unknown 'Ms Hazard').

A sign's **phatic** functions are the ways in which it constructs a *relationship* between addresser and addressee.

In its expressive and conative functions, the sign delineates a group including both addresser and addressee: the phatic effect of this is to mark out a sort of *community of communication* within which the exchange of signs is taking place. The phatic is what binds addresser and addressee together in the act of the exchange of signs. Conversely, though, in marking out a group like this, the phatic also excludes those who are not part of it. The phatic function works in terms of both inclusion and exclusion. It constructs social insiders and outsiders.

Some sort of phatic functioning is unavoidable in any sign activity. If an exchange of signs implies a common code within which the exchange can take place, then that exchange will on the broadest scale phatically include those with access to the code and exclude those without it. Whatever other phatic functions it might have, a letter in English will exclude non-English users. A particular way of speaking will bind a group together.

Phatic groups are generally somewhat more specific than this, however. One of the important phatic effects of the job application letter, for example, is to place Sam within that loose group of business-minded people, to suggest that he is already in spirit, if not in fact, part of the business community, aware of and working according to its values. The phatic community which the letter to Vivian sets up is much narrower: its references to the particular relationship between them, and experiences they share, tend to narrow that community down to two people.

> The conative, expressive and phatic functions are the sign's **functions of address**.

As Figure 1.3 shows, signs which are visual and representational may often display considerable complexity in their functions of address, particularly through the **gaze**. We shall be dealing with further aspects of the functions of address in Chapters 8 and 9 in particular.

Context

It only remains to say that all these functions depend on the social context of the sign. The social situations in which a sign is used may determine the appropriate content, type of sign and coding, who is being addressed, by whom and how, and the phatic community it constructs.

Figure 1.3 The gaze, the gift

To say that this advertisement is sent *by* a perfume company *to* women who are potential customers of its product would be to say little of the actual complexities of its address. The bodies of the man and the woman form a plane which contains most of the focal points of the photograph. It is marked out in particular by the man's face (exactly side-on, he is looking along this very plane), the woman's shoulders (emphasised by the pads of her suit) and her left arm, with its hand on her hip). The woman's body thus meets your gaze as viewer: she addresses you in her *bodily stance*.

Of the two characters, the man's attention is given wholly to the woman, but as her eyes, smile and pose show, her attention is directed away from him, at a right angle, towards the camera and thus seemingly directly out of the plane of the picture, towards the position of the viewer. The effect is that her eyes appear to meet your own; the picture looks back at you looking at it. He addresses her, but her *gaze* addresses you, and your act of looking at her. Her smile shows that in the phatic bond set up by the returned gaze, where each of you is simultaneously in the position of addresser and addressee, you are in complicity, sharing knowledge.

Somewhat in front of this plane the two bodies mark out, the woman's right hand is holding a bottle of perfume, whose Yves Saint Laurent label is clearly displayed facing the viewer. The *bottle* addresses you; the woman holding the bottle addresses you with her gesture. Her hand holds the perfume out from the plane of the two lovers, between them and you. It is a gift, for you. Her gaze emphasises the motion: while her eyes are looking directly at you, if she were looking in the direction her head is tilted, she would be looking directly at the bottle of perfume. Her eyes, making the offer, have gone from perfume to you. What she is giving you is what the perfume has given her: the affections and undivided attention of the man next to her, who is unaware of this complicity between the two of you, but whom you cannot help but see in the background plane every time your eye moves to the perfume.

(And who is this woman who addresses you, offering you not only a perfume but grand passion? Her *scarf* says it all, addressing you with its YSL logo: she becomes the manufacturer, the product itself, offering itself to you in a conspiracy of pleasure.)

A sign's **contextual** functions indicate the *situation* in which it operates.

One of the key questions to be asked of all the various conceptual models we develop in this book will be the extent to which they are capable of taking into account the complexities of contextuality.

The seven functions

Figure 1.4 shows how we can now summarise these various functions. There are several points we should note about them.

First, all these functions are necessary for any sign activity to take place. That is, a sign must:

- work within a system of references and codings;
- be able to be described in terms of formal attributes which allow one to distinguish it from other signs;
- set up relationships of address; and
- operate within, and vary according to, specific concrete situations.

Second, though all of them are necessary for there to be a sign, in any given sign certain of these functions may be predominant. The language of a scientific paper demands a high emphasis on the referential, but day-to-day work with colleagues in a laboratory will certainly require an emphasis on the phatic.

Third, these functions are never independent of each other, but are constantly interrelating within the sign. Some of the possibilities are:

- *Certain functions may work together very closely.*
  Expressively, the addresser of the second letter is constructed as fond, thoughtful, solicitous, reassuring, and looking forward to the addressee's return. Conatively, the addressee is constructed as an object of affection, hardworking, intelligent, deserving. Phatically, the letter constructs the relationship between addresser and addressee as one of close affection, even love. In this case, those three functions work together in a strongly cohesive way.
- *Certain functions may overlap to a degree.*
  In the job application, the referential and the expressive functions largely coincide: an application has to convey a certain amount of information, and that information has to be about the addresser. They do not entirely coincide, however. As well as conveying factual information about the addresser, the expressive function is also concerned with constructing the addresser as having a certain attitude—eagerness, earnestness, intelligence, politeness, etc.
- *Some functions may even work against others.*
  The second letter uses the same typeface and almost the same formal structure as the first, even though it is a personal rather than a business letter. Its formal aspects

Figure 1.4 The functions of the sign

FUNCTIONS OF
SIGNIFICANCE

referential
(content)

metalingual
(code)

formal
(form)

expressive (addresser)	**phatic** (contact)	**conative** (addressee)

FUNCTIONS OF ADDRESS

contextual
(situation)

This is an adaptation of a well-known model by the linguist Roman Jakobson. His original model, which is frequently cited in other textbooks, has six functions rather than our seven. Following Hymes's revision, we have separated out content and context. Our *formal* function is a reworking of Jakobson's *poetic* function: we have generalised its meaning somewhat, and renamed it to mark the difference (and also to avoid the implication that this function is synonymous with ideas such as a conative aesthetic pleasure, or the metalingual coding of a text as poetry). For similar reasons, our *expressive* function reworks what Jakobson calls the *emotive* function, which may misleadingly imply emotionality. (Think of a scientific paper: the addresser its expressive or emotive function constructs must be dispassionate and *un*emotional.)

thus tend to cue in the same metalingual codes as the job application—codes which in this case are not particularly appropriate. The letter recognises this, though, and even tries to defuse the possibility of an aberrant reading by drawing attention to, referentially and metalingually, the formal function and openly contradicting its effects. ('Sorry about the word processing' etc.)

- *One function may trigger off another.*
  The font and layout of the application letter are part of its formal function. This, however, immediately triggers off certain metalingual functions, which suggest what sort of letter this is and thus what sorts of codes might be appropriate to bring to bear on it.

Exercises

Examine the ways in which the following examples work, in terms of the seven functions we have developed in this chapter. How do the metalingual and formal functions work in with the referential function? What sorts of address are these examples making? What contextual determinants and effects are there?

Figure 1.5

Desk, teak laminate 1350 × 600, 4-drawer, steel frame plus chair, adj. height, swivel on castors, GC, $90 Macarthur 409 7658

Desk with 1 drawer, cupboard on side with shelves, has a few scratches on outside of hutch, VGC, $130 Lancaster 397 4014

Figure 1.6

Figure 1.7

For that Bright Future

OF WHICH THEY DREAM

At first, when the boy she was engaged to went into uniform, she merely wished for Victory. Now she *works* for it, works hard, to hasten the day when that bright dream of the future . . . his and hers . . . will all come true. Part of that dream, she's well aware, is his conception of her as the graciously lovely girl who will forever reign in his heart. For him, she resolves always to look her loveliest, so always Pond's two Creams are in her kit . . . . Pond's Cold Cream for soft-smooth cleansing, Pond's Vanishing Cream as a magnolia-petal base for her powder.

Pond's two Creams are sold at all chemists and stores in small and large jars, also in tubes for the handbag. Economy hint . . . buy the large jar, containing approximately 3½ times as much as the small jar.

POND'S

Distinguished American Beauties

Mrs. FRANKLIN D. ROOSEVELT Jr.

Mrs. ANTHONY J. DREXELL III.

Mrs. Franklin D. Roosevelt, Jr., distinguished member of America's First Family, has for years followed the Pond's ritual of skin care. "Since my boarding school days, I have used Pond's at least twice daily", she says. Her skin is damask-fine, soft, smooth.

Mrs. Anthony J. Drexell, III, a name which in America represents generations of culture, wealth, and distinction, is another devotee of the Pond's beauty ritual. Of her a famous Hollywood photographer said: "One of the most perfect natural beauties I have ever seen".

Figure 1.8

8.30 Billy (PGR) Comedy with Billy Connolly and Marie Marshall.
9.00 Married With Children (AO) Desperate for a date, Bud forms a fraternity in his own garage.
9.30 Raven (AO) Ski is hired by the curator of a museum to test its security system. Jeffrey Meek.
10.30 Nightline News program.
11.00 Star Trek, The Next Generation (PGR). Science fiction series.
12.00 Entertainment Report (AO)

Figure 1.9

Figure 1.10

Procedure:
1 Normal playback
   Press the PLAY button (1).
   • The PLAY indicator ▶ should appear in the display.
   • Eliminate noise bars by using the TRACKING control (2).
   • Adjust the picture with the SHARPNESS control (3), if
     needed.
2 Still playback
   To view a still picture, press the PAUSE button (4) when the
   VCR is in the normal playback mode.
   • The PAUSE indicator ▶ and ❙❙ should appear in the display.
   • If the VCR is left in the Pause mode for more than 5 min-
     utes, the unit resumes playback automatically to protect
     the tape and video heads.

Figure 1.11

Sources and further reading
The classic statement of Jakobson's model is in the first few pages of his
paper 'Linguistics and Poetics'. Here Jakobson's main purpose—which is
not ours—is to account for what he argues are the properties peculiar to
poetic language. Our model is a free modification of this, which draws also
on Dell Hymes's use of it in *Foundations in Sociolinguistics* (Philadelphia:
University of Pennsylvania Press).

2 Signs and systems

Building a model

In the last chapter, we suggested that signs do many more things than
merely refer. We briefly examined a few common situations in which
signs are used, and saw that in some of these the referential function is
not even necessarily an important part of what the sign does.

In this chapter, we will try to systematise some of these ideas
about language processes. We will develop a detailed **model** of sign
processes. As with all model making, this will inevitably involve
simplifying things somewhat, so there are bound to be aspects left
out. We will try to pay attention to where these simplifications occur,
but for the moment it should be stressed that this process may actually
be one of the strengths of model making. If for the moment we
concentrate on only two or three carefully chosen aspects of signs,
we may be able to provide a framework in which we can raise
interesting questions about how signs work.

The particular model we're going to construct is **semiotics**,
as it was developed in the work of the Swiss linguist Ferdinand de
Saussure, in his posthumous *Course in General Linguistics* of 1916.
Saussure's ideas have been taken up in many fields of the human
sciences under the general term of **structuralism.** Though we are
going to end up a considerable distance from structuralism and
semiotics, they will nevertheless be a very convenient point of
departure for us. While there is a tendency for Saussurean semiotics
to be formal and abstract in its approach, throughout this book we
will be progressively more concerned with the *social* contexts in
which signs are used.

It is important to emphasise that semiotics is, precisely, a model.
As we will use it here, it lays no claim at all to be able to explain
every aspect of sign practices. We simply claim it as a useful way of
picturing some of the things which happen in them. It is a starting
point, not the final truth about the sign; a set of tools which are
very useful for some jobs, but not necessarily for others. Part of
the skill, of course, always lies in picking the right tools for the job.

Semiotics provides an excellent framework for asking some questions about signs, but is less useful for asking others. We will consider these limits later on.

For our purposes, there are a couple of advantages in looking at semiotics in some detail here. First of all, it is a framework which is very frequently invoked in cultural studies, even when it is debated. You'll find the concepts we'll be developing mentioned almost everywhere in the literature. Second, semiotics is a very good example of just how much can be got out of a relatively simple model. It starts off from two or three assumptions about signs, but builds this into a model which has very wide descriptive power.

The initial abstraction: setting aside the referent

Our discussion in Chapter 1 has suggested that, even if it does seem the most intuitively obvious aspect of language, referentiality may not be a good place to start. Even the most common uses of language are altogether too complex to be summed up in terms of the simple relationship between a word and the thing it names.

As a first step towards constructing a theory of signs, then, we will take the apparently drastic step of leaving the function of naming to one side. That is, we are not initially going to assume we know anything about how the sound 'cat' comes to refer to a particular sort of animal.

This may seem odd, but remember this is purely a *tactical* manoeuvre, giving us a place to start. It is not intended to deny the obvious fact that the word 'cat' is in some way attached to a particular sort of animal, or that we mostly don't have any difficulty in using it that way. For most practical purposes, there is generally a reasonably clear link between word and thing (though perhaps not always as clear as we'd like). For the moment, though, we are not simply going to assume we know anything about what this link might be. While referentiality is certainly one of the *functions* a sign may have, one of its effects, it may not provide any explanation of how signs work. On the contrary, reference is one of the things we must explain about signs. If we start somewhere else, we may in the end be able to come back to the whole question of how words are connected to the world, but this time with some fresh ideas to work with. That is, instead of concentrating on the relationship:

$$sign \longleftrightarrow referent$$

we are going to concentrate on the *structure of the sign* itself.

Signifier and signified

What happens when something is perceived as a sign?

Take the sequence of sounds we write as 'cat'. Think about what happens when you recognise this sequence as a sign, not just a meaningless noise.

Two things happen simultaneously in your mind:

1 You have a **mental impression** of the sound 'cat'.
2 This sequence of sounds also invokes in you a certain general and abstract **concept**—in this case, the concept of 'catness'.

This may seem a simple, even obvious point to make, but, because it will be the basis of the entire system of semiotics we are going to build, we will take some time to discuss it before going on.

These two aspects of the sign have standard names. The mental impression of the sound is called the **signifier**, and the general concept invoked is the **signified**. In other words, one aspect of the sign does the signifying, the other aspect is what is signified. The relationship between the two is called **signification**.

We can generalise this distinction to other types of sign, such as the written or graphic signs in Figures 2.1 to 2.4.

> The **signifier** is the *sensory impression* of the sign: the mental image of marks on a page, or of sounds in the air, for example.
>
> The **signified** is the *abstract concept* the sign invokes.
>
> The *relationship* between signifier and signified, the way in which a sound impression 'points to' or invokes an abstract concept is called **signification**.

The two facets of the sign are often pictured like this:

$$\text{sign} = \frac{\text{signified}}{\text{signifier}} \quad \updownarrow \text{ signification}$$

There are several points to note here.

Signifier and signified are inseparable and simultaneous.

As shown in the diagram, signifier and signified look like two separable parts of the sign, as though you could somehow make a cut between them and peel one away from the other. In reality, they are simply terms which are useful for emphasising the two different ways in which a sign must behave in order to be a sign. Signifier and signified always go together. Compare them to the two sides of an infinitely thin sheet of paper. You can cut through the paper any way you like, but in doing so you will not in any way separate front from back.

Signifier and signified are abstract mental entities.

The sign itself is a mental construct, something which happens in our heads. What distinguishes a mere combination of sounds or graphic marks from a sign is a mental, cognitive activity. As a result, the two components of the sign, the signifier and the signified, must also be mental entities. This abstraction will allow us to formulate a very powerful and general concept of the sign.

First, consider the signifier. Every time I hear the combination of sounds we write as 'cat', I am actually hearing a quite unique combination. The word 'cat' as spoken by a man sounds different from the word spoken by a woman. Children sound different from adults. Geographical and class groups often tend to have their own distinctive accents. The same person will pronounce words differently according to where they come in a sentence, or the different functions they serve, or the comparative emphasis each is given. Say 'Cat? *What* cat?' and listen to the subtle differences between the two. Strictly speaking, each utterance is quite unique and unrepeatable. Even if you could make *exactly* the same sounds twice, the situation you'd be making them in would have changed.

Nevertheless, assuming a certain familiarity with accents and individual speech patterns, we tend to recognise the word 'cat' regardless of whether it's spoken by a Scots vet in a lecture, an angry Tasmanian breeder of rare mice, or a New York newsreader with a bad head cold. In order to do this, we ourselves, as listeners, make an abstraction from what we hear. In effect, we decide that certain features of the sounds we're actually hearing (pitch, individual variations, etc.) are really incidental and can be ignored. *What we are left with* after all these apparent incidentals have been stripped away is the signifier: the pure, abstract mental sound-impression 'cat'.

Something similar is true of the signified, too. The sign 'cat' doesn't signify because it invokes the image of this or that particular cat or type of cat: that would be the *referent*, which we've agreed to put out of play for the moment. The sign 'cat' signifies because it invokes a general and quite abstract concept of 'catness'.

In summary, the signifier is not the actual sounds heard, nor the actual graphic marks seen, but the *mental impression* of them.

Figure 2.1 The spoken word 'cat'

/kat/

Figure 2.2 A sentence written in chalk on a blackboard

The cat sat on the mat.

Figure 2.3 An amateur photo of a family pet

Figure 2.4 A magazine advertisement for cat food

READ *this* and you'll clearly see why
Whiskas® is good for your cat's eyes.

UNLIKE YOU, your cat can't eat carrots to help keep his eyes healthy. The fact is cats are
carnivores (meat eaters) by nature. So they can't absorb nutrients like Vitamin A found
in foods like carrots.

To keep his vision clear, your cat needs Whiskas every day. Being a complete and
balanced meal, Whiskas has all the nutrients your cat needs daily like Taurine and
Vitamin A (the nutrients for good vision). So every time he has his Whiskas, he's
keeping his eyes healthy. And because Whiskas has the taste your cat loves, you can
be sure he'll enjoy his meal every day.   *Whiskas knows cats best.*

® WHISKAS is a registered trade mark   © Uncle Ben's of Australia 1992   PATTS—W1831

Neither is the signified the actual thing referred to, but the *abstract concept* of the thing. The sign is not the actual mark or the sound, but a *conceptual entity*, the union of two conceptual others.

The signified is not the referent.

It's important not to confuse these two: they're quite different things, so different that they belong to two quite different orders of being.

The **referent** is something *other than* the sign, which the sign points to or stands for. It is an object in the world.

The **signified**, on the other hand, is an *aspect* of the sign, a pure abstraction, a concept.

It's precisely because there is a difference between the two that I can understand perfectly well what you are *signifying* by the word 'cat', even though I have never met the particular cat to which you might be *referring*.

The link between signifier and signified is arbitrary.

The signifier has no natural link with the signified. That is, there is no inherent and necessary reason that the sound-image or graphic-image 'cat' should automatically invoke the general concept of 'catness', or vice versa. The signified 'catness' can have other signifiers: the Latin word *felis*, for example, or a pictorial representation. The signifier 'cat', too, may have other signifieds than 'domestic feline'. It is also the name of a type of whip, a coal scow and a bit of nautical tackle. One signified may have many signifiers; one signifier may have many signifieds. Even though there can be no signifier without a signified (and vice versa), the two nevertheless slide around over each other with a fair bit of freedom. In other words, by their very nature, signs do not have a *single* meaning, but many.

This is not an absolute freedom: we could hardly argue that a sign can mean anything a user might want it to. Certain signifiers obviously do tend to get used in connection with certain sets of signifieds and not others (and vice versa), and this is not a matter for the individual user's choice. It is a decision that, as it were, has already been made for us by the language we speak and the conventions of representation we use. (The next chapters will return to this point, to examine ways in which meanings get stabilised or contested.) That the connection between signifier and signified is arbitrary is purely a matter of historical accident: there is nothing in the language system itself which would prohibit the possibility that, if history had been a little bit different, we would now associate different signifiers with the concept of 'catness', or different signifieds with the sound-image 'cat'.

Difference and value

We began by suggesting that a particular sign doesn't take on its meaning through the apparently direct link of reference, the relation between sign and object. Then we went on to suggest that even the more abstract link of signification (the relation between signifier and signified within the sign) is arbitrary. Because of this, the meaning of a sign cannot be due to some sort of essence of what the sign is in itself. There is no longer any such essence, since the sign is a sort of historical accident. How then *does* any sign take on meaning?

We already have the answer: from outside itself. We suggested in the first chapter that the meaning of a sign may depend on a variety of factors, including the situations and conventions in which it is used. The sign's meaning, that is, depends on what surrounds it: it is not a content hidden away somewhere 'inside' the sign.

Saussurean semiotics develops this idea in a narrower sense. Out of all the things outside the sign which may contribute to its meaning (everything we've called 'context', which potentially includes the entire situation and social world in which the sign is being used), Saussure only considers other signs within the system. That is, in the Saussurean system, a sign gets its meaning from *other signs*. The meaning it may get from things that aren't signs is not something with which Saussurean semiotics is concerned. Keep in mind that this is quite a restricted sense of meaning. We shall follow it for the moment, because even though it is restricted, the model we can build with it is still immensely suggestive.

If a sign gets its meaning from other signs, it works through a system of **differences** (from what it isn't), rather than of identity (with itself). It means something not because it has some fixed identity, but because it is different from other signs. We could put that in a succinct but paradoxical form by saying that what a sign *is* is due to what it isn't.

Let's make this more specific, by considering the case of our sign 'cat'. Again, we will consider both the signifier and the signified, in turn.

We determined above that the actual sound-sequence 'cat' can vary considerably, and yet still be recognised as a variation on the abstract, general sound-image which is the signifier. For this to occur, we need a system of sounds which can be distinguished from one another. If 'cat' and 'pat' are going to be different signifiers, we need to be able to distinguish between the sounds of 'c' and 'p'. What makes the sound-image 'cat' a possible signifier is not the qualities of the actual sounds themselves, but simply that we can distinguish them from other sounds. We can tell the difference between 'cat' and 'pat', 'mat', 'bat', and so on, or 'cat' and 'can', 'cap', 'cad', or 'cat' and 'cot', 'coat' or 'cut'.

Similarly, our general concept of 'catness' is defined in a network of differences. We can have a concept of 'catness' because we can distinguish this from other related concepts, like 'dogness', 'rabbitness', 'canaryness', 'fishness'. The sign 'big' takes on meaning only when it is part of a system which lets it be juxtaposed with 'little'. A big flea is of a different order of magnitude altogether from a big elephant or a big (or even a very small) supernova.

You will recall that signification is a *vertical* relationship between signifier and signified. What we are suggesting now as the source of the sign's meaning is a set of *horizontal* relationships between signifier and signifier, and between signified and signified. These horizontal relationships determine a sign's **value**. A sign's signification is a function of its value. The relationship between signifier and signified for any particular sign depends ultimately on the relationships all the signs in the system have with one another:

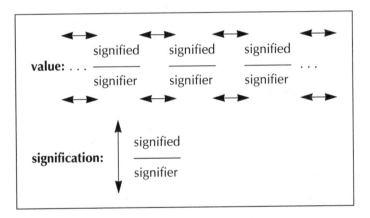

It may be useful to make a loose analogy with money here. A $10 note, say, buys a certain amount of one commodity, and a different amount of another. This is not because there is a direct and necessary relationship between an amount of money and an amount of a commodity: no law or principle says that $10 is inherently worth 9.2 litres of milk. The relationship between the two is due to all sorts of other costs: those of buying, keeping and feeding cattle, of hiring labour, maintaining machinery, and processing and distributing the product. These in their turn depend on many factors: the cost of hiring labour, for instance, is determined by factors such as the cost of living—to which of course, the cost of milk makes its own contribution. The cost of milk is rather like the vertical relationship of signification. The link between the signified commodity and the money which signifies it actually comes from the horizontal relationship it has with all the other costs in the economy.

Indeed, the very term *value* which we have been using to describe signs comes, of course, from economics. Semiotics is basically an economic model of sign processes: it sees exchange as their essential feature.

System and acts

In discussing the signifier and signified, we have emphasised that neither of these corresponds simply to the actual sound or mark, or to the thing itself: both are abstractions. We are now going to make another, potentially very useful abstraction.

We have just decided that the sign's meaning doesn't arise within it, but from the entire system of relationships within which it exists, giving it value. The object of the semiotics we are building up here will have to be not the individual sign, but the entire system which gives any individual sign its meaning. Semiotics will be concerned not with individual or specific acts of sign use, but with the systems within which they operate, and on which any particular case of sign use must be based. We will not be interested in everything which can be said in English, for example, but in the structures of English which allow us to say these things.

This allows us to make a valuable distinction. In studying sign use, the problem is the sheer volume of material. The number of possible things that can be said in English is for all practical purposes infinite. Even to list the available words with a brief description of each takes some twenty large volumes of the unabridged *Oxford English Dictionary*. The number of meaningful statements into which these can be combined is enormous. Clearly, for purely practical reasons we can hardly take this almost unimaginably vast mass of statements as our object.

But this mass is not entirely chaotic. It has regularities. What if these statements are all produced according to a relatively small number of effective *rules*? If statements follow rules, then a knowledge of how the rules work should actually let us produce any possible statement: in effect, it will tell us everything we need to know about statements, and do it a lot more economically. While listing all possible English statements might be an infinite task, a list of the rules of English grammar fits pretty comfortably into a modestly sized book. Let us assume, then, for the sake of the model we are constructing, that *all actual sign usages follow conventional rules*.

This may be something of a simplification of the situation. Although it has certain advantages for our model, it may often be more useful to think of these regularities in other terms than rules that must be followed. Real sign practices may be more complicated matters. We shall take this up again in Chapter 9, but for the moment the hypothesis that signs follow rules will let us take a valuable step forward.

If sign usages are rule-bound, we can separate the domain of signs into two conceptually distinct areas. We will give Saussure's original French terms for them, since there isn't a single pair of English words which makes quite the same distinction, and you'll find that most English texts on semiotics just adopt the French. They are:

---

parole (or **utterance**, or **speech**):
a given act or artifact of language, such as a spoken utterance, a conversation, a postcard, a novel, or a course handout; and

---

langue (or **code**, or **system**, or **the language**):
the system which enables such acts of *parole* to be produced.

Saussure also uses the term *langage* to refer indiscriminately to either of these, so in effect:

$$langage = langue + parole$$

Parole is made up of actual, concrete sign uses in the real world, and is potentially infinite. *Langue* is finite, but also abstract, something we infer behind the examples of *parole* we can observe. *Parole* has meaning only to the extent that it manifests, or is constructed according to, the system of *langue*. Semiotics is concerned with reconstructing the *langue* which underlies certain types of *parole*. We shall also have to ask about the relationship between them: how is the system *used* to produce utterances?

According to the semiotic model, a sentence, for example, makes sense to the extent that it is constructed according to a system (grammar). It is important to note that this system doesn't have to be what's often called 'good English usage' (which is really just the way in which certain dominant groups construct *their*

English usage). It may be local, dialect, patois, jargon, slang or whatever. The important point is that each of these does have its own system of regular and conventional uses, to which users' utterances broadly conform. To understand the utterance, you have to know something of the system.

Codes

We can sum up this concept quite simply. In practice, a single sign is capable of taking on many different meanings. This depends on the **code** or sub-system within which it is used and interpreted.

Take an example. I shake my head from side to side when asked a question. In most cases in Australian usage, this is a quite obvious act of *parole* which signifies 'no'. In the system of bodily gestures of which it is a part, it is contrasted with a nod which means 'yes'. But meaning depends on the system of gestures. In some other cultures, a shake of the head stands for 'yes', and is contrasted with other gestures meaning 'no'. The important thing is not whether the gesture of 'yes' is a shake or a nod, but simply that it has a consistent meaning within the system.

Another example: in Western cultures, white stands for purity, and is traditionally worn at weddings, but in Chinese culture, white is a colour of mourning, and is worn at funerals. Meaning, then, is not the product of the sign itself but of the code within which it is used.

Even within any given code, any number of **subsidiary codes** may also be operating. These may overlap, or may be relatively separate from each other, even conflicting. Any example of *parole* may invoke and work from several different sub-codes at the same time. It will be useful to return to this point later, when we come to consider genre.

Though this may seem altogether different from the model introduced in Chapter 1, what we have developed so far allows us to talk about some of the features of the previous model in much more detail. We have suggested, for example, that the meaning of a given sign comes from the code within which it operates. Another way of putting this is to say that *codes provide positions from which it is possible to speak or to mean*. To use terms we developed in Chapter 1, we could say that *codes construct possible positions for addresser and addressee*. What's more, since codes are social constructions, shared by a group, the positions they provide for addresser and addressee are necessarily social positions. Even though it tends to a rather formal analysis of signs, Saussurean semiotics nevertheless seems to open up possibilities for thinking of language in more fully social terms. We will discuss this shortly.)

Synchrony and diachrony

A code is in effect a description of the state of the sign system at any given instant. It is something like a cross-section of the sign system along a time axis. As a result, we can characterise it as a **synchronic** structure, and a semiotics like the one we have been developing, which studies sign systems by taking such a cross-section of them, we could accordingly call a **synchronic semiotics**.

Such a study necessarily leaves out many of the ways in which signs work. In considering them only as a system frozen in cross-section, it may have little to say about their historical aspects, or the ways in which such systems inevitably change with time. On its own, synchronic semiotics can have little to say about why the English spoken in London today is different from that spoken there 500 years ago, or how the film Western has changed over the last fifty years, or how fashions or car design have altered in the last ten. The aspects of signs which are time-bound rather than a product of a synchronic system are, by contrast, called **diachronic**.

The organisation of the system

It is all very well to say that sign acts are the result of a structured system, but we are left with the problem of how that system might be structured. To complicate things, we are after a general theory which will work for all systems of meaning. Take our previous examples, Figures 2.1 to 2.4: is it possible to find principles of construction common to all of them?

The sentence (Figure 2.2) perhaps has the most obvious structure. It is made up of a number of clearly demarcated *elements* (words), which are *arranged* in a certain way, according to the rules of English grammar, so as to produce meaning. Both of these contribute to the overall meaning. Alter either the elements or the way in which they are arranged, and the meaning changes or even vanishes. 'On the mat sat the cat' means something very similar (but not exactly the same: Jakobson's model might suggest ways of pinpointing these differences). 'The dog sat on the mat' or 'The cat slept on the mat' are also meaningful, but in different ways. 'The mat sat on the cat' sounds rather improbable, but we can dismiss it only because it has a basic minimal intelligibility. Precisely because we clearly know what it means, we can consider it as different from the usual behaviour of cats and mats. The arrangement 'the The on sat mat cat', on the other hand, doesn't have even that intelligibility.

Is this true of the other examples? Take the advertisement of Figure 2.4. Is its overall meaning the result of both a set of elements and the ways in which these are combined? There may not seem to be anything as strict as a grammar at work here, but it is not too hard to isolate a basic set of elements whose arrangement is also crucial to the meaning. A convenient way of dividing up this advertisement would be to say that there are three basic elements: the photograph of the cat in extreme close-up, and taking up the top two-thirds of the page; the written text, taking up most of the bottom third; and the photograph of the can of cat food at bottom right. There would be other ways of doing this, and quite a few further subdivisions we could make, but for now let's take these three as a minimal set of elements. Does the way in which they are arranged affect the meaning?

Imagine how different the advertisement would be if the photos of the cat and the can of food swapped size and position. In its original full-page, full-colour magazine form, with the cat's eyes an electric yellowy-green and the whole face almost the same size as your own, the ad itself gives the arresting effect of staring back at you. Swap the order of the elements and that effect is altogether lost.

How about Figure 2.3, an amateur photograph of a family pet? Even here, we could argue that the meaning of the photograph comes from a certain set of elements (at very least, these would be the cat itself and the surroundings in which it is shown), and the way in which these are arranged (the cat is roughly central in the photo; it is also in front of the setting, not obscured behind it: those two aspects are, after all, precisely what leads us to call this a photo of a cat, rather than a photo of a garden path). And in Figure 2.1, the spoken word has clearly been broken down into three elements, the sounds /k/, /a/ and /t/, which are combined according to the possibilities of English-language phonetics: recombining them as /akt/ would have produced a different meaning altogether, whereas the arrangements /tka/ or /kta/ would have been nonsensical.

A commutation test

The concept of value lets us formulate a useful **commutation test** for determining, in a rather *ad hoc* way, what the significant elements of a given array of signs might be, what contribution they make to the overall significance, and what effect their particular arrangement may have. Simply imagine what happens when one of the elements is changed, or the relationship between any two. The extent to which this imaginary change alters the overall meaning suggests the extent to which the original element is contributing to the array's meaning. It makes a big difference to the cat food advertisement if you swap the cat and the can, so we could expect the layout to be a big contributor to what the signs can mean.

Note that this commutation test is purely a preliminary step. It helps identify elements and relationships, but as yet it tells us nothing more about them, other than that they are significant to various degrees. It doesn't say anything at all about how they come to be significant, or what the implications of that might be. It is not yet a proper semiotic analysis, but it does provide a very useful basis for one, by giving a rough-and-ready idea of where to look.

Paradigm and syntagm

We can formalise these considerations by saying that *langue*, the code or system of signs, is organised along two axes: *selection* and *combination*. On the first axis, elements are selected. On the second, the elements which have been selected are now combined according to certain rules. Another set of names for these is the *paradigmatic* and *syntagmatic axes*.

A **syntagm** is an ordered array of signs *combined* according to certain rules.

A **paradigm** is a set of signs, any of which are conceivably *interchangeable* within a given context.

Paradigms are not fixed; they are determined by the criteria of the context and topic. Elements of the same paradigm can be substituted for one another in a given syntagmatic context. In the two statements, 'The cat sat on the mat' and 'The dog sat on the mat', 'cat' and 'dog' both belong to the paradigm of *domestic mammal*. If the cat is mine and the dog belongs to the people next door, I may decide that they don't belong to the same paradigm at all (which would be *my pet*), and wonder what next door's dog is doing on my cat's mat.

In general, the less easy it is to substitute a given element for the original term, the more distant that element is from the original paradigm set. If we broaden the paradigm set from *domestic mammals* to *mammals*, we start to get the possibility of less and less likely syntagms ('The dugong sat on the mat'). The further away we move, the less likely the syntagms we get. If the paradigm set is simply *nouns*, we have possibilities like 'The generalisation sat on the mat'. If we broaden it out even further to, say, *prepositions*, we might just end up with nonsense ('The of sat on the mat').

A syntagm, then, is the result of using a conventional rule to combine a series of elements from various paradigms:

> **elements of paradigms + rule = syntagm**

Here we find the beginnings of a solution to a possible problem which arose earlier on. We said then that the link of signification between signifier and signified is arbitrary, and that therefore by their nature signs do not have a single fixed meaning; instead, they have potentially multiple and shifting meanings. How is it then that in our everyday lives we use signs as if their meanings were stable— as if we know what they mean? Why doesn't every attempted communication break down into a morass of ambiguities?

The answer is simple enough. If any individual sign may have several *possible* meanings, the actual utterances in which a sign is used tend to narrow somewhat the field of *probable* meanings. In isolation, the word 'cat' may equally well mean a domestic mammal, a whip, a coal scow, a bit of nautical tackle, a two-hulled boat. . . In fact, however, words never occur in isolation. They always occur in some context, and generally within some sort of syntagmatic statement, and this tends to narrow greatly the probable range of meanings. If the word 'cat' occurs in a syntagm such as 'The cat is on the mat', it is much more probable that the cat in question is the domestic mammal rather than the boat. The context and situation may make one particular meaning or set of meanings more probable again: it may not be the domestic mammal I mean if I say this sentence while wondering just where in the dungeon I left the thumbscrews, or while staring at the coal barge which has just crashed in through the wall. Paradigms provide a plurality of possible meanings, while syntagms tend to narrow these down according to context. Paradigms expand; syntagms contract.

Semiotic systems in general

It is surprising how many activities can be described in this way. A recipe, for example, is a set of instructions (rules) showing you how to combine certain elements from a paradigm set of 'ingredients' so as to produce the desired syntagmatic dish. Ordering food in a restaurant, you select elements from a number of paradigms ('appetiser', 'main course', 'dessert', etc.) and combine them according to certain customary rules (generally only one dish from each category, and following a given order). An outfit of clothing worn on a particular day is a syntagm combining elements from various paradigm sets ('shoes', 'hats', etc.) according to a code of dress which may vary according to time of day, occasion, economics, and—of course—gender.

'Errors of syntax' are always possible. I can utter a non-sensical 'sentence' like 'The the sat mat cat on', or combine the three letters into an illegitimate 'word' like 'tca'. To ice a fruit cake before cooking it and then to add the fruit later is also, in the semiotic terms of this analogy, equivalent to producing a badly constructed statement: it goes against all the conventions (or 'grammar') of cookery.

Figure 2.5 Paradigm and syntagm

elements of paradigm	+ rule	= syntagm
words	grammar	sentence
ingredients	recipe	finished dish
clothes	codes of dress	complete outfit
items on menu	sequence of courses	order to waiter
playing cards	rules of game	sequence of play
letters, numbers, operators	algebra	equation
folds	origami	paper animal
genes	genetic code	you

Does this mean that all these activities—preparing a meal, wearing clothes—are in some sense activities of signification: that is, that they are not just matters of satisfying a biological need or shielding oneself from sun or cold, but activities which produce meanings? Try the commutation test suggested earlier: does a bottle of cheap red wine carry the same meanings as a French vintage? What would it mean to eat your dessert first? Does an evening gown mean the same thing regardless of whether it's worn by a man or a woman?

It is perhaps not yet clear from our model just where these different meanings might come from, or how they might function—but the model certainly seems to indicate the possibility of explaining such variations. Although it comes initially from the specific case of language, semiotics does seem to be broad enough to be able to describe quite non-linguistic social phenomena in terms of signification. Now we must try to describe just how such complex social meanings are produced. To do that, we shall first have to look at various ways in which signs within systems can interact with each other.

Exercises

1 Saussurean semiotics is based on a linguistic model. When Saussure defines signifier and signified, for example, he has spoken language in mind. Does this model work as well with graphic signs? (You may wish to refer back to the various graphic signs reproduced in this and the previous chapter.)

Can we, for example, argue in the case of a photograph that the signifier and signified have only an arbitrary link? What precisely would 'arbitrary' mean in such a case? (Recall here that there is a careful distinction to be made between signified and referent.) How can we isolate individual signs from the continuum of a photograph? Does the commutation test help here?

2 Figure 2.5 suggests some activities and processes which can be understood in terms of semiotic system: that is, in each case there would seem to be a basic set of elements which develop meanings when they are combined according to the rules of a system. What other examples could be added to this list?

Does the idea of a system of rules work in quite the same way in each of these cases? Do the rules always have the same importance? What are the different effects, for example, of an incorrect syntagm in a game of cards (an illegal play) and an incorrect syntagm of clothing (odd socks, a colour mismatch, runners worn with a suit)? Can the application of the rules always be described simply as correct or incorrect? If not, what other factors should be taken into account, and how do you think the Saussurean model might accommodate them?

Sources and further reading

The principal source for much of the material dealt with in this chapter is of course Ferdinand de Saussure's *Course in General Linguistics* (London: Duckworth, 1983 [1916]). Though the *Course* is undoubtedly this century's most influential single text in linguistics, it has a complex and somewhat uncertain status: published in 1916, three years after Saussure's death, it was compiled from various sets of lecture notes by two of his former students. It's an approachable and interesting work, necessary reading if you're going to do advanced work in semiotics, structuralism or post-structural theories, and well worth looking at anyway. There are two translations available: the more recent, by Roy Harris, has the advantage of being able to draw on the 1972 critical French edition, which thoroughly revised the text from the original notes. It does, however, provide some opportunities for confusion. Rather than translate *signifié* and *signifiant* as the familiar *signified* and *signifier* (the terms we've used here), it chooses to translate them as *signification* and *signal*.

Jonathan Culler's *Saussure* (New York: Cornell University Press, 1986) is a brief and very approachable introduction to the *Course*. For a more advanced discussion, see Roy Harris's *Reading Saussure* (London: Duckworth, 1987).

Saussure's *Course* is primarily linguistic, though he does suggest the future possibility of a general theory of signs to which he gives the name *semiology*. In his *Elements of Semiology* (London: Cape, 1967), Roland Barthes provides a sketch of what such a generalised science might be, supplementing Saussure with the work of later linguists such as Benveniste, Hjelmslev and Jakobson. Despite its title, this is not an introductory text: it's brief, but demanding, though a book the advanced student will want to investigate.

Terence Hawkes' *Structuralism and Semiotics* (London: Methuen, 1977) is addressed mainly to students of literature, but it provides a clear and useful introduction to Saussure. The various essays in *Structuralism: An Introduction* (edited by David Robey, Oxford: Clarendon, 1973) are also helpful.

3 Interactions of signs

An individual sign gains its meaning from its value in a system of signs. Signs invariably invoke other signs. Within paradigmatic sets and syntagmatic sequences, signs may associate with, or substitute for, each other in potentially very complex ways. In this chapter and the next, we will start to examine some of the basic mechanisms by which this can happen. We will then be in a position to start examining something of the social nature of signification.

Metaphor

Perhaps the most obvious way in which one sign can substitute for another is by *comparison*, or **metaphor.**

> A **metaphor** is an implicit or explicit *comparison* between signs.

'To make a pig of yourself' is a metaphor. It doesn't imply that you actually turn into a farmyard animal, but that your behaviour is in some way *like* that of a pig—perhaps that you're eating a lot, very fast and somewhat noisily. What is *described* is you; the paradigm into which you have been placed is that of 'things with disgusting eating habits'; what you are described *as* is another member of that paradigm, the pig.

Everyday speech is full of metaphor, ranging from the inventive ('as much use as pockets in socks') to the banal ('to make a pig of oneself', 'to follow like sheep', 'sour grapes', 'lion-hearted', 'to go flat out', 'to have egg on one's face', 'to be caught with one's pants down', 'a dog-in-the-manger attitude'). Nicknames may often be metaphorical. Australian Prime Minister Paul Keating has been called 'The Undertaker' by his enemies. The nickname suggests that he is *like* an undertaker, either in the way he looks (tall, thin and always formally dressed) or in what he does (his actions and policies become a metaphorical burial of a dead Australian economy). What aspects of Margaret Thatcher, Bob Hawke and Malcolm Fraser were metaphorised in the nicknames 'The Iron Lady', 'The Silver Bodgie' and 'The Prefect'?

Metaphors may be visual as well as verbal. Figure 3.1, for example, compares the process of making a meal to that of making a movie. What is described is the familiar and perhaps mundane process of cooking, but it's described in terms of the somewhat less familiar and possibly more exciting process of shooting a film. The effect the metaphor has is to inject one sign with some of the meanings of another: the everyday process of preparing a meal is invested with some of the glamour and excitement of Hollywood.

Figure 3.1

Figure 3.2 is somewhat more oblique in its comparison. Here, some aspects of the large picture on the left are being compared—and transferred—to the small one on the right. It may not be obvious what Stilton cheese has to do with arriving by boat at a deserted shore somewhere on a vast lake or fjord at sunset, but the title running across the large picture makes the link: 'Stilton makes any meal a special occasion.' What they have in common is that they're both 'special occasions'. (Note here how the caption has almost acted as an 'equals' sign, in that it's suggested just what the similarity is. Without it, the similarity might well remain a mystery.) By means of metaphor, a lump of animal fat has been invested with qualities of adventure, romance, escape—and whatever other qualities we might argue the large picture as signifying.

Figure 3.2

From the examples we've examined, it would seem that metaphor can have an interesting function of **transference.** That is, it can in effect transfer certain qualities from one sign to another, which is thus invested with properties it might not originally have had. Tomatoes are not inherently glamorous, and nor is cheese in itself adventurous.

Metaphors have both paradigmatic and syntagmatic effects.

Paradigmatically, they substitute one element of a paradigm set for another. To take a previous example, if you refer to a greedy person as a pig, you effectively place them in a paradigm set of voracious or disgusting eaters, and substitute for their name that of another member of that set. The paradigm sets may be obvious and familiar, or unfamiliar and more demanding of thought. Depending on how the paradigm set is chosen, metaphor can be used to describe the unfamiliar in familiar terms, or—going the other way—to describe the familiar in less familiar terms. The first can work to explain or illustrate. A child's science book, for example, might describe the human body as 'burning' food. This explains a complex and unfamiliar process (the breakdown and absorption of biochemicals) by placing it within a broader paradigm (chemical reactions in general) and from that substituting a simpler and more familiar example (burning). The latter case is more a strategy of defamiliarisation. In Raymond Chandler's *Farewell, My Lovely*, for example, the detective-narrator Philip Marlowe describes a big man as 'standing out like a tarantula on an angel cake'. The effect here is one of humour (and at the risk of missing the joke, the paradigm set is 'things that are out of place'). Indeed, entire genres of jokes may rely on metaphoric transpositions of paradigms ('What do X and Y have in common?').

Syntagmatically, metaphor sets up a proposition. In effect, it says, 'Since X and Y are both members of the same paradigm set, they are equivalent.' X and Y act as the subject and complement of a statement of identity. Because you and a pig are sloppy eaters, you are effectively a pig.

Metonymy

Metonymy covers a much more diverse series of processes than metaphor.

A **metonym** is an *association* of terms. One sign is associated with another of which it signifies either a part, the whole, one of its functions or attributes, or a related concept.

The general process of association is called **metonymy.**

To refer to a car as 'a motor' or as 'wheels' is a metonym which substitutes the name of a part of the car for the whole thing. When Prime Minister Paul Keating's public statements about Australia's severance of ties with Britain were described in the press as outraging *the British*, the opposite metonymic substitution had occurred: the whole for the part. While the statements doubtless outraged some—or even many—British people, they hardly outraged all.

Similarly, a television news shot of troops and tanks in a desert may metonymically invoke the Gulf War. It is one of the many scenes from the Gulf War, but is used to stand for the entire conflict: part for whole. To call a tall person 'Lofty' is to refer to them metonymically by an attribute. Your signature is also an attribute which metonymically stands for you: a metonym with legal status. To address Bill Clinton as 'Mr President' is to refer to him metonymically by his function.

Metonyms may be quite complex chains of association. Take, for example, 'The Crown', as in *The Crown vs Jane Smith*. Ms Smith is clearly not being sued by millinery. Instead, 'crown' is an *attribute* of its traditional wearer, the monarch; the monarch's *function* is nominal head of the British legal system; and lastly, 'The Crown' comes to stand for that legal system itself (*part for whole*). Metonymic links may be very powerful and subtle, and we shall have cause to return to them again when we consider myth in Chapter 4.

As with metaphor, *visual* metonymy is also common. Again, advertising is a good source of examples. In many Western nations, tobacco advertising is no longer permitted. In others, it is controlled in various ways: advertisements may not show the actual products themselves, or they may not show people using them. In some cases, they may not even show the *packaging* of the product. As a result, cigarette advertisements have often made particularly ingenious uses of metonymy to overcome some of these constraints while still remaining within the letter of the law. In each case, the impermissible sign (the cigarette itself, the packet, even the brand name) is invoked by a metonymic sign associated with it.

The well-known series of advertisements for Benson & Hedges cigarettes show quite clearly one solution to the initial problem that one cigarette looks pretty much like another, no matter what the quality of the tobacco: they concentrate instead on the embossed gold foil packet that is the company's trademark. In fact, thanks to the success of this campaign, the trademark is so well known it is no longer necessary even to show the cigarettes themselves. The packet becomes a metonym of the contents; indeed, it even becomes a 'truer' sign of the company than the product itself.

Once goldness and the distinctive script of the brand name have been established as its signs, they can become more and more removed, not only from the actual activity of smoking (which has never figured in these ads anyway), but even from any representation of the packet. In other ads in these series, the packet starts becoming a sort of visual pun on other objects: a mantelpiece, an easel, a float in a swimming pool. In still others, the key elements of goldness and script have been cut adrift from the packet altogether, and have become elements in an elaborate and seductive visual puzzle. The cunning campaign has resulted in an ad which is instantly recognisable, but for a product it nowhere mentions by name, depicts, or even shows the packaging—all by a progressive process of metonymy.

The most minimal and effective examples of this process are the famous Silk Cut ads, which rely on sumptuous photography and (again) a visual pun: the elements are silk, of the same colour as the Silk Cut packet, and a cut. Where the Benson & Hedges ads truncated and dislocated the elements of the name of the product, here even the name is absent. The only thing which identifies the photograph as an advertisement—let alone as an ad for cigarettes— is the compulsory health warning. This reveals it as a cigarette ad precisely because it cites that one, metonymic feature characteristic of all such ads.

Metonyms too work both syntagmatically and paradigmatically. They suggest, but do not state, the completion of the whole whose attributes or parts have been signified. The metonym provides the paradigmatic example, the one which sums up the entire paradigm from which it is selected.

Metaphor and metonymy: a detailed example

Metaphor and metonymy are each quite simple concepts in themselves, though, as previous examples have shown, they are each capable of considerable elaboration and subtlety. Between them, these two mechanisms alone account for a surprising complexity of meaning.

Figure 3.3 shows a news photograph with its caption. It is not a particularly unusual example of local news photography, either in its subject matter or its execution. This is precisely why we have chosen it here: its very ordinariness will provide a useful demonstration of the sheer complexity of ways in which everyday meanings are constructed. That is, we are *not* interested here in finding some deeper and hidden meaning to this photo. What we want to do with the concepts we've developed so far—and particularly metaphor and metonymy—is to look at the obvious and widely accessible meanings, and ask how they come to be obvious. As we go through the discussion, ask yourself if this is in fact what we're doing. The semiotic concepts we're using may be still relatively new to you, but is the meaning they describe familiar already from the photo?

Figure 3.3

Taylor family all groomed for victory

AFTER a landslide change of voting favouring the Liberals in the Groom by-election on Saturday, the new member, Mr Bill Taylor, his wife Jan and son Nick, 17, were all smiles yesterday.

One of the first things to note is that the photograph doesn't simply function referentially. It does a lot more than show us what the new member for Groom and his family might look like: it doesn't simply identify them for us, like a passport photo. It seems also to make various statements, about family life and public life, about being a politician: to suggest that being a politician, or a member of a family, *means* something in particular. In fact, the photograph even seems to equate the two. This is a picture which is ostensibly about the winner of a by-election, but it shows a family.

We can see how this works by starting off with the simple breakdown suggested in the last chapter. Can we simplify the picture somewhat, into a more manageable array of a small number of significant elements?

One fairly obvious way to do this is shown in Figure 3.4. What we've kept is four basic elements: the family group, the election poster, the setting, and the words which frame the picture. In a moment, we will break each of these down further, but they are an adequate starting point. (We are, after all, trying to describe and analyse this picture as extensively as we can with a minimal number of terms. The simplest models are often conceptually the most powerful.) When we diagram it in this way, it is easy to see the way in which the photograph is setting up a *metaphor*. The family group is on the left, the election poster is on the right: imagine a large 'equals' sign suspended between them.

Figure 3.4 Signifying elements

Let's look at each of the three groups of pictorial elements in turn, bringing to bear on them the suggestions made by the fourth group's verbal anchorage.

Family

Take the largest and most prominent single group of elements first: the group of three people which takes up almost two-thirds of the width of the picture. Why, without any independent knowledge of the member for Groom, and even without reading the accompanying captions, do we see this as a family group? (Try a commutation test to see which aspects of the photo give this as a meaning. Would you read a single-sex group as family, for instance?) We make the *inference* of 'familyness' from features such as the particular combination of ages and sexes represented, the intimacy implied by the proximity of the various figures to each other, their stances and facial expressions, and the positions of their hands. All of these are *signs* of 'familyness' available in the photo for us to read. Even if the three figures were in fact professional actors, totally unrelated to each other, who had met for the first time minutes before the photo was taken, we would still tend to read the signs they are giving out as overwhelmingly those of 'familyness'. Reading the photo, we may have no idea whether these people actually form a family or not; but we *are* certain that this is a very clear *coded representation* of a family. In the terms we used in the first chapter, we can say that the *addressers* this photo constructs are a family, regardless of whom the people who posed for the photo might be. We can read more than that, too. This is just as obviously a *happy* family, and their happiness is coded in just the same ways. The *addressers*, that is, are a *happy family* (regardless of what the actual people who posed for the photo think of each other). This addresser-family is all but independent of the actual Taylor family. It is something the picture constructs out of common social codes: proximity means close ties, a smile means pleasure, etc. In posing for their photograph, the Taylors are playing a certain set of (addresser) roles provided for them in these codes.

This means that the family depicted in (or rather, constructed by) the photograph can mean something more than the Taylors alone. This is a public photograph, to be seen by an audience who for the most part have absolutely no personal knowledge of the Taylors. If it carries meaning for such an audience, it can only be because it draws on aspects of 'familyness' which are public, not the particular property of the Taylors alone. (Compare this photograph with one from a private family album. Even though album shots too are generally highly coded, they may require a detailed commentary in order to make full sense to someone not in the family.) In a sense, this photograph is also a photograph of *the family in general*, as it is imagined and coded within the particular society from which it comes.

This is *metonymy* at work. *This* family stands metonymically for *the* family, as an idealised type. It plays on all sorts of received ideas about how families are imagined to be. As the clothes and the setting make clear (about which, more later), it is a middle class family. It is a family with both parents, not one split by divorce or death. It consists of a dominant father and a mother who submits to his authority: look at the protective position of the arms of the two men. The son defers to his father (he is somewhat less prominent in the picture), but is ready to take on that masculine role himself (his arm duplicates the protective gesture of his father's). What's more, their smiles and proximity say that they are content with the roles they play, and are proud to display them publicly. Whatever the Taylors who are the subjects of this photo may be like, the family which semiotically addresses us from the picture is one which is entirely without dissent or unhappiness.

Something quite remarkable is happening here. This picture has all the force of an exact and precise depiction of the real: it *is* a photograph, after all, and what it depicts is presumably exactly what was happening in front of the camera at the time. But through these processes of metonymy, it is also at the same time a depiction of something almost entirely imaginary, which has never existed as such: the perfect family. What we can see here, in this perfectly banal photo, is something of the immense power of signs to *produce*, or *simulate*, the real.

Poster

We shall return to this. But now we turn to the next-largest group of signs, the **poster.** Like the picture as a whole, it is made up of both pictorial image and anchoring verbal text. The anchorage allows us to recognise it immediately as an electoral poster, even though it is in a situation in which we would not normally expect to see such a poster displayed. The essential anchoring information is in the three words in large type: the names of the candidate, the party and the electorate. Where the first grouping of figures says *family*, this set of elements says *politics*, and in just the same metonymic fashion. If this poster works, it is not because it imparts any information about Bill Taylor's expertise, abilities or policies, but because it metonymically represents him as *the politician* in abstract, the *ideal* politician.

This is done largely through camera angles. The camera is

slightly above the level of the subject's face, so he is looking very slightly upwards: that is, this addresser is somewhat lower (or shorter) than the viewer, and hence does not dominate the addressee. The addresser is deferential (he is, after all, soliciting votes). And the entire shot is taken in three-quarter face: the subject is facing slightly away from the camera his eyes are looking at, as if there is also an entire world beyond the frame of the photo, in which he has been engaged, and from which he has torn himself in order to meet the addressee's gaze. It's as if the electorate calls, and he listens.

Bill Taylor, of course, is the common element in both the family grouping and the electoral poster, and that both strengthens and complicates the implied metaphoric equation of the two. He frames the picture on both left and right:

family grouping = electoral poster

We have also determined that each of these groups may metonymically also stand for more abstract qualities: this family for *the family*, and this man for *politics*. This now leaves us with the interesting equation:

family = politics

What this picture is doing, then, is using metaphor to explain something which is relatively unfamiliar (politics) in terms of something more familiar (the family). The nation and its governance are just like a big family. There needs to be a strong and effective head, and there also needs to be willing acceptance of his headship from the others, over whom he exercises his just and natural authority. If Bill Taylor knits the two groupings together, that is because:

Bill Taylor's role in the family = Bill Taylor's role in the electorate

As he is to the family, so is he to the electorate. The family and the electorate are made to appear as basically continuous: the rules and structures which govern one also govern the other. We can see that he is a successful father of a happy and approving family. Can there be any doubt (the photo asks) that he will go on to represent Groom with the same success?

Setting
This is also where the third group of elements, the setting, comes in. The photo is shot within a house, presumably the Taylors'. Though there is not much detail available, we can make out some signifi-

cant features of its style. The weatherboard walls, high ceilings and skirting board all mark it as a distinctively Australian style of architecture: a high-set Queenslander, possibly from around the turn of the century. Designed as spacious family homes, these houses are highly desirable properties, and a sign of nationality, class and tradition. This house signals those who live in it as authentically Australian, as continuing a tradition of Australianness, and as members of the comfortable middle classes. Metonymically, again, it thus comes to stand for *the traditional Australian family home.*

As the family home, it is private space: in fact, the very seat of the private. Note that it is also an enclosed space, without visible windows: the outside world does not belong in here. But on the other hand, *the private* (the family) is only one side of the equation, balanced by *the public* (the political). Looking again at the picture, we will find that this apparently enclosed space is indeed open to the outside in all sorts of ways. The photograph itself, after all, is eminently public: not the sort of thing one might expect to find in a family album, but exactly what one might expect to find in a newspaper. And the poster, to take another example, seems quite out of place here: surely it should be displayed on a front fence or on a telegraph pole, rather than on the candidate's wall. It is a bit of the outside public world which has intruded into this private space. Notice also where it is hanging. It appears to be on a door, either in a hallway or the front door itself: that is, in that intermediate area of the house between the public and the private, the hallway that receives strangers on their way into the house, and holds the family's coats and umbrellas for their own excursions. Look at the clothes the people are wearing: the man's white long-sleeved shirt with tie and the woman's necklace are articles of apparel which belong to working or public life rather than in the home. They stand at the threshold of their own house in greeting, welcoming the addressee into that part of their private life which, with the advent of the photographer who has carefully arranged this scene, will now become public. At the same time, in greeting us only at the threshold, they withhold the privacy and sanctity of *the family.*

Caption
Finally, we should consider the fourth grouping, which comprises the caption and the brief story text. This acts as an **anchorage** for the picture as a whole: it serves to stabilise the possible meanings by metalingually cuing in relevant codes as a frame for interpretation. To point out what an essential part this cuing has already played in our interpretation, all we have to do is show what happens with different cues, as in Figure 3.5.

Figure 3.5 Changing the anchorage

ALL GROOMED FOR VICTORY

BRAVE IN DEFEAT

Bill Taylor, one of the many sitting members likely to lose his seat in yesterday's landslide election surprise, is philosophical about his future. . .

SPITTING IMAGE

Mr Andrew MacLeod has a problem which won't be over until Saturday's by-election—and even then may stay to haunt him, if the polls are any indication. Mr MacLeod is an uncannily close double of the Liberal candidate, Bill Taylor, even though the two men are not in any way related. The resemblance is so close that Mr MacLeod is often mistaken for Mr Taylor in the street. 'It gets embarrassing,' he says. 'I've never even voted Liberal.'

STANDING FOR WHAT SHE BELIEVES IN

Mrs Jan Taylor, wife of Mr Bill Taylor, the Liberal candidate for Groom, rose bravely from her wheelchair yesterday for the first time in six years to go to the polls and cast one of the votes she is sure will bring her husband victory.

Connotation and denotation

Because the relationship between signifier and signified is an arbitrary one, there is nothing in the nature of the sign itself to tie a given signifier to one signified alone. We all know from our own experience as language users that words are capable of having more than one meaning, and even of changing their meaning with time. Instead of a signifier paired to a single definite signified, the sign can more accurately be pictured as having a *spread* of signifieds, which we will call its **connotations.**

> The **connotations** of a sign are the set of its possible signifieds.

> **A warning!**
> Don't get the terms *connotation* or *connotative* confused with the *conative* function we discussed in Chapter 1. The two are quite different in meaning and use.

Used in this way, connotation emphasises the plurality of the signifieds.

This is by no means the only usage of the term you will come across if you continue work in semiotics. For a brief discussion of these, see the 'Note on usage' at the end of this chapter.

Metaphor and metonymy, as we've just been discussing them, are processes of connotation: they are ways of generating a spread of signifieds around a given signifier. Connotations need not be true in any sense: a cigarette advertisement which juxtaposes the name of the product with a group of happy, active young people makes 'health' into a connotation of tobacco. Connotations of the same sign may even utterly contradict one another: after all, another connotation of tobacco is 'cancer'.

Connotations may be plural, but this does not mean that they are a matter of individual subjective preferences. Like all meanings, they arise through codes which are ultimately shared and social. Connotations are not simply what you personally make of a sign: they are what the codes to which you have access make of the sign. Connotation is highly structured, if in a very mobile and flexible way, and one which lets us see clearly some of the means through which the social and the sign interrelate. Through connotation, the entire social world enters the systems of signification.

The link between a signifier and its signified is effected by a code, *langue*: change the code in which a given signifier is to operate, and the signified alters too. As we know, codes are social formations, shared and contested by what we could think of as communities of sign users. Social positionings such as class, gender and ethnicity make it more or less likely that a given sign user will have access to a certain code, and thus to a certain range of connotations. (We say 'more or less likely' because this is not a relationship of simple determinism, as if any of the above factors consign the bearer of them to a permanent position within sign systems. We will elaborate on this in Chapter 9.) What's more, some codes are more prevalent than others, available to more and larger groups. Not surprisingly, the specific connotations such a code carries thus tend to become the dominant ones of the relevant signs, and to gain a sort of stability within the spread of connotations of that sign. To users of that particular code, those particular meanings will tend to appear obvious, or natural, or even simply true.

We can picture the spread of connotations of a given sign as a set with somewhat fuzzy edges. They are fuzzy because it is in principle impossible totally to exclude the possibility that any given signified can function as a connotation of the sign. (Even though the probability of the situation ever arising may be small, it's possible to think of a situation where *calculus* is a connotation of *custard*. Advertising, after all, has exploited many stranger connotations. All it takes is a code in common, or the link provided by metaphor or metonymy.) Within that set, there will be certain large clumpings for the dominant connotations, and a number of smaller concentrations. The set of connotations has something like a gravitational field: some of these possible signifieds are likely to appear of more central significance than others, or to have other connotations clustered about them. Such clusterings of meanings indicate codes. At the centre of the field are the most stable meanings of the sign, which we will call its **denotations.**

> The **denotations** of a sign are the most stable and apparently verifiable of its connotations.

Precisely how such denotations come to crystallise out of the mass of connotations is a process we shall reserve for later investigation of concepts such as **hegemony** and **legitimisation** (see in particular Chapters 8 and 9). For the moment, we will simply suggest that the relative stability of a denotation may come about in a number of ways:

1 when a certain common range of meanings is *prevalent*—that is, attributed to the sign by a number of the codes in which it operates;

2 when any of the codes in which it functions is *dominant*; and, in particular,

3 when the sign works within certain *objective* or *scientific* codes.

It is important to emphasise that though denotations may be relatively stable meanings, they are not fixed. Like all meanings, they are produced in a differential play of values among signs and codes, not by a simple correspondence of signifier and signified. Denotation's stability is purely a relative matter, and for this reason there can be no clear and absolute distinction between denotation and connotation: the difference is quantitative rather than qualitative.

Like all connotations, denotations may and do alter with time. At various times in the past, for example, the sign *woman* has included such denotative meanings as 'frailty', 'irrationality', and 'deceitfulness'. These have been denotative rather than merely connotative, because they have fulfilled each of the above criteria: they are prevalent and dominant meanings, which have at times been supported by authoritative religious, moral, medical, psychological and even scientific codes. To take another example, Figure 3.6 shows some of the ways in which eighteenth and nineteenth-century science was able to assert European racial superiority: that is, to assert that a *denotative* meaning of *African* and *Asian* was 'inferiority-to-Caucasian-ness'.

As such cases suggest, denotation is inevitably bound up with historical and social factors, even in the case of those most objective of discourses, the sciences. Denotations need not even be true in any simple sense, but nevertheless, by the very fact of their being denotations they have certain **truth-effects**: they demand to be taken as true, and claim the privileges we reserve for the true. It is not surprising, then (and again, we shall return to this later, in Chapters 8 and 9), that denotation is something over which there may be intense struggle.

We must underline the distinction we are making. This is an argument about *denotation*, which is a matter of signs and the ways in which they work. It is not an argument about *the real*, which is what is assumed to pre-exist our investigations and awareness of it, even though it is known only through those investigations. To say that denotation is historical is not to say that the real is merely what a dominant consensus makes it out to be. It's rather to make a

Figure 3.6 Powers of denotation: Two examples of racism at work in nineteenth century science.

(a)

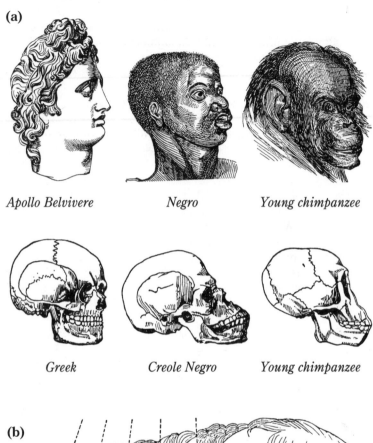

Apollo Belvivere　　　*Negro*　　　*Young chimpanzee*

Greek　　　*Creole Negro*　　　*Young chimpanzee*

(b)

more modest argument that the sciences can lay claim to un-ambiguous, objective meaning only because they build up a very elaborate and rigorous discursive apparatus to ensure it, and that *this apparatus*—which includes not only scientific language, but all the signifying practices and situations which make science possible, from replicable laboratory procedures to questions of pro-fessionalisation, careers and funding—is historically variable. What such an apparatus does is *legitimise* certain denotations, by provid-ing criteria for deciding which, amongst all the possible meanings of a term, are to be treated as valid. The very complexity of scientific language itself testifies to the difficulty of pinning signs down to single meanings. They have a constant tendency to escape from these meanings.

Denotation is what is often thought of as the 'literal meaning' of a sign, the obvious and true first-order signification which comes before and is independent of any secondary, later accretions, like connotations. What we have been suggesting is something rather different: that denotation is not so much the *natural* as the *natural-ised* meaning of the sign. *Denotation is a process of naturalisation.* Denotation, as Barthes puts it, is the last connotation: it is the persistent shape which only gradually emerges in the space marked out by connotation. Recall the news photograph of Figure 3.3, which is denotative only through a screen of connotations.

There are some unexpected implications of all this. Since denotation is only one of the meanings of the sign, but one which comes to stand for all the others, *denotation is a form of metonymy* (an individual example substituted for the general case). As we shall see in the next chapter, this means it is also aligned with myth. Far from being a non-figurative, literal sign use, denotation is always (so to speak) a figure of speech.

Note on usage
The way we have used the terms *connotation* and *denotation* is not necessarily the one you will find in other textbooks, though it is both a logical outcome of the Saussurean model and a way of getting round a number of conceptual difficulties in other accounts. Though connotation and denotation are terms which are common to a number of areas in philosophy, linguistics and literary criticism, they are used in a variety of ways, without any necessary agree-ment among the various areas.

Here, we have used **connotation** to refer simply to the entire spread of possible signifieds of a given signifier, and **denotation** for the most stable of those connotations. Other writers (such as Fiske, Hall, Hartley, O'Sullivan) define connotation more narrowly as *a* *sign whose signifier is itself a sign.* This gives a two-tiered linkage of signs, like this:

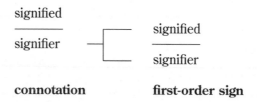

| connotation | first-order sign |

Hamlet, for example, is a complex sign capable of acting in this two-tiered way. Its signifiers are English words, and their (first-order) signified is a story of revenge and tragedy. But *Hamlet*—the entire complex sign—also functions as a signifier to evoke a whole series of connotations. On this second-order level, *Hamlet* signifies 'drama', or 'literature' (and in particular, 'English drama' and 'English literature'). Through the figure of Shakespeare, it signifies 'genius'. Put these together, and it connotes 'great art'—and so on.

This way of defining connotation comes from the work of the Danish linguist Louis Hjelmslev; it is best known in English through Roland Barthes' adaptation of Hjelmslev in his *Elements of Semiology*. Barthes and Hjelmslev use the term **denotation** correspondingly to mean a sign whose signifier is *not* a sign in its own right. For them, a denotative sign is one which doesn't enter any further into the process whereby a sign's meaning is generated by its inter-relationships with other signs. Follow the chain of connotative linkages back, and eventually you will always arrive at denotation. Denotation, in this view, is a 'first-order' sign, and connotation is 'second-order'. Denotation logically precedes connotation: first there must be denotations, and then there can be connotations. Denotations thus appear as something like the 'real meaning', the official or dictionary definitions, with their firm link between signifier and signified. Connotations will correspondingly seem somewhat 'less real', imaginary or illusory meanings.

The problem with this, as Barthes was to argue later in his career, is that, as we have just seen, this sort of fixity of meaning is just not possible in a Saussurean system. In this system, signs take on their meanings from their relationships to other signs, and this produces meaning as an effect of signification. For the Hjelmslevian denotation, though, just the opposite is the case: the denotative sign doesn't gain its meaning from other surrounding signs, but purely from the vertical relationship of signification between signified and signifier. It is hard to see how this can be contained within a

Saussurean system. Barthes' response to this later in his career was to reverse this model, in the way we have outlined in the main text. Rather than see meaning as starting from denotation, Barthes now gave priority to connotation, of which denotation would be nothing more than a special case.

Before we leave the subject, consider a variation on the diagram for connotation. Is there a second-order sign whose *signified* is a first-order sign (rather than the *signifier*, as is the case for connotation)? A sign whose signified is another sign is a sign 'about' another sign: that is, a **metalingual** sign. Most of the sentences in this book, for example, are metalingual. This sentence is metalingual.

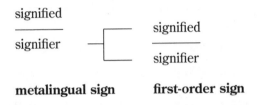

metalingual sign   **first-order sign**

The idea of a metalingual function is already familiar to us from the model we considered in Chapter 1. As you'll recall, there we suggested that *every* utterance has such a function to a greater or lesser degree. And here we run into a similar objection to that we found in the case of connotation and denotation. If the Hjelmslevian version of denotation implies a sign where signifier and signified are joined without the mediation of the entire system of *langue*, so too does the first-order non-metalingual sign. The Saussurean idea of system would lead us to expect that there are no signs which are not *both* connotative *and* metalingual in Hjelmslev's sense. If that is the case, then the distinctions named by each term are largely imaginary ones.

In short, rather than the hierarchy implied by Hjelmslev's schema of connotation and metalanguage, we wish to emphasise that:

1 all signs are plural and connotative; and
2 all codes are to some extent metalingual.

Exercises

1 Analyse how metaphor and metonymy combine to generate meaning in Figures 3.1, 3.2, 3.7 and 3.8. Use our analysis of the newspaper photo in Figure 3.3 as a guide. How do metonymy and metaphor work together to invest what is depicted with certain significations?

Figure 3.7

2 How do the connotations of the Australian flag differ according to the various codes through which it is read? Does an Australian flag flying over Sydney Cove in January 1988 suggest different readings (i.e., invoke different codes) from a similar flag flying over a government office, a British football ground, or a destroyer in the Persian Gulf in January 1991? How are its particular connotations likely to differ, depending on whether you are white Anglo, white non-Anglo, Aboriginal or Asian, Australian-born or migrant, Australian or non-Australian, monarchist or republican?

3 We have concentrated here on two broad types of graphic sign: the news photograph and the print advertisement. What other signs and processes may be described in terms of metaphor and metonymy? How might the name of a designer work on an item of clothing, or that of an author on a book cover? Certain activities are often represented metonymically, as a matter of

Figure 3.8

course: the man with the guitar, for example, is often used to stand for all popular music (rather than, say, a woman with a guitar, or a person behind a mixing desk, or an accountant). What are some of the possible effects of representing a complex social process metonymically, through a single feature?

Sources and further reading

Denotation and connotation are concepts which come primarily from Louis Hjelmslev, *Prolegomena to a Theory of Language* (Madison, Wisconsin: Wisconsin University Press, 1969) where they are grafted onto a basically Saussurean apparatus. Roland Barthes' *Elements of Semiology* (London: Cape, 1967) draws heavily on Hjelmslev, and is the main source of the use of this distinction in cultural studies. Both of these are difficult texts, and are not recommended for introductory studies. Barthes' later, briefer and much more approachable reconsideration of these terms and the relationship between them is in 'Change the object itself', from *Image–Music–Text* (London: Fontana, 1977). One of the classic texts on the semiotics of advertising is Judith Williamson's *Decoding Advertisements: Ideology and Meaning in Advertising* (London: Marion Boyars, 1978).

4 Texts and textualities

Why a text?

To consider the different sorts of meanings that signs generate we emphasised the paradigmatic axis of meaning. Both signifiers and signifieds take their values and meanings from sets of possibilities. A signifier can always have more than one signified, and a signified may be linked to a number of signifiers. Because of these multiple possibilities, a sign's meaning results from its contrast to other meanings it might have.

The sign has such meanings for various groups of people in various social contexts—the words 'herb' or 'weed' signify something quite different to weekend gardeners than to fans of reggae music. Of course, someone might be both a gardener and a fan. In that case he or she would use the sign 'herb' in different ways depending on the situation (though it is not hard to imagine a sentence where both meanings would be used).

Signs link together to form texts, so the notion of text involves ideas of syntagmatic combination as well as paradigmatic choice.

A **text** is a combination of signs.

Obvious types of texts are a sentence someone writes or a fashion outfit someone wears. Each of these texts has paradigmatic and syntagmatic features. The words and clothes can be thought of as signs, and they join together to form a *verbal* text and a *fashion* text.

In the sentence a number of choices are made: which words to include (there are always synonymous words or phrases that could be used, and choices that are made seem to be based on a number of factors such as convention, decorum, code and connotation as well as the writer's vocabulary); and what codes and rhetorical strategies to use (for example, will something be said straight or ironically, flatly or persuasively, and so on). Paradigm choices of words will depend on which strategies are employed and which

67

functions are dominant. They will also signify these strategies and functions to readers.

As these sorts of choices are being made, the words are also being joined into a sentence. Syntagmatic rules apply to how the signs can be combined. In the case of language, grammar is a key set of such rules. The sorts of choices and rules that are available change through time as well as according to the social groups the writer belongs to, and is addressing. Different groups use different grammars and different syntagmatic rules. A sentence like 'Good grammar is a sign of good character—not!' is an example of rhetorical strategy, word choice and combination working together to produce an unexpected meaning. The sentence invokes a traditional idea about language only to attack it, and the unconventional grammar registers the attack as much as the final word and punctuation choices. The choices and the rules of combination work together to produce the text's meanings.

We can see the same double process going on in producing a fashion text: choices of shirt, pants, socks, shoes, even (if absolutely necessary) a tie. All the items then have to be combined. The point would be not only to make sure that you don't put the socks on your ears, but that everything 'goes together'.

The syntagmatic rules and conventions for dress may be quite subtle. Questions of 'taste' come up. We could think of fashion taste as a set of connotations, signified by certain clothes, that a group considers suitable for specific social events or occasions. Different groups will have different ideas of what is suitable, and members of one group may try to challenge the ideas and taste of another group. This chapter is being written on Melbourne Cup day, and one fairly safe bet is that at least a few of the boys in the public car park at Flemington racetrack will be wearing top hat and stubbies. Part of their day's fun is to challenge the conventional combination of dress choices that members would make. Their outfits will rework more orthodox fashion texts.

What do we gain by calling the way someone is dressed a 'text'? There is a series of advantages if we are trying to think about how culture works:

1 By rethinking fashion as a type of text we can apply semiotic concepts to it to see what sorts of social meanings are involved in a particular outfit.
2 We can relate fashion to the ways that other kinds of social texts work to convey meanings and ideas to people. (As we will see, fashion is an important part of the way advertising and news work; it is not only advertised or newsworthy in itself, but can signify many social meanings and values in relation to other issues.)

3 We can consider how different groups use certain styles of dress and the meanings they connote in order to distinguish themselves from other groups; fashion is one of the main ways of producing group and personal identities.

Overall, then, the key effect of thinking of something like fashion as a text is that we break through any façade of naturalness it may have. We realise that fashion, like any text, is always *socially constructed* to have certain meanings and to do certain things (such as creating an identity or impression). All textual construction occurs through the two processes of paradigm choice and syntagmatic combination.

Cultural studies suggests that we can learn a great deal about how a society functions by examining its different customs, structures and institutions, as well as the verbal and visual texts it produces, through using semiotic concepts of textual analysis. By *textualising* these various cultural areas and events, that is, by thinking of them as comprising choices of signs that are combined into larger groups or patterns, we can start to uncover the attitudes and beliefs that motivate social actions and then go on to think about their effects.

The textual approach to culture is not the only way of thinking about how it works. Other approaches have included seeing culture as a game (as we shall see), or as a drama; instead of using semiotic theories, different kinds of economic, political or religious schemes have been used. Often these sorts of approaches can be useful supplements to seeing culture as text. Yet as we hope to show in this and subsequent chapters, once we have taken on board the basic semiotic concepts we can start to analyse a vast range of cultural texts and activities. We can investigate our own habituation to the meanings that surround us and through which we live.

Practising analysis

Before we develop these ideas on texts and textuality, let's try a little textual analysis. The aim is to see how the semiotic concepts that were introduced in the previous two chapters can help us uncover the processes of social meaning that go on in everyday texts. It is not only literary texts such as novels, plays and poems that express interesting and often complicated themes and ideas. As we saw in the last chapter, similar processes of meaning go on in all kinds of social texts—from films to ads to news stories—and semiotic theory provides a set of concepts through which these processes of meaning can be traced. We can start by looking at another magazine advertisement, Figure 4.1.

Figure 4.1

The ad is for Dunhill cigarettes. To analyse a text like this one, we have to move between the text's paradigmatic and syntagmatic axes, first considering the possible meanings of each of the chosen signs and then noting how they combine and whether they reinforce one another's meanings. What are the key signifiers in this text? The colour gold, the open cigarette packet, the sheet music and clarinet, the gold lighter, and the phrases 'Dunhill DeLuxe' and 'Always in good taste' seem to make up the important signifiers.

What are some of the possible signifieds? The colour gold, as well as signifying 'a precious yellow metal, highly malleable and ductile, and free from liability to rust' (*Macquarie Dictionary*), can signify wealth and status. The sheet music looks complex and classical, and along with the word 'Always' seems to signify timeless taste and classiness. The open packet and lighter suggest accessibility.

All of these signifiers are already **connotations**. The signs are being related to certain codes of meaning over others. Wealth, taste and status codes come into play far more readily than health, mineral and music codes. An important reason for this is the *syntagmatic effect of combination*. When placed together, the different signs emphasise the codes they have in common. Codes that are not shared fade back into (but do not disappear from) the text. In our example, metallurgical meanings may be signified by the gold, but they do not seem to relate to classical music or cigarette codes. This syntagmatic cross-referencing among signs and codes activates some meanings and sidelines others.

A second factor involved in considering which codes of meaning are active in the text is their *familiarity* to readers. The signs in the Dunhill ad are used in many other social texts to trigger off similar codes of taste and status. In the next chapter, on genre, we will consider that just as signs in one text refer to one another, so they relate to each other across separate texts, and the texts themselves can also refer to each other. For the moment, however, the point to note about the familiarity and repetition of taste and status codes through signs such as gold, classical music and accessibility is that, for many readers, they transform these connotations into **denotations**. The semiotic link between gold and status or classical music and taste does not seem to be just a possibility—a single connotation from one code—but the true, timeless meaning of the sign.

With these denotations operating, the text has a further semiotic effect. By being linked to gold and classical music, as signifier Dunhill no longer merely connotes cigarette. It metaphorically denotes lasting status and taste, and its apparent accessibility—the open pack, the handy lighter—seems to put these socially valued ideas within our g(r)asp.

There are other things we might note about this text. Its spatial structure is important, with the cigarette packet centrally placed, the cigarettes leading our sight to the music, and the lighter guiding us to the slogan. There is also a kind of semiotic contest going on in the text: it includes an official warning that confronts the other signs but seems to be overshadowed by them. Furthermore, we could consider how the text's signs and codes are informed by valued social ideas, but at the same time signify those values and quite possibly reinforce their appeal to readers. *The text is both produced by and reproduces cultural attitudes.* In these various ways, our analysis would develop by continuing to explore the exchange of meanings between signifiers and signifieds, and the interaction between choice and combination, paradigm and syntagm.

Social texts, social meanings

In considering how this advertisement is working we followed a particular analytical procedure. It involved a sequence of steps:

1 We located the key signifiers in the text.
2 We proposed a range of possible signifieds for each of the signifiers.
3 We identified the connotations and social codes to which the signifieds were relating.
4 We noted which of these connotations seemed to become the naturalised, true meanings in the text. Another way to put this stage is that we tried to recognise the signs' denotations. These denotations worked together to give the text its denotative meaning. (Sometimes this meaning is also called the text's 'literal' or 'surface' meaning, and later we will rethink what these terms imply.)
5 We considered that these denotations might reinforce familiar social structures of thought. We tried to derive the larger systems of cultural beliefs and attitudes which the text seemed to represent.

It is worth thinking a little more about this last step. When signs and connotations appear 'normal', this is because the text presents itself as truthful, and as a vehicle for eternal or natural beliefs or outlooks. In connoting ideas as such, the signs disguise the particular social influences that underlie the relevant codes. If this effect occurs, we can say that the text is participating in a cultural process of **myth**.

Myth is a set of signs which implies extremely familiar and influential social structures of thinking. Frequently it has traditional, historical acceptance. Later on in Chapter 8, we will develop the notion of myth in relation to questions of ideology. At this point, however, it is useful to introduce the concept because it enables us to start to talk about the social functions and effects of textual meanings.

Myth emerges in texts at the level of codes. It conceals its identity as one social meaning for a text's signs, among many, and seems instead to be the only, natural meaning. It parallels the way that, at the level of signs, denotation operates as the 'truthful' connotation.

Myths are naturalised codings of social meanings and values. The extreme effect of myth is to *hide* the semiotic workings of a text's signs and codes. The denotations appear so true that the signs seem to be the things themselves. In Figure 4.1, myth guarantees that Dunhill cigarettes do not merely signify status and taste, they *are* status and taste. Myth turns social signs into facts.

Since signs and codes are produced by, and reproduce, cultural myths, the processes of textual meaning must be seen as central to social thought. Texts become kinds of social activity. Semiotic analysis reveals the potential effects of such activity. Another example (Figure 4.2) may clarify these points.

The key signifiers in this advertisement include the colours, the vegetables, the tins of soup, and the words 'natural', 'freshest tasting' and 'sprouted'. The dominant signified seems to be nature. Together, the vegetables form a metonym for nature. The colours and images of the vegetables are transferred to the labels, which also then signify nature. The tins of soup operate as metaphorical signifiers of nature, and metonymic signifiers for the Campbell's company, and even for society itself.

The text sets up a contrast between the natural and the cultural: fresh vegetables versus tinned soup. But this opposition seems also to be dissolved through the soup, and by extension through Campbell's. Like the brand name, which sounds like both a family and a company, the tinned soup is a double sign—of nature and culture. Its denotative value of 'soup' compresses and reconciles two, supposedly opposed, signifieds.

This reconciliation works in other ways through the text. First, there is the arrangement of signs. The abundant supply of vegetables and the rows of tins make up a neat picture, almost like a school photograph. Indeed, the tins organise the excess of the vegetables, seeming to impose some sort of order upon them. But it is not a destructive order. The tins signify the best features of nature combining with the best aspects of culture. Campbell's all-natural soup harmonises nature and culture, and does so not by manufacturing but by 'sprouting' a new product.

Figure 4.2

THE FRESHEST TASTING
RANGE OF SOUPS HAS JUST SPROUTED
THREE NEW VARIETIES.

Introducing All Natural French Onion, Creamy Cauliflower and Garden Tomato & Vegetable.
Made from the freshest ingredients available. From Campbells. Naturally.

CAM636

There are some important myths about nature in this text. Nature is positive but wild; nature and culture seem to be opposed. Culture, however, is able to control nature, reduce its excess and make it beneficial for people. This text picks up on a long tradition of social thought and texts concerned with the links between nature and culture. It represents a positive image of their relationship—that culture brings nature to fruition. It is possible to see this myth determining the signs and codes of many other texts, particularly ones denoting social progress. Such texts, in turn, can work to justify and endorse programs of research, development and change. Textuality translates into social action.

Textual analysis and production

The kind of analysis applied to these two advertisements comprises a basic set of steps which can be used to study many types of texts and their social meanings. A simple diagram shows how it works:

Textual analysis
signs → connotations and codes → denotation → myths

As can be seen, the analysis moves from locating specific signs, to examining the structures of social myths. We can make several observations about this approach. It involves the following assumptions and makes these connections:

1 The basic premiss of textual analysis is that *all signifiers have multiple signifieds.*
2 Signs' connotations are always related to *codes* of social values and meanings. (Remember that a code is a set of values and meanings shared by users, the producers and readers of the text.)
3 Each text is a syntagmatic combination of signs, with their related connotations. So texts are always linked to *social codes.*
4 The *connotations* emphasised by different readers depend on their social positions, that is, the class, gender, race, age, and other factors that influence the way they think about and interpret texts.
5 Socially preferred connotations become *denotations*, the apparently true meanings of the signs and the text for readers.
6 Denotations represent *cultural myths*, sets of beliefs and attitudes which readers of texts may be invited to accept as true and natural.

It is useful to think of this sort of analytical process as one that gradually *unpacks* the text. In a way the process reverses the structure through which social texts are produced or 'packed'. Texts are always produced in social contexts; they are always influenced by and reproduce the cultural values and myths of those contexts. The prevailing myths and cultural beliefs determine what a text's key denotations, codes and connotations, and signs will be. Even if a text contradicts those beliefs, and publicly announces its disagreement—as, for example, graffiti often do—it is still being influenced by them. So at this point, we can say that the process of textual production in many cases looks something like this:

Textual production
myth → denotation → codes and connotations → signs

This process also has a couple of implications. On the one hand, the influential myths and cultural attitudes seem to affect the structure and meaning of texts. Myths underlie texts' meanings and values. On the other hand, because the myths do underlie the text and seem to be natural, they remain hidden within the text. They are not noticed because they invite acceptance as social truths. Say someone is reading a magazine and sees one of the advertisements we analysed earlier. This person's understanding of the text would be influenced by the cultural myths that structure the signs, though he or she need not be conscious of that influence. The text addresses the reader as if the values underlying its signs were natural and normal, and invites the reader to read the text in those terms. As we will see, much of this process of **socialisation** takes place through texts and their functions of address.

Myths structure texts but, for many readings, they remain unrecognised. It is these naturalised, invisible myths that the analytical process we mapped out earlier tries to unpack. Hence there is a twofold relationship between text and myth:
1 Cultural myths structure the meanings and values of the text.
2 The text hides the myths which structure it.
It is this double process of the structuring and hiding of cultural values in texts that semiotic analysis aims to reveal.

The surface or literal meaning is only the tip of the textual iceberg. Its image of finished meaning requires a lot of semiotic work to be done, in the exchange of signs, connotations and values. Yet that image can be so powerful and convincing that it conceals all the work and ends up looking real. There is more to reality than meets the eye.

Social readers, social reading

For a number of reasons, texts never exist abstractly. As we have seen, they work through semiotic processes, such as metaphor and metonymy, where social meanings are exchanged and social codes interact. They don't make the real present but *re-present* it through certain codes and signs.

Furthermore, texts are always read by someone. The notion of text always implies an audience; there is always an addressee—a role usually filled by a group of readers (or viewers), less frequently a single reader. What we need to do now is to consider the various ways that different texts produce social meanings for readers. What's going on when we read a text?

Let's begin to answer this question by having a closer look at some examples of the relationships between social attitudes and texts. The myths that influence texts are not simply true or false. Rather, they are processes of thought that both structure and get represented in texts, and thereby often reproduce and reinforce certain values and beliefs for readers. In this way reading texts becomes a social practice.

Initially, we can consider a couple of texts which seem to reproduce Western myths and codes about African and Oriental cultures. In the first, an advertisement for Revlon products (Figure 4.3), the exotic difference of the Oriental world is emphasised. There is a blurring of Western time, as well as a mixture of slightly contradictory concepts, such as the forbidden and the elusive. There is a dreamlike superimposing of images. The fan could also work as a gender metonym, suggesting Oriental women's modesty and seclusion.

These verbal and visual signs come from codes that represent the Orient's cultural difference. But difference from what? The Western world, of course. In reverse, and as it represents the East, the text also works to stabilise the norms of the addressee's Western culture as the known, the familiar, the everyday. Further, as the sign of the fan suggests, there is even a sexual contrast being hinted at—the feminised Orient and the masculinised West—and through the Revlon product this archetypal but exotic femininity can be transferred to Western women.

A second advertisement, for Sony audiotapes (Figure 4.4), reinforces related myths of cultural contrast. The woman's ear signifies the otherness of African cultures for Western readers. The text triggers dominant Western myths and codes for representing this foreign culture. They have positive and negative meanings—colour, vibrancy, inner rhythm, but also excess and distortion. We can also note the emphasis on the woman's body, from the elongated earlobe to the sensual facial expression, her lips parted, eyes dreamily half-closed. As in the Revlon advertisement, Western conceptions of race and female sexuality

Figure 4.3

combine to depict the cultural 'other'. Again, the Western product packages this 'exotic-ness' and can make it easily attainable.

The principal signs and codes in these texts pick up on a social grid of understanding which is founded on a basic cultural and mythic opposition—that between 'us' and 'them'. Although the 'us' are not personally represented in these texts, they are involved in two ways: first, through the intervention of the product, and second, and of greater textual interest, as the texts' addressees. Both

Texts and textualities **79**

Figure 4.4

DECORATE YOUR EARDRUMS.

    SONY.
THE ONE AND ONLY

texts are structured towards the perspective of a Western 'us', who are positioned to understand the signs, and hence the importance of the product, in certain very Western ways.

It is important to study the way texts set up these sorts of contrasts: us–them, West–East, culture–nature, masculine–feminine. Earlier it was noted that the key codes in a text are activated by the syntagm's reinforcement of its signs' connotations. We can now develop another angle on the textual process: *signs (and codes) are often contrasted, with values and meanings working in opposition to each other.* The text encourages readers to privilege one set of values and meanings over the other. In the above examples, we don't simply note the West–East contrast. The text positions us to prefer the West.

These kinds of textual oppositions can be thought about in three related ways:

1 The oppositions are part of the text's *structure*: a text is constructed through the contrasting relationships between key signs.
2 These structural oppositions and contrasts organise and signify the text's meanings.
3 The text positions the reader to value one side of the opposition, with its related meanings, over the other.

These three points suggest some of the results of semiotic analysis. By looking at the structure of signs in a text, we can begin to understand how its social codes of meanings, values and related cultural myths are represented and organised in ways that affect people's thinking.

Let's return to an earlier text to examine the interplay of semiotic oppositions and similarities with social values in more detail. Revisiting the Taylor family, still happy after Bill Taylor has won a Queensland by-election (Figure 3.3), we can see how much further our analysis can now go. Quickly to recap: the key signs include the three people (all touching), the smiles, the clothing (especially the pearls and tie), the election poster and the Queensland-style family house. There is a complex mixture of signs from interpersonal (gesture and expression), fashion, family, political, even architectural codes.

The connotations of these signs are already located within social codes of meanings. We don't know these people but we read them as a family—the ages, physical closeness, the overall similarity to other family photographs we have seen. Their specific, personal identity (or the name of the electorate) is not particularly important to the codes being used. The heading could just as easily read 'The Groom Family All Tailored for Victory'—the details could change but the codes would still work in the same way. Their dress signifies middle class status, their stance and expressions a contented closeness. On the surface, the naturalised denotation is of a happy, middle class family. The mother is subservient, framed by the man's arms, but central. She mediates between father and son. The positive myth of the family obviously has a strong influence on the text.

There seem to be a number of other myths working through the photograph that link this idea of the family to politics. To trace the way they work, remember we have to view these figures as signs used in a text, not as real people. The Taylors do exist, yet we are thinking about them not in terms of their daily lives, but as they are represented in a text. They are like characters in a soap opera or a movie: they look real (even if their pose seems rather artificial), but what is more important is that they signify certain ideas about people, behaviour and society to us.

Accordingly, we can see that Bill Taylor works as a metonym for a traditionally patriarchal, political system. He is a father *and* a politician. There is also a series of metaphorical transfers between Taylor's denotations in the family and political codes. Straightforward denotations of the paternal Bill Taylor are translated into a political code. The good father becomes the good politician; the close, happy family becomes the contented electorate. There is an equation between the two Bill Taylors in the text—the political one on the poster and the family one embracing his wife and son. The text sets up an opposition and then synthesises it.

The mythic effect of this fused, double sign of Bill Taylor is to naturalise patriarchal politics through linking it to a seemingly natural, truthful image of the family. The politician becomes *our* father. The text is organised according to these two mythologies—family and politics—but through its readily recognisable codes and denotations, it also seems to conceal the way these myths express versions of family and state where the father is dominant. In particular, the family myth seems to hide or disguise the text's political meanings. At the same time, it positions the readers to accept this representation of politics. For if we reject it, it seems that we are also rejecting the ideals of the happy family.

To suggest the broader social extent of this intermixing of family and political codes we can compare a still from a TV news story on a political anniversary for the former Australian Prime Minister, Bob Hawke (Figure 4.5). This political event is represented through signs of a marriage anniversary. There are various metonymic and metaphorical exchanges between signs of Bob Hawke as husband and Prime Minister, and Hazel Hawke as wife and country. Other key domestic signs include the cups of tea and the fireplace. As in the Taylor text, there is a central shot of the political family, this time in front of the hearth. As the setting for these shots, the Lodge fuses domestic tranquillity and political power.

Figure 4.5

In all the last four texts, opposition between the sexes has been an underlying myth that structures the signs and codes. We have seen this kind of opposition in an earlier example in the book, the Yves Saint Laurent advertisement (Figure 1.3). Note the contrasts that run through the differing body positions and patterns of address. A set of male-related signs confronts a set of female-related signs. The connotations within each set reinforce one another. The social meanings of maleness and femaleness define one another through their opposition to each other.

Hence the structure of this text is in itself meaningful. It is not merely a spatial organisation of signs. The structure replays patriarchal myths of male control, female subordination and sensuality. The text positions the reader within these myths. The male in the photograph frames the woman and looks upon her as does the reader.

We can consider the interplay of myths in these texts in further detail. As noted earlier, in the Taylor and Hawke texts, the family myth seems to bail out the politics myth, by making it more palatable or acceptable, and even by pressuring the reader not to reject the apparent denotations of family contentment. What is at stake in this process of using one myth to support another? What does it tell us about the way cultural myths work in texts?

The myth of politics is not unequivocally positive. Especially in Queensland after 1988, when the findings of a commission of inquiry into official corruption were made public, texts concerning politics reverberated with connotations of impropriety and dishonesty. A deep paradox in political mythology was brought into the open: politics is both good and bad, respected and denounced; politicians are forthright leaders and shady schemers. These paradoxical meanings reveal an important aspect of the way all cultural myths are structured and function in texts. *No myth is unambiguous or singular.* Like signifiers and signifieds, myths are at least binary and often multiple, quite possibly in contradictory ways. Compare the Campbell's soup advertisement: nature is depicted as providing for culture or needing to be controlled by culture. In the Sony text, the female other is both desired and confronting.

Other myths which everyday texts often suggest include that the passing of time leads to progress and improvement or to the earth's ruin and judgement day; that the child is an innocent who needs protection and nurturing, or an anti-social figure who needs to be disciplined and educated. In the texts we have been studying the family may be read as a restrictive patriarchal unit or a nest of support and contentment, politics as the basis of society or its corruption.

The myths that influence social texts are often *oppositional*. They can be interpreted in different ways and are frequently in conflict with various counter-myths. Like the connotations of signs, the codes that fill texts have multiple rather than singular meanings. Consequently, the social values represented by texts are often ambiguous or contested. Depending on the social group and context of the readers, as well as the codes that are operating, differing cultural myths and values will come into play as a text is read. And since these myths and values are equivocal in meaning, so the texts that represent them are socially ambiguous.

We can draw four conclusions about the ways that myths and social meanings work in texts:

1 Myths and values are never ultimately fixed in meaning; they are varied and often split into conflicting versions of myth and counter-myth.
2 Members of different social groups will read and respond to cultural myths in different ways; a myth's structuring function and effect for a text is not always predictable.
3 Meanings and values are not simply contained by a text; they emerge as the text is read by socially positioned readers.

4 Reading texts is a social activity. We can best think of reading as a process of *social negotiation*, wherein the values and myths represented by a text may be taken up and either agreed to, reinterpreted, or opposed by readers. The meaning of texts is never fixed; it, too, is multiple and gets negotiated through social values.

Dominant, negotiated and oppositional readings

A text like the photograph of the Taylor family thus works in a somewhat contradictory way. On the one hand, it is composed of codes of social meaning so conventional that they seem natural, and many readers who are familiar with these codes and signs are unlikely to interpret them in surprising terms. There is a dominant or preferred set of meanings on the photograph that would re-inforce positive social myths about the family and politics. In this case readers accept the addressee position the text offers.

On the other hand, differently placed readers—ones less ready to accept the codes and signs denotatively—will interpret this text in a variety of ways. Some may question its mythological images of family happiness and unity; some may dispute its political values. Such readers reject the offered addressee position. The text's dominant or preferred social meanings and myths can be agreed with or challenged.

Accordingly, we can say that an actual reading of any text can involve the acceptance or the rejection of the addressee positions it offers. The addressee position can itself be negotiated or contested. And because of this possibility, varied readings and interpretations of texts are always possible.

To cover these possibilities for interpretation, a number of theorists have developed a threefold model of social reading. The point is not so much to prove that people read precisely in one of three ways, or that texts have exactly one of three meanings. Instead, the most useful way to apply the model is as a further phase of the analytical procedure. Once we have moved through the basic steps of semiotic analysis and uncovered the complex play of meanings among the signs, once we have identified the key social codes and related them to cultural grids of beliefs and attitudes or myths, we can use this threefold model to propose the various and changing ways that a text can operate in its contexts of address—the ways in which it is read and used by people.

Like any text, then, the Taylor photograph sets up dominant or preferred meanings which can be interpreted in at least three ways:

1 **A dominant** or **preferred reading** in which readers reproduce the preferred meanings concerning family, fathers and politics.

2 **A negotiated reading**, in which readers question some of the specific connotations and codes of the text but still accept its overall mythologies. For example, certain readers may reject the approving middle class, Liberal Party connotations of the photograph, but accept a patriarchal model of the family and politics.

3 An **oppositional reading**, in which readers would challenge the middle class connotations and codes as well as the patriarchal myths that are depicted. The difference between negotiated and oppositional readings thus takes place where codes trigger conflicting myths.

There are undoubtedly many more ways in which this text could be interpreted by different groups of readers. Social factors such as age, gender, class, ethnicity, educational background, and so on, are powerful influences on how people read. Moreover, no single factor is the ultimate key to the way someone responds to a text. Readers' responses are complicated social actions which vary over time, depending on where and with whom the text is read and thought about, as well as the motives for reading it. Nonetheless, this three-part model of reading underlines the point that texts do not contain fixed ideas but are involved in people's negotiations with, and responses to, the social values and attitudes represented by dominant and preferred meanings. Again we can see that reading is a social activity that entails working through and responding to connotations and myths.

The concept of preferred meaning suggests that although textual meaning is socially variable, texts often seem to set up a certain interpretation for readers—a certain addressee position. Readers may accept, question or oppose the preferred meaning and the position it entails. Indeed, it seems unlikely that in most cases readers completely take the preferred meaning on board. Some degree of negotiation would always seem to be involved, because of the complex range of factors which influence the act of reading. Where the stakes of negotiation move from codes to myths, reading becomes a contest over social values.

A clear example of the way texts try to tie down their meaning can be seen in the way captions work in photographic texts. We can call this function of the caption **anchorage**, as it tries to anchor the text's meaning, that is, to tie down the connotations and codes that the visual signs are generating and orient them towards certain versions of the underlying myths. Anchorage is a feature of news photographs, but we could also compare the effects of the title of a painting, especially a non-realistic painting, or a reporter's voice-over, accompanying a piece of TV news footage. *Anchorage can work to fix the addressee position of response to such texts.*

The effects of anchorage are, of course, not absolute. In the first place, in news texts the visual signs are often far more striking than the verbal ones—one of the main reasons for using them. Second, and more relevant to our understanding of textuality, *the anchorage itself constitutes another text*, with its complex interplay of signs, codes and readings. Anchorage may even increase rather than reduce textual interactions and interpretations; it rarely finalises them.

Consider one of the most infamous social texts of recent times, the video of Rodney King being bashed by four Los Angeles policemen. For many viewers, the text's meanings seemed clear, yet as the legal defence and jury finding in the first trial showed, this text could be negotiated in unpredictable ways. As an amateur video, cameraman and addresser more or less unknown, there seemed to be no way of working out the text's preferred meaning. The connotations became complex as many codes were triggered by the video—law and order, police brutality, violence against blacks. Behind these were still more complex myths of justice, morality and racism.

The controversy over the verdict enacted an intense response to the signs' possible meanings. A single preferred reading was not possible. More and more texts were produced—film of other violent acts, interviews with experts, eye-witness accounts, recollections of social unrest in the 1960s, and ultimately, a second trial. None of these texts reduced the complexities, for each drew on different codes and was open to conflicting interpretations.

The King video shows that in social terms textual meaning neither originates in the sender's mind nor is fixed by a single receiver. The text's many meanings, its **polysemy**, were the condition of its circulation through the local, national and international communities. In each site, and for each group of readers, the significance was perceived very differently. The video was then used to justify specific structures of social, legal and racial attitudes and became the immediate pretext for a range of social actions from protest to law enforcement. As noted earlier, not the least of its effects was to initiate a continuing cycle of other texts.

Texts are combinations of signs with multiple, social meanings. These meanings derive from cultural codes and myths. While texts may often seem to represent a preferred meaning, this meaning may be accepted, negotiated or opposed by different social groups of readers. Indeed, because the condition of a sign is its polysemic potential, we could say that a text's meaning never has a single origin or final destination. It is always an effect of different readings. This process reveals that textuality and reading are always social activities. The important question for us is no longer simply what texts mean, but how they are used.

Exercises

1 Many types of social gatherings can be analysed as texts. Try to examine the structure and meanings of such events as a barbecue, a concert or a party by using the semiotic concepts introduced in the last three chapters. What are your text's key signs? Do they work metaphorically and metonymically? What are the different sorts of readings that people make of these texts?

2 Your university or college campus—from the overall layout to the design of individual lecture theatres and seminar rooms—can also be analysed semiotically. Which cultural myths do the oldest buildings on the campus seem to represent? Do more recent buildings suggest changes to these myths? How could the lecture theatres or seminar rooms be analysed? What are the connotations of the students' seating arrangements in contrast to the position set up for the lecturer or tutor?

3 Collect a series of magazine advertisements that depict family groups. Note the key signifiers for the different family members. What are their connotations? Find some family advertisements from twenty or thirty years ago, and analyse any changes to myths of the family.

Sources and further reading

For a general discussion of the different metaphors that have been used to discuss culture see Clifford Geertz's essay, 'Blurred Genres: The Refiguration of Social Thought' in his book *Local Knowledge: Further Essays in Interpretive Anthropology* (New York: Basic Books, 1983).

Roland Barthes' *Mythologies* (New York: Hill and Wang, 1987) offers a general outline of the notion of myth introduced in this chapter. Barthes also provides numerous examples of how to use the concept in cultural analysis. Other examples of this kind of analysis can be seen in John Fiske, Graeme Turner and Bob Hodge, *Myths of Oz: Readings in Australian Popular Culture* (Sydney: Allen and Unwin, 1987).

There are numerous works that discuss the models of textuality and reading introduced in the chapter. For a clear summary see Graeme Turner, *British Cultural Studies: An Introduction* (Boston: Unwin Hyman, 1990). Stuart Hall's essay, 'Encoding and Decoding' (in *Culture, Media, Language: Working Papers in Cultural Studies, 1972–79*, London: Unwin Hyman, 1980) provides a more complex account. David Morley's books, *The 'Nationwide' Audience: Structure and Decoding* (London: British Film Institute, 1980) and *Family Television: Cultural Power and Domestic Leisure* (London: Comedia, 1986) apply theories of reading to television viewing.

5 Genre and intertextuality

Textual relations

One of the key effects texts have is to provide a context in which other texts are read and experienced. Surrounding texts influence readers' responses to any particular text. They suggest *metalingual* cues through which a text's codes may be recognised, understood and often questioned. And they link up with the *contextual* function through which a text indicates the context in which it is operating.

To continue to examine the social meanings and effects of texts, we therefore need to expand the kind of close semiotic analysis practised in preceding chapters. This type of analysis can disclose the interplay of signs and cultural values at work within one text. It can also suggest the various readings of, and attitudes to, the subject matter that is depicted. These are important steps to take if we want to investigate how a culture functions and how it is represented. But these steps need to be supplemented by considering contextual and metalingual interactions between texts that also affect the processes of textuality, address and reading.

Up to this point our focus on the possibilities of reading a single text has sought to explain one of the basic conditions of social communication: that every text is understood in different ways by different groups of people at different times. To understand this we mapped out the general polysemic potential of signs and texts. Such a focus must, however, be broadened, since one text never functions in total independence from others. We could compare the way a sign never operates by itself but generates meanings in contrast to, and combination with, other signs. The relationships among signs are central to their significance. Processes of meaning are also affected by the relationships among texts. We have already seen examples of this in the impact of anchorage on news photographs, where visual and verbal signs work together. Our analytical method needs to be able to address the effects of these connections.

Texts can interrelate in a wide range of ways, from imitation to confrontation. In general terms, these relations come into play when a text reproduces or refers to the paradigmatic selections and the syntagmatic combinations of signs from other texts. Reproductions may be more or less exact. At one extreme, the same signs can be used in the same order and elicit the same sort of interpretation or response from readers.

Take, for example, the movements and gestures of a military parade. The actions are selected from a strictly defined code of bodily signifiers and signifieds. The movements of each soldier make up a separate text. (We could also take a larger perspective and consider the parade itself as a text and each soldier a sign within it. This parade would be related to other parades as well as to other kinds of group behaviour. Texts are elastic, and their frames or boundaries can always be redrawn by readers.) As each soldier snaps to attention, the commanding officer sees a precise reproduction of connotations of authority and obedience. As more soldiers repeat the move, this authority and obedience are naturalised within the context of military life.

A set of complex interactions takes place among these soldier-texts: all reproduce the connotations separately, yet in doing so they construct a group effect. Each soldier signifies individually *and* contributes to establishing a cumulative meaning. In one sense, individual significance is dependent upon the group. The action of a single soldier—the snap of the salute, the click of heels—realises meaning through its resemblance to the actions of the others. Because it is similar, connotations of obedience and authority are immediately set up. In turn, the significance of the one text contributes to the overall effect and helps represent a mythology of discipline. Each successive salute seems to reinforce the truth of disciplinary values.

If a soldier trips or refuses to salute, the significance of the act is underlined by its contrast to the others. This contrast may also serve to disrupt the meaning of the other salutes, of the parade as a whole, and of the mythology it represents. One text could change the significance of the whole group by altering either the choice of signs or their combination. Even without making such overt paradigmatic or syntagmatic changes, a single text may always receive negotiated or oppositional readings which would question the seemingly settled body of connotations, meanings and values that it and the other texts have. The hundredth perfectly executed salute convinces a watching pacifist of the madness of military culture. Although this response is the opposite of the commander's, it is nonetheless the links *between* the soldier-texts that allow their apparent meaning to be challenged.

This example illustrates some of the key features of textual relations:

1 Most importantly, it suggests that the relationship between one text and others is always reciprocal: that is, the single text and the group affect each others' meanings.

2 The group provides the context of codes—the choice and combination of signs—within which the text is placed and read.

3 Some aspects of this context may act as metalingual cues to the preferred meanings of the signs, though whether these meanings are taken up will depend on readers' acceptance of that context.

4 A text can always be read against rather than within context, or the reader may connect it to a different set of texts—the tripping soldier could be removed from the set of parade texts and linked to a set of anti-military texts such as protest rallies and sit-ins.

This last point indicates a further feature of the reciprocal relations between one text and others. While the group of texts with similar codes does provide a context for the single text, it is one that remains dependent on the contribution of each text and of readers' responses to it. The relevance and coherence of the group codes are reinforced by every text that can be read as following them. Instead of confirming the codes, however, a text may disrupt or change them, and thereby affect the group meaning. Additionally, some readers may see one text as enacting this kind of disruption even though other readers continue to view the text as reinforcing the usual codes.

These possibilities suggest that textual groupings and their social meanings are not static. They can change through a single text's reworking or adapting the conventions of sign choice and combination. And they can also be altered through the activities of readers, whose interpretation of, or response to, a text may challenge the previously accepted meanings of texts like it.

Three elements are thus particularly important in thinking about the relationships between texts. These are:

1 The **texts** themselves, in terms of the selected and combined signs and their metalingual function.

2 The **intertext** of references that texts set up amongst themselves.

3 The activities and responses of different groups of **readers**.

Text, context and reader are the central concepts to be kept in mind when examining interactions among texts. In the rest of this chapter we will examine the different operations and effects of these interactions and the way these concepts are involved in them.

Genre

A **genre** is a grouping of texts which are similar in structure or subject matter.

Genre has often been used simply as a means of categorising texts. If they are considered to share enough characteristics they can all be placed in the same genre—plays like *Hamlet*, in which a good prince dies, are called tragedies. This use of the idea is fairly limited, and we will attempt to expand on it.

Genre is not simply a cataloguing device, but instead names the ways in which texts can relate to each other. As emerged in the previous section, the relations between texts—what makes them seem similar or not—are complex and variable. Furthermore, these relations depend not only on a text's internal features. They are also constructed through the social readings that may be given by different groups.

As was recognised in our discussion of texts in Chapter 4, all elements of textuality are cultural activities, from the selection of signs to the options for reading and relating them to different social experiences. Genre is no exception. In fact, because the premisses concerning a text's genre entail questions of sign choice, reader response and so on, genre is pre-eminently a cultural concept. Generic issues relate to all aspects of textuality as social process. They involve the conventions, and so also the exceptions, for thinking about texts in terms of:

1 *Textual production*, including semiotic factors such as sign choice and combination, as well as the technical and institutional features of a medium.
2 The ways that people can *read, interpret and use* texts.
3 The *relations* between texts and whether they affect each other in terms of contrast or similarity.
4 The *cultural conditions and contexts* in which texts are used and the effects of their use.

In short, considerations of genre deal with the *social functions* of texts.

Because it presumes that different texts and readings are always related, a further implication of the generic approach is that neither a text nor a reading can be unique. They both form part of a network of social meanings and values. No text is the absolute first to present certain ideas, just as no reading is the first to present a certain opinion. A text always re-presents ideas in a particular form or style. A reading always responds to a text in terms of certain pre-existing social values. One of the main revelations of generic analysis is of a text's and a reading's lack of originality. Their ideas and signs will always have appeared elsewhere. They come to a text trailing signifieds and values from previous uses.

This lack of originality is neither a defect nor a symptom of an unimaginative text or response. Rather it marks the interplay of attitudes and beliefs at work in the textual process. As we will see, such repetitions and interplay add to the social meanings of encounters with texts.

One of the aims of the generic analysis of texts is to investigate this interplay. By tracing the relationships among texts, we can examine differing social responses towards the subjects being represented. This kind of textual comparison and contrast reveals that such variation has two dimensions:

1 It shows that the connotations and myths triggered by signs change over time. That is, generic considerations can uncover the *historical process* of social meaning.

2 By comparing texts and responses from the same time period (or from a relatively restricted period, say of a couple of years), one can begin to gauge dominant and alternative ways of understanding a particular topic. In this case, generic analysis reveals the *contemporary structure* of social meaning.

These two dimensions may interact to produce further effects. For example, generic variation may also suggest conflicts or contradictions within a structure of meaning and so point to the beginnings of change in attitudes and values. In that case, comparisons between texts and readings would show a contemporary structure of meaning being transformed into historical process and change.

Hence there are a number of advantages in introducing the concept of genre into the analysis of social texts. In the first place, genre foregrounds the influence of surrounding texts and ways of reading on our response to any one text. More specifically, it confirms textuality and reading as functions rather than things, and shows that they take place within two kinds of context. The first is the context of *other texts* and the cultural values and myths they represent; the second is the context of *social readings, interpretations and responses* to these values and myths. Just as a text's structure is influenced by similar texts, so readings are shaped by traditions and trends of response. Genre exemplifies the fact that reading and producing texts are social actions.

Finally, the concept of genre suggests that texts, readings and the myths they support and enact are historically placed. Analysis based on comparison and contrast is the premise of the generic approach to textual relations, and it enables us to measure against each other the changing representations of, and responses to, cultural values and beliefs. In considering effects of genre, our understanding of texts can move beyond the static analysis of single objects and begin to see that textuality, representation and reading participate in unfolding processes of social and historical change.

Reading genre

These processes can best be studied by focusing on a particular genre and examining its textual and contextual effects along with the range of readings that confront it. As a genre, media news illustrates many of these important points.

Let's begin by considering the opening sequence of the ABC television news. Before the first item commences, we hear the stirring theme music, a set of aural signs that connote importance, drama and, as the theme rises to a crescendo, viewers joining together to form the 'Australian public'. While the music sounds, we see moving, computerised pictures of the globe, which suggest the hi-tech, dynamic, international world that is the subject of an equally hi-tech, dynamic, international coverage.

Figure 5.1

As the images change, there is a recurrent focus on Australia, the colours of the Australian flag, and the flag itself. Again, there is a double connotation—of the importance of Australian events as news in themselves and of an Australian perspective on international happenings.

The sequence then includes a series of visual headlines. The newsreader, who has not yet appeared on the screen, explains the significance of these brief shots. In this case, they cover the national economy, state politics (the news is broadcast in Queensland), and an international event in which Australia is involved—the war between Papua New Guinea and Bougainville secessionists. Following these scenes, a computer graphic version of the ABC logo is presented. Finally, as we see in Figure 5.1, the newsreader introduces himself, with a series of phatic comments and facial expressions, and then begins the first story.

This segment of the news can be framed as a text in itself. Most of us would probably find it very familiar: that is, we identify it *generically*. The precise set and order of the signs may be different to those we have seen before: the headline stories are not the same every night; the newsreader changes every now and then; the ABC production team might refashion the logo or update the images of the world and the soundtrack. The other networks have varied 'signatures'—different logos, themes and newsreaders. Nonetheless, as experienced TV viewers, we easily identify the kind of text. Paradigmatic and syntagmatic variations do not disrupt the generic structure of 'the news'.

By responding to the text in terms of its genre, we are able to distinguish it from other texts in the surrounding social and TV discourses. This kind of response suggests the basic notion of genre as a means of categorising texts. If the generic factors are considered more closely, however, a wide range of interpretive and cultural effects can be observed. For in recognising a genre, readers are subject to an array of socialising factors.

One of the first steps involved in recognising the text as news is to acknowledge the significance of the reported events. Not everything that occurs in the world is considered newsworthy; indeed, the media use a set of **news values** to decide the events that are to be covered. According to these values, events that are negative, that involve élite persons, that may affect the audience, of which film can be shown (for TV news), and so on, are suitable to be shown as news. They fulfil the media's criteria of what is 'newsworthy'. News values designate what is to be included as news. They are generic markers of the signs that can be used.

In defining which occurrences can be signified as news, news values also reinforce cultural values. The principles of news selection work generically and socially. The selected subject matter is assumed to match social concerns. Since the events are given news coverage, their importance is emphasised. They are transformed into *issues*. The reported issues are then reinforced as central, social concerns. The process is circular—social concerns define the issues which reinforce the concerns. Each story then develops such concerns either by noting the general importance and relevance of the events or by offering specific judgements and interpretations of them.

As they recognise these events as 'news', viewers are being offered generic and social judgements of what is meaningful to them. An acceptance of this position suggests the potential influence of a genre's socialising effects. The address and conative function of news texts can have a powerful impact on the audience.

The first of these effects, then, is that the news *tells us what is important*. As noted earlier, the media use a fairly strict set of values to decide what constitutes 'news'. Events which may be of the utmost interest to some social groups are simply not included.

A second effect is that the news *represents the events in specific ways*. A recurrent structure of reporting is used. It has a couple of key features. First, the news relies on official figures—government, administrative, professional and other appointed speakers—to give the **primary definition** of an event from the perspective of the organisation they represent. Then, once the primary definition has set up the terms of the story, a single opposing view (usually that of a rival group) can be included. The effect of this inclusion of the two sides of the story is twofold: because it is the subject of conflict, the importance of the issue seems beyond question, and alternative views on the issue are excluded. Either one side or the other is 'right', and the issue remains fixed in the terms offered by these two groups.

These two aspects of news reporting—*choice of subject matter* and *structure of representation*—make up the genre's key paradigmatic and syntagmatic features. These aspects do more than simply set up the conventional appearance and content of the news. They also work to position viewers in relation to the events in specific ways. The selection of stories, along with their primary definitions and closed for-or-against structure, invites viewers to interpret 'the world' in specific terms. The opening of the ABC news suggests that these terms revolve around a notion of 'Australianness'. Although the text does not explain or define this notion, the colours, flag and images of the country give the events a significantly Australian connection.

Hence these generic features not only tell us *what* the news is, they also suggest *how* to read it, the kind of perspective we can adopt. At a general level, this viewpoint is structured as 'in the national interest'. In specific stories, however, it is also based on the perspective provided by the primary definitions. Viewers are positioned to depend upon, and consent to, those expert opinions.

A further socialising pressure derives from these generic traits. In instructing readers and viewers on what is newsworthy and how it is to be understood, the news genre fits them with a cultural identity. This identity is both conative and phatic, being based on a shared way of representing and viewing the world. The textual processes of connotation and myth set up a strong phatic identity of addresser and addressee. They invite a preferred reading of the news, through which the audience may accept the selection and interpretation of material as their own choice. If the invitation is taken up, the various national and social positions implied by the material are adopted. With the opening of the ABC news, this means another member of the 'Australian viewing public' is produced, as he or she is greeted by the smiling face of the newsreader.

At the same time, the generic processes of the news are naturalised. The processes of selection and representation arranged through news values and primary definers may go unnoticed. Instead, myths of the truthfulness of the subject matter, of its inter- pretations, and of the objectivity of the genre are reinforced.

The reading position that the genre sets up may be rejected, either totally or partially. Audience members might find that the social viewpoint of the news alienates or oppresses their perspective. In a few pages we will discuss some examples of this possibility by seeing how generic structures can be questioned, and then rejected or revised by readers. Genres, as ways of representing the world, can be contested and changed.

Generic change

Since it implies a kind of group identification, the notion of genre may suggest that textual relations are based on stability and that genres exist because textual relations are constant. The potential influence of the news outlined in the previous section also seemed to suggest that generic effects realise cultural stability; the positioning of the viewer as 'Australian' would reinforce enduring myths of the nation and of citizenship.

By examining a series of generically related texts, we can, however, start to see that genres do not only work to tie down social meaning. The choice and combination of key signs may also alter as one genre is affected by interactions with others. The responses of different groups of readers can exert pressure to change key patterns of meaning. Accordingly, we may need to rethink our initial definition of genre. In short, we can think of genre as a body of signs, texts, meanings and responses which are constantly being reworked. Rather than denoting settled social meaning, a genre's seemingly stable point of significance forms a launching pad for revisions.

By looking at generic effects in one medium we can observe the recurring signs and codes, and then start to trace the range of shifts that can occur. Look at the following series of photographs of businessmen from *The Australian* (Figure 5.2). One of the features of this genre is its focus on men. Most of the pictures are taken from the business section of *The Australian*, although some are also from the main news section. The different texts appear to quote and imitate each other. Their cross-referencing seems to stabilise the way they can be read, reinforcing preferred meanings and social values.

What are the recurring signs and codes? In most cases the camera is pointing slightly upwards at the figure, who makes eye contact with the reader by gazing downwards. The figure is in the centre of the frame and his face is well lit. He is dressed in a work 'uniform', usually a dark suit, though sometimes in such pictures more active gear such as an industrial coat and hard hat are worn. The accompanying written texts, though not included here, are invariably about the figure's commercial successes.

Perhaps most striking is the figure's relaxed but controlled pose, leaning either backwards, at ease in the surrounds, or forwards in concentration. The background is also relevant. It seems to signify the business setting in which the figure is expert—an aeroplane or ship, a boardroom or desk with computer. Against this, the authoritative pose connotes mastery and expertise. We might also note the prominence of the hands throughout the pictures, connoting a readiness to work and an ability to seize opportunities and success.

The recurring signifiers and connotations suggest a set of positive codes of masculinity and commerce. They invoke and reinforce a cultural myth of the businessman as hero. Economic success is naturalised as the output of a poised, male individual. The combination of visual style (pose, camera angle, lighting), the characterisation of a single figure featured against these backgrounds, and the hard or business news context in which the texts appear, distinguishes the genre. (The contextual function is important; if these pictures were presented in a satirical article on men's fashions, the connotations would change dramatically.) Again, the relationship

Figure 5.2a

Figure 5.2b

Figure 5.2c

Figure 5.2d

Figure 5.2e

between the photographs and the genre is reciprocal: each text is influenced by the generic rules in the way it is put together; the generic rules are reinforced by each text.

As noted earlier, the rules also affect the way the texts can be read. With the same codes and conventions being used and re-used to depict businessmen, the preferred meanings are more closely tied to cultural myths of masculinity, individualism and commerce. It becomes more difficult not to see these connotations, texts and genre as natural and true. They interact to establish a socially authoritative representation of the world and of people in it, including the positioning of readers.

There are various ways in which this particular genre can change. The first is related to *social context*. Since signs and codes work in such a context they are affected by changes within it. Such effects are also reciprocal: a genre develops according to prevailing social conditions; transformations in genre and texts can influence and reinforce social conditions. In both cases the transformations are part of a historical process of cultural change.

For example, the next photograph is of a businesswoman (Figure 5.3). It was not placed in the business section but framed as part of a 'human interest' story. This location suggests that the

Figure 5.3

image of woman as business leader constitutes an exceptional case within the genre. Nonetheless, the genre is flexible enough to represent and include such a figure.

Many of the same generic signs we noted earlier are reproduced here: the upward camera angle, the assured but comfortable stance, power dressing, the work environment, the symbolic aspect of being on top of the world. A notable difference is that the woman does not meet our gaze. She looks up, connoting future prospects—her own, the company's, perhaps the future of other women in the corporate world. Such shifts within the genre register changing social conditions, with the entrance of more women into domains and activities that had been exclusively performed by men.

While the gender of the business figure may change, the other myths that link commercial success to heroism and individuality have not altered. If the gender code is emphasised, the text could be read as signifying a step forward for women in certain respects. If the business code is underlined, then the genre's expansion could be viewed as a sign of the extended cultural reference of commercial success, which can now apply to women as well as men. The augmented genre may signify the strengthening of the business ethos through the community rather than any revision of it. Generic change can itself be interpreted as symptomatic of different cultural trends.

A further way in which a genre can change is by interacting with *other media and genres*. Paradoxically, one of the basic rules of genre seems to be that it is always breaking its own boundaries, with key signs and codes often cutting across to other contexts. As various kinds of texts interact with each other they recycle signs, codes and social values of different genres. These are transposed to a different setting and assume a new reference. Once again, the effects of such movements are hard to predict. Social myths may be more strongly reinforced and naturalised by being represented in a wider range of texts. On the other hand, the values that a genre tends to advocate can be disrupted or questioned through the contextual shift.

We can see an example of the extension of the myths of business success and masculine individuality in the advertisement in Figure 5.4. In part, its connotations derive from the genre of news photographs previously considered. Many of their features are recycled: the prominent hand, not ready to work but already grabbing the fruits of its labours (a celebratory gin and tonic, or perhaps a reinvigorating mineral water); individuality; business dress; black and white photography; a view, from on high, over the metropolis. The major change is that the businessman does not face the reader. Instead, we are positioned to see with him. We come close to sharing his successful identity. Yet the angle of our view is not quite his; the desired identity eludes us. Of course, the text suggests, we can get a lot closer by obtaining an American Express card.

Despite the shift in the codes and signs from news to advertising texts, the myths about masculinity and success continue to be emphasised. A set of intertextual effects may also be triggered by the shift. For it seems that both genres, advertising and news, are quoting from each other, moving signs from one setting to another. The effects of such moves are not always predictable and can, in fact, work in quite contradictory ways.

For example, the apparent objectivity of the news images may be transposed to the advertisement and serve to make the positive results of possessing a credit card indisputable. At the same time, the repetition of the images in the advertisement may reveal that in addition to providing information the news photographs are also selling something—a cultural system based on economic success and individuality.

This last point suggests that in addition to supplying signs and codes, thereby supplementing their social meanings, different

Figure 5.4

genres may react *against* each other. The connections between texts need not lead to a synthesis of values and meanings, but to contests between them. This notion of conflictual textual relations is the last outcome of generic interaction that we will consider. Genres also participate in conflictual dialogues. In so doing they open up opportunities for readers and viewers to question and rewrite the myths and values they represent.

Dialogism

Just as signs interact within texts, and texts interact within genres, so genres interact with one another. At times, these interactions can be relatively harmonious, and the genres' meanings can combine with or reinforce one another. It is also possible for there to be degrees of difference or contradiction among genres. When such differences emerge, a unity or synthesis of the genres' meanings is precluded.

These differences can occur in various ways. As we saw in the previous chapter, a cigarette advertisement promising prestige and status can be challenged by a medical warning. Two genres clash within the one text, and it will be readers who decide which genre is more significant. The contradiction here is quite obvious. In other cases, conflicts of meanings may not be so prominent. They will result from the interpretations of certain groups of readers who, in relating the text to their social values and attitudes, challenge meanings that other groups might immediately accept. In this instance, conflicts of meaning may arise as the two (or more) groups of readers struggle to maintain their interpretation of the genre.

Texts and readings interact as if in dialogue with each other. When a group of readers uses certain texts it fills them with meanings related to its social position. Their readings debate or agree with the texts. As part of their response, readers then produce their own texts, ranging from raised eyebrows, to spoken comments, to published articles and books. These readings and texts will be more or less different from those produced by other groups. A dialogue of social values commences between readers and texts and among different groups of readers.

Texts and readings are an important site for the expression of differing social viewpoints. This kind of textual **dialogism** is another of the basic conditions of social discourse. It is also a fundamental aspect of social action. Texts and readings are used to impose cultural dominance and to offer resistance. Genres play an important role in this dialogic process. In the interaction and conflicts among genres we can see the connections between textuality and power.

If we now turn to a particular set of genres and texts we can start to see these social processes at work. Let's consider all the texts and genres related to a specific *social institution*. In official terms, they will have a hierarchical organisation, with some genres being privileged as more important, more relevant, and even more truthful than others. (At this point we want to consider the kinds of interactions that go on among institutional texts and genres.

Chapters 7 and 8 contain a more detailed discussion of the cultural and ideological workings of institutions, and the discourses that they produce.)

For example, running through the social institution of the *law* is an expansive set of genres and texts. At the top of this institution certain genres are employed: political statutes and decrees; decisions by attorneys-general; court rulings; findings of commissions of inquiry; pronouncements by law societies; statements by police officials; academic research reports, and so on. Through a combination of subject matter, style, the roles of the authors and speakers, and the contexts in which they are produced, these genres have the broadest social authority. The figures who produce these sorts of texts—politicians, judges, commissioners, and other official spokespersons—are the primary definers of the legal institution. They establish official definitions of the law.

These figures also establish which genres and texts are most important in running an institution. The genres they use exert great power in setting up the terms through which the rest of us can think about legal issues and texts. The more these genres are used, the more strongly the positions of the primary definers and of others involved in the institution are entrenched. As seen in an earlier section, the social impact of these genres and their definers is frequently intensified by the address of the news media to the community.

The hierarchy of legal genres and texts does not, however, stop at these levels. It moves from there to include media reports on the law; consultations between clients and lawyers; arrests and orders issued by police; courtroom dramas in books and on screen; two people chatting about the enforcement of drink driving laws while they wait at a taxi rank; groups protesting about cuts to legal aid funding; people complaining on talkback radio about old-fashioned judges, and so on. Although each of these texts belongs to a different genre, all of them refer to the same social institution. Yet they do not all represent it in the same way or with the same effects. The connotations of the 'law' range from positive to negative, and the influence of the different genres on other people varies considerably.

There are also specific kinds of interaction going on among these genres. There is a tendency for the official genres to represent a shared conception of the law as a 'pillar of society'. They might at times disagree on the best way to fortify the law—a royal commission might challenge the views of politicians—but none of these genres questions the necessity of supporting the law.

In contrast, we might note that the last few genres mentioned above—private conversations, public protests and comments—

contest primary definitions of the official texts. They question the authoritative versions of the legal institution and propose their own rival definitions of what the law is and how it operates.

Although genres are often organised hierarchically, the hierarchy is *never* totally fixed or accepted. Instead, there is a continuing process that actively reads and responds to institutions as they are depicted in official genres. Part of this process is also to offer alternative definitions in other texts. These kinds of interactions between genres represent power relationships within the social system which are continuously being worked out. These interactions take place not only over the ways that social institutions operate but also over how they are represented and who is entitled to speak about them.

Hence the interaction of social genres is like a dialogue in which speakers are always negotiating their positions and identities. A clear example of this process can be seen in the following exchange between a patient and a doctor. It reveals much about the genre contests that construct the social institution of medicine:

> **Doctor:** Good morning, Mrs Johnson. I'm Doctor Spencer.
> **Patient:** Good morning, Doctor. I've come as I'm sure I have a, um, hormonal imbalance. I seem to have symptoms of . . .
> **Doctor:** Just about every woman I see thinks she has hormonal troubles nowadays. Now why don't you just describe the problem. I'll do the diagnosis.

The exchange sets up a relationship of social power between the two speakers. The doctor initiates the dialogue, first by establishing both speakers' social identities through assigning titles and names—'Dr', 'Mrs' (and note the doctor, not the patient, uses names). The doctor also imposes two roles—one who knows and one who doesn't. In this scheme, only the doctor has legitimate knowledge. He or she reacts sharply when sensing that the patient has usurped some specialised language. The implication seems to be that the patient, in starting to use the doctor's speech genre, threatens the power hierarchy of the medical institution. She is rapidly silenced as the doctor seeks to restrict the sort of speech she can use and thereby control the situation.

This exchange also reveals that dialogues between genres do not merely reflect relationships that pre-exist in the community. Rather, they are one of the key avenues through which these relationships are founded, reinforced or challenged. In the interaction and contests between genres, questions of social power are worked through.

We can see the way that genres and power interact in more detail by looking at two items from ABC TV news (Figures 5.5 and 5.6). This time the institution that is being represented is the national economy. Initially we may note that one of the main effects of news on the economy is less to inform viewers than to reproduce the order and primary definitions of the genres used by politicians and 'experts'. We could say that the referential function is less dominant here than the metalingual and phatic functions, which work to support the official hierarchy of who can speak authoritatively about the community, and in what terms.

Figure 5.5

JOHN KERIN
Treasurer

The spoken text uses the news genre's standard signs and connotations to establish this authority. First, it sets up a national identity for viewers, and foregrounds supposedly shared viewpoints and experiences. Collective nouns help to realise these phatic effects: 'Australia has', 'we are now closer to living within our means.' Second, it employs a specialised vocabulary to imply the truth of this account of the nation. The metalingual and formal functions are at work here: 'monthly surplus on goods and services', 'seasonally adjusted balance of payments'. Lastly, in typifying the way that the news genre organises material, the text sets up a single primary definer as the official source of knowledge, 'Treasurer John Kerin' (Figure 5.5). But it then places this definer in conflict with another authority, 'the Opposition'. The meanings of the story are pinpointed by these two figures.

In the same news bulletin, a later story on age pensioners who are protesting at their social situation, contests the settled meanings and definitions that have been presented. It does so in two related ways: by varying the standard generic pattern of news stories, and by introducing different speech genres to depict events. The introduction to the story does not establish a common identity for viewers by using 'we', but depicts one specific group, 'Australia's growing band of disgruntled pensioners'. The primary spokesperson for this group is not an official primary definer with a public identity. It is an unknown man, who proceeds to use a colloquial, personal style of speech to offer an alternative version of the economic situation (see Figure 5.6). He contrasts 'the people in Canberra' with his social group which is 'fed up' and is seeking 'a better deal'. He mixes genres, juxtaposing official and everyday terms, making the former seem incapable of registering personal experience: the experts' reliance on the 'CPI cost of living index' is 'balderdash'.

Placed together, the two texts reveal a number of important points about the social functions of genres. First, they reflect the hierarchical structure of genres that is used to represent and organise a social institution like the economy: the authorities define a reality on which others subsequently comment. Next, they show that a single genre, such as media news, never works entirely in a singular way. It is marked by degrees of variation that may pressure its conventional cultural impact. In this case, the second story clearly remained within the genre of news, but in doing so it questioned the adequacy of the institutional hierarchy and primary definitions that the bulletin had already represented by depicting an alternative viewpoint. This viewpoint used a different genre to depict the state of the economy.

Finally, the texts reveal the processes of *social negotiation* that occur as different genres interact. The contrast between the phrases 'balderdash' and 'CPI index' suggests two distinct ways of conceiving a social situation. The pensioner seems to use the official phrase in order to deflate its meaning and importance through his colourful, colloquial dismissal of it. The dialogic clash of generic styles makes a strong social point.

One of the most significant means through which genres and texts register the exchange of social values is the way they refer to, or depict, each other. In this example, the older man's quotation of the official terms enables him to critique them. In

Figure 5.6

repeating these terms, he undermines them. Through analysing these kinds of *intertextual* links, echoes and repetitions—the way one text uses other texts to make its own points—we can trace the shifts in social values that are taking place. As we have seen, texts constantly cite and quote other texts, and in removing their generic norms to new contexts they adapt their meanings and implications.

This dialogic, intertextual process is exemplified by *parody and satire*. In parodying the style of another text—be it the jargon of specialists or the uniform of officials—the new text critiques the other's social perspective. The practice of graffiti is a revealing example of the way texts re-use others in articulating critical social ideas. Graffiti rework and reclaim public places, turning them into spaces for private performances and interpersonal conversations. They challenge social institutions by rewriting their codes and connotations, using satire and irony to transform their meanings.

Graffiti on advertising billboards are perhaps the clearest example of this kind of intertextual challenge. They re-evaluate the text's generic structure to uncover the absurdity of a product's link to paradise or the violence of its attitude towards women. Graffiti set billboard ads against themselves, and in so doing reveal that the interactions among texts and genres are always a form of social action.

Exercises

1 Genre can often work as a compact form of communication, relying on a few recurring signs to enable readers or viewers to recognise a text. By examining the opening sequence of three or four TV soap operas, try to identify the key signs that distinguish the genre. What sorts of social values and myths do these signs signify? Write a parody of the openings that questions those values.

2 Identify and analyse some examples of teenage sub-cultures that adapt the fashion genres or uniforms of official social groups.

3 Sketch out the hierarchical organisation of a social institution such as the university department in which you study or the place where you work. What kinds of genres and texts are produced at the different levels?

Sources and further reading

Many works on genre discuss the concept in relation to literature and film. One of the clearest introductions to traditional literary genres is Heather Dubrow's *Genre* (London: Methuen, 1982). A more complicated but important discussion of genre, especially in relation to film, is also called *Genre*, by Steve Neale (London: British Film Institute, 1980). If Dubrow tends to assume genres are relatively stable things, there is also a growing body of work which concentrates precisely on their instability, and the ways in which genres lend themselves to complex and sometimes transgressive permutations. See Anne Freadman and Amanda Macdonald's *What is This Thing called 'Genre'?* (Mt Nebo, Queensland: Boombana, 1992) and Freadman's 'Untitled: (On Genre)', *Cultural Studies* 2 (1), 1988.

Some of the key ideas in this chapter derive from the work of the Russian literary critic M.M. Bakhtin. Bakhtin's work is quite complex, but the essay 'Speech Genres' in the collection *Speech Genres and Other Late Essays* (Austin: University of Texas Press, 1986) is accessible. Two recent studies apply many of the key notions of genre and intertextuality to examining popular television, film and fiction. These are John Fiske, *Television Culture* (New York: Methuen, 1987) and Tony Bennett and Janet Woollacott's more complex *Bond and Beyond: The Political Career of a Popular Hero* (London: Macmillan, 1987).

For detailed analysis of the news media, see Stan Cohen and Jock Young's collection of essays, *The Manufacture of News* (London: Constable, 1973), and John Hartley's *Understanding News* (London: Methuen, 1982).

6 Narrative

Texts and time

One of the key points that our study of textual relations has revealed is that texts are not part of a static structure of social meanings. By looking at genres of texts we can see the ways in which signs, connotations and myths develop over time. They are influenced by changing cultural beliefs, and they represent such changes to readers and viewers. Especially in the case of popular, mass media texts, these changes are fed back into wide sectors of the community. They are responded to in various ways by different groups, who not only interpret the texts but produce new texts about them. In this continuing process of textual reading and production, the history, or histories, of a society unfold.

Genres and texts, then, are located in time. We can use this diachronic angle to supplement our analysis of their synchronic structures. But there is also another way in which the notion of time is central to textual and generic processes. Texts and genres are not only situated in social time, they *depict* the passing of time. Time is a key semiotic element in many genres. It works paradigmatically and syntagmatically, being used as sign as well as a means of structuring ideas.

Consider one of the simplest types of 'time texts': a before-and-after advertisement. Time itself is not the signified product but is a metonym that indicates the product's effects. In addition, time is also being used to arrange other signs in the text—the straggly

---

Narration consists of the processes and effects of representing *time* in texts.

A **narrative** is any text that functions through these processes and effects.

---

split ends of 'before' are transformed into 'after's' bouncy, shiny hairstyle. The way time is used here confirms that the paradigmatic and syntagmatic axes of texts always work in tandem. Time is a structural and meaningful component of many texts.

Narratives are everywhere in the social texts that surround us. We are all very competent in the cultural skills of producing and analysing them. This makes them an important topic for the study of texts and textuality. As was the case when we analysed texts and genres, in this chapter we will try to slow down familiar, everyday narrative processes in order to examine the ways in which they set up certain patterns of meaning to which readers and viewers respond.

Because narratives are used in many different kinds of texts and social contexts, they cannot properly be labelled a genre. Narration is just as much a feature of non-fictional genres such as news, documentaries and biographies as it is of fictional genres such as popular romance, spy thrillers and TV situation comedies. It is also used in different kinds of media—from language in a novel, to visual images in a film, to the old and new building designs in a city centre which may tell the stories of the community's development.

Narration is not specific to one type of text over others. Indeed, one of the most interesting aspects of narrative processes is that they cut across distinctions between, for example, fiction and non-fiction, verbal and visual texts. The concept of narrative enables us to pursue the analysis of many textual structures. It is one of the main strategies used by seemingly very different texts to represent reality. Further, by studying the stories that social groups produce, we can gain insights into the way their culture functions.

Narrative is a way of organising cultural signs. We can think of it as a textual *mode* rather than a genre: one that depicts events and ideas by foregrounding their movement through time. The reference to time is, however, only one of the important aspects of narrative. As we will see, there are many variations in narrative structures—different ways of telling and retelling events—all producing distinctive effects and possibilities of response. Because of these possibilities and their widespread use, the study of narrative offers numerous insights into the social interactions that occur when texts are produced and read.

Narrative movement

One of the first distinctions between texts that we can rethink by using concepts of narrative is the contrast between continuing texts like novels and films and seemingly static or unchanging texts like magazine advertisements, photographs and pictures. The latter also allude to the passing of time and events. By tuning into the way such texts incorporate narrative elements, we may gain a fuller understanding of the meanings they represent. Narrative structures often intensify the kinds of generic and textual effects we have been considering.

The advertisement in Figure 6.1 has a number of links with the set of business and economic texts and genres we were analysing in the previous chapter. Recurring features include the use of black and white photography, eye contact between viewer and the male figure, and a specialised vocabulary with terms such as 'superannuation' and 'Balanced Pool Super Fund'. These signs combine to portray the modern 'businesskid', an adult-child who seems to be both vulnerable and in control. His hybrid nature triggers the cute humour that is often a central code in the advertising genre.

As well as being a portrait, the text also sets a narrative in motion. It tries to tell a story by taking a number of specific steps. First of all, it proposes a *chronological and causal chain of events* that moves from the present into the future. It envisages the progression of time and calls for action to be taken: 'You must provide now for your later years.' Secondly, the text introduces *characters*: the businesskid Rex, who is to take action, and his 'partner', on whose behalf he is to act. It foresees the course of a person's life, suggesting novelistic and biographical genres which are also rooted in narrative. It even establishes a *goal* or *climax* for this life: 'a decent lifestyle'. Finally, the text passes judgement on the quality and personality of its central character: Rex is potentially an heroic figure, a decision maker who will respond actively to the social imperative to 'make a decision', and thereby ensure a happy ending.

We can see that this narrative structure is closely tied to cultural myths such as the potential of childhood, the equation between financial and moral success, and an esteem for masculine action. Economic issues are translated into an optimistic tale of individual success. With the intertwining of a narrative pattern, this portrait of a single figure becomes a culturally suggestive text. It tells a story that moves in two ways: as a progression from past to future, and as a persuasive model to be imitated.

Figure 6.1

You Can't Ignore Superannuation

Your superannuation decisions are amongst the most important you will ever make – **no matter how old you are now.**

Why? Think about it. In retirement you will be content if you have enough money for a decent lifestyle. With less than enough money **there is no escaping that you will not be content** (and most probably concerned for your partner's welfare if you are not around).

You must provide **now** for your later years.

You must seek responsible **performance** to keep up with inflation and **you must take advantage of the tax deductions** the Government offers.

Potter Warburg Asset Management offers a wide range of investments created specifically **for personal and company superannuation.**

Our Balanced Pooled Super Fund achieved the highest return of any Australian super fund in the extremely difficult period from November 1987 to February 1991.

Make an important decision now. Review your superannuation position and ask for more information on Potter Warburg Super Trusts and a Prospectus on **008 331 335,** Melbourne **(03) 655 2100,** or return the Reply Paid coupon (no stamp required) or ask your investment adviser.

Join the tens of thousands of Australians who invest with Potter Warburg Asset Management and look to retirement with greater confidence.

To: Reply Paid 1361
Potter Warburg Asset Management Limited
Level 16, No 1 Collins Street Melbourne VIC 3000
Please send me more information on the Potter Warburg Super Trusts.

Mr/Mrs/Miss/Dr _____ First Name _____ Initial _____

Surname _____

Address _____

_____ Postcode _____

Tel: (H) _____ (W) _____

Applications can only be made on the form in the current prospectus.   ACN 006 165 975

Growing Stronger in Australia

The narrative structure seems to accentuate and complement other textual and semiotic features in three main ways:
1 It offers a **time frame** over which the signified connotations and myths will come into play.
2 It reinforces a network of social meanings by transforming events into *actions* performed by **characters** (in our example, myths of personal achievement support those of social and economic success).

3 It adds the enjoyment of a story—through the use of characters and forecasts of their actions—to the text's signs.

The narrative gets us in. We like stories.

Narrative pleasure and desire

By alluding to news and biographical genres, the 'Rex' text is able to address readers via a network of positive connotations. It depicts economic and personal values in a rosy light, and encourages us to read them in that way.

The narrative elements intensify these positioning effects. They invite readers to join the story and try to foresee its outcome. We could do this in a few ways—by empathising with the main character or by putting ourselves in his place, or both. Of course, many readers will also refuse the narrative's invitation and turn the page or criticise the values that are connoted. But for those who read the text affirmatively, Rex's story offers a certain degree of pleasure. The question of whether he will make the right decision seems happily anticipated by hints of his success.

One of the most powerful signifying effects narratives often have is to offer different kinds of **pleasure** to readers and viewers. These pleasures may arise in a number of ways, and we have already seen some of them at work: the chance to observe or even identify with a particular character, watching or sharing their prospects and experiences; the satisfaction of seeing events and situations resolved. We will return to these particular aspects a little later when we consider narrative structure and point of view in more detail.

Readers enjoy and anticipate narratives. There are two pleasures involved, a kind of double **desire**: the motivation to follow a narrative and the satisfaction from doing so. Readers both desire narratives and respond to them through desire. This may range from curiosity, to yearning, to lust. Even where readers might, as we will also see, reject one ending and seek to replace it with others, the enjoyment derived from narrative may still be at work. In fact, the desire for narrative pleasure seems to stimulate readers' efforts to re-tell and re-work stories.

The advertisement in Figure 6.2 is a good example of a text provoking various kinds of desire. It has an enigmatic quality and seems to raise questions rather than give information. Who is she? Who is she waiting for? Whose car is it? Where is this scene? What does her expression suggest? It puts readers to work, forcing them to weigh up contrasting possibilities. She is alone; she is waiting for somebody; she surveys the scene; she looks for someone; she

Figure 6.2

squats with relaxed authority; she crouches submissively; she leans on the car possessively; she leans on the car for support, and so on.

The text does not resolve these alternatives but rather triggers a desire to know the answers. The referential function is not fulfilled but remains in process. The process is a social one, as our path to knowledge is routed through contesting cultural myths about gender and women. For the moment, these seem to concentrate around the woman in the picture. Is she a powerful or a dependent figure?

The desire to know the answer motivates our engagement with the text. But how does the text stimulate this desire? The ambiguity seems to arise because it looks as if the picture has been taken from a larger syntagm. We try to imagine a framing context that will help us to interpret these signs. And we mainly develop this context out of other texts with which we are familiar. Our previous reading of narrative genres comes into play, and we search for metalingual cues through which we may comprehend this one.

The signs here seem to constitute an episode from a narrative, perhaps a movie. In this case, answers to our questions might or might not be resolved by what takes place in the next scene (if there is a next scene; this could be the last shot), or by what has happened in an earlier one (we might just have seen her companion hop into a truck with someone else).

These possibilities inspire our interest. Our familiarity with road movies and love stories provides interpretive options, but the text seems to suspend them. The verbal anchorage does little to diminish curiosity. Instead it may increase our uncertainty. It offers a name—the product's of course, but might it also be hers? Is she the answer we are looking for? Our wish to know her and to know the answer to the narrative seem to be fused. (In an effect that many narratives construct, the female character becomes the *object* of our reading. We will return to this effect in the final section of this chapter.)

The story stays up in the air. The narrative provokes multiple desires as it draws us into the signified world. It interweaves our reading with questions that concern the narrative (What's happening? What's going to happen?), while also having sexual undertones (Who is she? Who is she with? Or is she alone?), as well as personal allusions (Where do I, the reader, fit in? Am I part of this story?). The questions remain open, and because of this the address to us is all the more powerful. Our desire for knowledge seems to be inscribed *within* the picture.

In structuring traces of character and plot into this allusive form, the text triggers a complex kind of cultural desire. (Since it is an advertisement, the preferred goal of this desire is, at one level, the product: the clothes will give us all the answers.) It is less the signs in themselves that are provoking than the range of inter-textual and generic references they set in process. Such provo-cation hinges on the way the signs are put together. The structure of stories, and of ways of telling them, is a key aspect of the narrative process. Structure orchestrates readers' reactions and positions their responses.

Narrative structure

The two texts we have been considering have quite different structures. The first one implies a happy ending, with the trans-formation of Rex into an active, successful man. The second defers, perhaps rejects, this kind of neat conclusion. As we saw, both kinds of structure offer readers different kinds of pleasure. This type of variation in endings or **closure** is only one aspect of possible variations in narrative structure. Let's now examine these possibilities more closely.

The first point to make is that as a structure, a narrative can be seen as built out of smaller units. In this view:

> A **narrative** is a structured sequence of events in time.

This is a very basic definition, but it will prove useful since it will allow us to examine not only the ways in which narratives are assembled, but also the ways in which they unfold and conclude.

The next point to note is that, like all texts, narratives have a structure of **address**. They, too, have an addresser and an addressee.

> Narratives are told by *narrators* to *narratees.*
>
> The **narrator** is the narrative's *addresser*
>
> The **narratee** is the narrative's *addressee.*

We will develop these ideas later on. But from the start we should note that the narrator is not the 'real life' author of the text, and the narratee is not the 'real life' reader. Rather, as is always the case with addresser and addressee, narrator and narratee are *textual positions*. They are *roles* that a narrative sets up to be occupied by writers and speakers, readers and audiences, as well as by the host of other voices and characters that appear throughout the text.

For the moment we will concentrate on the idea, that a narrative is a structured sequence of events. One particular sequence is used by many narratives. It has three phases: starting from a point of stability or equilibrium, the story moves into a phase of disruption before stability is renewed:

equilibrium ⟶ disruption ⟶ equilibrium

This three-part structure corresponds to another basic notion of narrative form: that a story has a beginning, middle and end.

Many genres employ both these structures. Their combined use provides one of the first angles through which, as was noted earlier, we can start to examine the parallels among apparently different types of social texts.

For example, news stories are based on an occurrence or event that breaks through or stands out from a background of the everyday and the ordinary. In practice, everyday life is not constantly stable but, as we will discuss in Chapter 9, endlessly varied. Nonetheless, the news media posit this kind of uniform background to contrast with the events and issues they cover. The reported event corresponds to the disruption phase of the narrative pattern. The disruption may concern an outstanding success but mostly it deals with some kind of crisis or dispute. As we noted when discussing generic news values in the last chapter, news events are mostly negative.

News contrasts such events with the everyday background. In so doing it reinforces the norms of daily life. News events are the exceptions. Once they are recognised as such, they no longer threaten the background. The act of reporting an event signifies that it has been recognised and fitted into the usual routine. In this way the news restores equilibrium to the narrative of everyday life.

Specific news stories also have a narrative structure. Two characters—the primary definers—are pitted against each other, and their contest is narrated to us by the newsreader or reporter. In some cases, a story will run for several days, having a number of 'chapters'. But in the main, news media tend to feature stories that are compact, one-off narratives, with closure already realised when the story goes to air. The longer the story and the less certain its ending, the more difficult it will be to arrange it into the three narrative phases.

One of the most popular cultural texts also using the three-part structure is the TV situation comedy. Usually these programs are set within a family home or use a quasi-family group in settings like a workplace, school, even a desert island or spacecraft. Regularly they commence with things going along smoothly until one of two kinds of disruption occurs: either one of the family members threatens to leave or re-organise the group, or an outsider arrives and jeopardises the group's integrity and unity. (Often there will be a sub-plot in which a mini-version of the disruption also arises.) In the course of the narrative, the threat is contained. The episode closes with the narrative and the group once more in happy stability. The same pattern then emerges in the next episode. Sitcom characters are nothing if not consistent in their behaviour.

This narrative pattern changes when we turn to another popular TV genre, the soap opera. The difference suggests one of the central generic contrasts between a TV series and a serial. Sitcoms exemplify the former, where the narrative pattern is reproduced from episode to episode. In soap operas, there is a series of narratives, each involving a different group of characters in a different setting. The soapie cast is larger than a sitcom's, and the titles often introduce either a community—a street or a neighbour-hood—rather than a family, or the type of workplace that is open to a wide range of characters, such as a hospital.

The soap opera defers closure. It always aims to have a number of narratives in process, cutting across the boundaries of each episode. A particular storyline can be resolved, but the others will remain up in the air, somewhere in the disruption phase. This usually gives the soapie narrative a slower rhythm than the sitcom, with total resolution never being realised.

The three genres we have surveyed all use very deliberate narrative structuring. While news stories and sitcoms follow the three-part pattern quite directly, soap operas draw out the disruption and resolution phases. Each genre regularly contains narratives within narratives. (Even a news or current affairs show can be considered a single story about 'the world'—the narrative of everyday life—with lots of sub-plots all told by one narrator, the newsreader or presenter.)

In all three cases, the narrative is usually located in the present, although flashbacks are sometimes used. Events are represented either as they take place or after they have occurred. These genres rely on a stable relationship both among the events they depict—basically one of chronological order—and between when the events occur and when they are narrated.

Such relationships can, however, vary and create different effects. The basic three-part structure we have considered so far can be complicated by changing connections between the order and timing of events and the way they are told. These kinds of variations in narrative structure can significantly affect audience response.

Story and plot

The distinction between *what* is told and *how* it is told is an important aspect of narrative structure. There are parallels here to the separation we made regarding the structure of the sign. Just as a sign comprises a signifier and signified, so narrative comprises two elements: **story** and **plot**. Plot is analogous to the signifier, and story to the signified. (Other terms are sometimes used to name these same elements; for example, plot is often called *discourse*, which is a term we have reserved for another meaning in Chapter 8. The point is not the term, but what the distinction between plot and story can tell us about the way narratives work.)

> **Plot** is *the narrative as it is read, seen or heard* from the first to the last word or image. That is, like a *signifier*, it is what the reader perceives.
>
> **Story** is *the narrative in chronological order*, the abstract order of events as they follow each other. That is, like a *signified*, story is what the reader conceives or understands.

The links among the story's events are usually temporal *and* causal: events at the beginning of a story not only happen earlier in time than those in the middle and at the end, but also bring about or cause these later events.

The order of events in the plot and the story can be quite different. Familiar examples of this kind of variation would include flashbacks or leaping forward in time. These occur in the plot—a character reminisces about the past or is projected into the future—but not in the abstract story, which still follows chronological order. For example, during the 1980s, a number of American movies came out, such as *Back to the Future* and *Peggy Sue Got Married*, that began in the present, with the main characters then being transported back to the 1950s by devices including a time machine or a traumatic bump on the head. In terms of plot, the narrative moved from present to past to present. But in terms of story, events moved in one direction only, from past to present.

By making the distinction between story and plot we are able to analyse many of the narrative strategies used to create effects for readers or viewers. A movie like *Peggy Sue Got Married* is able to depict a current situation and then move us back to see how it developed. It shows us alternative narrative possibilities that then evaporate as the main character chooses one man over another for the 'big date'. We can not only enjoy seeing how Peggy Sue's present life came to be, but also ponder what might have been 'if only'.

Suspense thrillers are another genre that often set story and plot against each other. The plot omits an early event, such as a crucial rendezvous between two characters, before revealing it at the end in order to conclude the story. Some crime narratives offer a variation on this pattern. The key event, like a murder, occurs just before the plot commences. The story, that has begun before we read page one or see the opening shot, and the aim of the plot, is to recapture what happened in this lost scene.

In all these cases, the alternating plot-story relationships are used to intrigue, frustrate and flatter readers' knowledge. In this context, the pleasures of narrative derive from the comparisons we make between what we (think we) know about what's going on, and what various characters do or don't know.

The plot-story connection is one of the main ways in which questions of narrative knowledge—who knows what— can be linked to ideas of social power. Narratives frequently show us that the one who knows the full story, in spite of any false leads which the plot may throw up, remains in control of the situation.

Events and closure

So far, we have been dealing with larger-scale aspects of narratives: their entire design and patterns of inclusion and exclusion. But the analysis of narrative structures can also become microscopic. Rather than assessing overall features, we can focus on their component parts—their events. Indeed, the most interesting types of narrative analysis take a double approach: they try to see how different sections of the narrative interact to produce its wider shape and effects.

> **Events** are the basic units of a story. They constitute the paradigm choices that are combined into the narrative syntagm.

For the sake of analysis, the textual frame can be e
movie, a single event can be bracketed off from the rest i
ined in detail. All the techniques of textual, generic and
analysis can be applied: that is, we can consider this ev
text, study it, and then relate it to other events in the movie. The
availability of movies on video makes it possible to analyse one
event frame-by-frame, each frame constituting, as it were, a complex text in itself.

We can think of an event as a *dynamic* part of the story; it
changes a situation. Events then combine into sequences to build
up the story. The story, as noted, may be made up of more than one
sequence of events, such as a main plot and a sub-plot.

There are two major kinds of events:

1 Some events *advance* the action by opening up alternatives: a
stranger walks into a room; a telephone rings; there is a knock
on the door.
2 Other events do not open up alternative actions but *expand* or
delay their results: two people turn around at once; a character
has to unlock the door to get to the phone; or he has just fallen
asleep.

These two types of events, advancing and delaying the action, move
the story through its equilibrium and disruption phases.

The way in which both kinds of events are combined affects
the *tempo* of the narrative, the pace at which situations are
introduced and resolved. Alternating these types of events builds up
suspense, that sense of not knowing what is about to happen. The
use of suspense is one of the strongest ways of involving audiences
in a narrative. In response, they attempt to use their familiarity
with the genre—the conventional sorts of things that happen and
characters who appear in it—to predict what will take place.

Events bring the narrative to its **closure**, resolving the
possibilities that have been opened up in the middle phase of
disruption.

> **Closure** is the restoration of narrative equilibrium.

The classic closure is of the 'they all lived happily ever after'
variety. The narrative's resolution often has great influence on
readers. The way things turn out seems to pass judgement on
preceding events, deciding who was really guilty and innocent, or
who was truly in love, or that things are better now, or have
returned to normal.

Accordingly, it is with narrative closure that the greatest pressure for the text's preferred reading may be activated. This pressure applies not only, say, to nineteenth century novels or Hollywood romances where, after many scenes of nefarious doings, hero and heroine are united in a marriage that promises contentment and children, and seems to symbolise broad cultural renewal. It also relates to hints of social integrity implied in a news report on violent events occurring in another country, and to claims of progress that emerge in a documentary on the latest scientific advance. In such celebratory endings, narrative closure works as a powerful means of both expressing positive cultural myths and positioning readers to accept them.

As for all texts, the readings that respond to these forms of closure will be social interpretations of the values and myths that have been raised. The narrative's preferred meaning is only one possible response. It can be contested both by the audience and by the viewpoints of different characters within the narrative. As we will discuss in the last section of this chapter, like genre, narrative also functions in a dialogic way.

Characters and characterisation

We noted earlier that events take narrative through its three phases to resolution. This process is accomplished as **characters** carry out the events. It is important when analysing narratives that we don't think of characters as 'real people'. For us, the woman in the Simona advertisement is not an actual person. She is a syntagm of different signs that connote a certain figure of woman. This figure will then be read in different ways by different groups of readers.

Similarly, characters in a narrative, whether in a fictional or non-fictional genre, are combinations of signs whose meanings may be more or less varied. These signs signify personality traits through characters' actions, speech, and external appearance. *Flat* characters don't change as the story progresses, whereas *complex* characters develop new traits as the story goes on. Examples of these sorts of character development are quite easy to think of: on the one hand, the virginal heroine of a Victorian melodrama sustains her innocence despite the schemes of the moustache-twirling villain; on the other the figure of Ripley in the *Alien* movies calls on previously unknown qualities to overcome the monsters.

A character's *proper name* works as a metonymic sign for the full set of attributes. If the narrative is widely known, the name may even be used in everyday speech to characterise other people: 'He's got a bit of Mad Max in him.'

Different characters perform various functions in events and sequences of events. Thus another way of identifying and analysing characters is according to *what they do* in the narrative structure rather than *who they are*. There are two basic functions: character as *doer* or *receiver*. Conventional characterisation tends to depict male characters as doers and female characters as receivers. Consider our Victorian virgin. She is on the receiving end first of the villain's misdeeds, and then of the hero's brave feats. One of the interesting features of Ripley's characterisation in *Alien* is the way she develops as a female doer. (In contrast, her macho companions all succumb to the aliens; their apparent 'doing' role contrasts ironically with her ultimate effectiveness.) Ripley becomes an increasingly complex character as her function in the story becomes more active.

Like other aspects of narrative, such as plot and closure, characterisation often illustrates the ways in which narrative works through *conventions*. The various genres of narrative, from news and documentaries to novels and films, tend to rely on well-established semiotic codes to represent characters. We have suggested some of these already, such as passive female characters and active male ones, the moustache-twirling villain or the blond hero. The scientist in a white lab coat depicted in many documentaries and advertisements, or the well-dressed, smooth-talking politician who regularly features in news bulletins, also spring to mind.

These kinds of character conventions reproduce **stereotypes**: mythic figures who represent a concentration of attributes that social groups consider ideal or contemptible. Stereotypes are not true or false; they are used to depict sets of social values in the form of negative and positive characters. They are generic figures, and readers who are familiar with the genre may recognise them from only a few details—clothes and make-up, a certain speech style or ethnicity. Stereotypes seem to have a wholly denotative meaning. (We will consider some of the ideological effects of stereotypes in more detail in Chapters 7 and 8.)

The thirty-second television advertisement from which the pictures in Figure 6.3 are taken is notable for the speed with which it establishes contrasting characters. These figures are stereotypes of nice and devious women respectively. Even from a couple of frames we can see that through stereotypical traits of dressing style, the use or absence of make-up, body language and facial expressions, the text depicts characters who enact a complete narrative. It moves from the stability of friendship through the disruption of desire and betrayal, to closure with boyfriend-stealing treachery on the verge of being discovered. (A reassuring moral,

Figure 6.3a

Figure 6.3b

fused with the dependability of the advertised tampons, is finally announced.)

As this example illustrates, stereotyped characterisation frequently works together with a conventional narrative structure to denote and reinforce dominant cultural attitudes and beliefs. Female character is here based on a good girl–bad girl opposition, and both versions are oriented towards a 'cute' guy. Myths of women's morality, sexuality and jealousy are recapped and reproduced.

Through such stereotypes and conventions, the *social motives* of narrative may come into play. The processes of characterisation and plot do not only tell a story. They pass judgement upon the cultural values that underlie the narrative's events. Every narrative is told from a **social perspective** or **viewpoint** offered in the reading. When engaging with these narrative viewpoints, audiences do not simply accept the given representation. They subject it to the range of social readings and interpretations that other kinds of texts receive. Indeed, responses to narratives exemplify in many ways the active involvement of readers and audiences in the production of social meaning.

Point of view

So far we have been thinking of events and characters as signified aspects of the story. They can also be thought of in terms of their signifying roles in the plot. The narration of events and characters involves the selection of some signifiers over others and their combination into certain patterns. As suggested in the previous two sections, these moves follow generic and conventional lines. At the same time, the choices that are made reveal a narrative **point of view** specific to the text. In order to analyse the social meanings that a narrative represents, we need to identify the viewpoint that these kinds of choices construct.

This viewpoint entails all the issues of address that are central to the circulation of texts: the setting up of addresser and addressee positions and the interaction between them through the phatic function. *Narrative point of view is a specific kind of textual address.*

As noted earlier, the act of narration implies a narrator and a narratee. These are roles that the text constructs. They do not exist before the text. Rather, they offer ways of telling and responding to the events and characters that are narrated. (It is possible when analysing narratives to speculate on what the 'real life' author meant and what 'real life' readers are thinking. Studies of literary narratives are often preoccupied with such questions. We have seen throughout this book, however, that the intentions of the author or sender make up a very limited part of the meanings that texts generate. And we have also seen that senders and addressers may be very different things. Here, we are more interested in the possibilities of cultural meaning and response that social texts, including narratives, open up.)

As a textual effect, the narrator can function through various sorts of relationships to the story he (or she) is telling. These variations involve both events and other characters. The narrator might tell the story before, during or after the events have taken place. He might or might not be a character in the story. If the narrator is not a character, he may tell the story by surveying all the events and characters from an external viewpoint. On the other hand, he may use a single character's perspective on events or introduce a number of characters' perspectives.

These multiple viewpoints may be synthesised, working to confirm each other and leading to a united closure. Or the narrator may contrast different characters' viewpoints with one another, thereby precluding the kind of fused resolution that is predominantly used in a popular narrative genre like the family sitcom. The narrative may end with the disruption unresolved.

All these structural possibilities and variations would affect the narratee positions offered by the text. They influence the ways readers will respond to, and interpret, the narrative. For example, if the narrator is a character in the story, we might suspect that his or her narrative is loaded, or even biased. The narrative may not be deliberately weighted, but because of the narrator's involvement it might show only a limited or partial knowledge of events and of other characters' thoughts. If the narrator isn't a character in the story and seems to use various characters' perspectives on events, we might conclude that the narrative recounts events accurately.

On the other hand, the narrator might favour a single or some particular characters' viewpoints over others, and this could prompt us to be a little sceptical about the narrated version of events. Our responses can be further complicated by the relation between the time of telling and the occurrence of the events. Predictions may seem less reliable than reports on completed incidents.

These different effects in the narrator's relationship to other characters and events can come to work as generic conventions. Factual narrative genres such as news and history use narrators who survey a range of characters' views and tell the story after some of the events, or the whole sequence, have occurred. These structural cues are naturalised signs of 'the truth'. Yet their denotative effects are no less conventional or constructed than the hazy ripples and violins of a movie which signify the start of a narrative flashback, after a character has lost consciousness.

Narrative negotiations

Narrative is no exception to the social process of reading through which all signs, texts and genres are open to negotiated and oppositional responses. Although the narratee may be placed to produce a preferred reading, there is no guarantee that such a reading or position will be adopted. The points of view of narrator and of characters can be questioned. This can happen internally, externally, or through a combination of internal and external challenges.

First, the text can present rival viewpoints within the narrative. A number of characters may test the ideas of the authoritative characters. In the news, protesters may force their views into a story by loudly contradicting the primary definers, even if the report focuses only on the latter. In family sitcoms like *The Simpsons* or the older *Leave It to Beaver*, the children, often supported by the mothers, consistently show up the opinions of fathers as at best misguided, at worst mean. Such texts have internally dialogic structures through which characters in the text disrupt the dominant perspectives of narrator and main characters.

Second, readers or viewers may dispute the depiction and closure of events and characterisation. They read the story in negotiated or oppositional terms. The official white narrative of Australia's settlement—the brave actions and resourcefulness of the founding fathers—has been strongly and successfully contested by Aboriginal readers. They challenge it in various ways: critiquing the portrayal of white figures as heroic and of Aborigines as savage or aimless; rejecting a plot that began in 1788 and has highpoints such as Federation and the Bicentenary, and a closure implying continued social progress. (In some ways the Aboriginal reading is compelled to be 'external' since one effect of the white narrative is to erase Aboriginal characters.)

Third, the external and internal challenges to narrative point of view may merge. Negotiated and oppositional responses to narrative texts are mostly of this combined mode. A group of readers may reaccentuate the role and views of supposedly minor characters and feel that these either constitute the narrative's central events or undermine its key features. They read *against* the story's apparent closure. Such are the response and actions of Aborigines who see in Australia's post-1788 history a continuing tale of the survival of their cultures despite deadly oppression.

These active readings of narrative structure and characterisation become, in effect, *rewritings* of the narrative text. As we have seen with other kinds of texts, narratives are the scene for negotiations over meanings rather than readers' acceptance of the pre-determined significance and structure of events and characters. The pleasure and desire that narrative triggers thus arise as much from the powers of readers and viewers to re-tell and re-narrate the stories that surround them as they do from responding to circuits of identification and suspense that texts set up.

Some of the strongest examples of the re-telling of narratives are the responses of women to patriarchal narrative structures. Responses comprise a wide range of textual genres and activities. They include: feminist film and literary criticism that questions and attacks the way conventional plots use female characters to indulge the desire for sexual power of male characters and readers; narratives in which these conventions are revised, rejected, rewritten and refilmed to foreground women's perspectives; and the whole spectrum of active readings of patriarchal and feminist narratives that women constantly perform in everyday experience.

There are many instances of these kinds of response. We can indicate a few. Feminist criticism has re-read the 'married and lived happily ever after' finale of narrative fiction, film and much journalism as signifying female characters' re-enclosure in patriarchal systems. Film and art theory especially has paid attention to the way women's bodies are dissected and depersonalised for the gratification of male visual desire.

In contrast to conventional depictions of women, a film like *Thelma and Louise* adapts standard 'buddy' and 'road movie' motifs to represent women's experience. The journey of the two main characters allows them to evade and invert many of the constraints of patriarchal culture and develop a strong personal relationship.

Finally, much critical attention has also been paid to the way many women read popular romance fiction. They rework the apparently sexist narratives into stories that not only provide pleasures such as seeing a man come fully to appreciate the heroine's personality, but also offer imaginative and intellectual support for the day-to-day domestic routines and family lives that the readers lead.

These various strands of feminist analysis have been prominent in underlining the point that narrative genres have a central role in social experience. Narrative texts constantly represent a wide range of cultural myths and meanings to readers. But perhaps the more significant effect emerges through the opportunities narrative gives for readers to tell and retell their own versions of social stories.

Exercises

1 Collect a number of strip cartoons or jokes. Identify the plot-story distinction within them. How is this difference related to the humour?
2 Choose one magazine and one TV advertisement. Reconstruct the narrative which each represents. From whose perspective are they told? How do these perspectives relate to the narrative closure that is realised?
3 Retell a sitcom episode from one of the minor character's viewpoints. Do different social values come into play? Does the narrative closure have to be rewritten? What kinds of different audience responses will be elicited?

Sources and further reading

There are many studies of narrative processes and structure available. Three of the more accessible ones are Shlomith Rimmon-Kenan, *Narrative Fiction: Contemporary Poetics* (London: Methuen, 1983); Michael J. Toolan, *Narrative: A Critical Linguistic Introduction* (London: Routledge, 1988); and Steven Cohan and Linda M. Shires, *Telling Stories: A Theoretical Analysis of Narrative* (New York: Routledge, 1988)

For accounts of narrative structures in television and film, see John Ellis, *Visible Fictions* (London: Routledge and Kegan Paul, 1982); Robert C. Allen (ed.) *Channels of Discourse: Television and Contemporary Criticism* (London: Routledge, 1987); and Steve Neale and Frank Krutnick, *Popular Film and Television Comedy* (London: Routledge, 1990)

The opening chapters of Sander L. Gilman's *Difference and Pathology: Stereotypes of Sexuality, Race and Madness* (Ithaca, New York: Cornell University Press, 1985) study the cultural function of stereotypes. Bob Hodge and Vijay Mishra's *Dark Side of the Dream: Australian Literature and the Postcolonial Mind* (Sydney: Allen and Unwin, 1991) offers a critical reading of Aboriginal and white representations of Australian culture.

There are also many studies of women's re-readings and re-writings of narrative and other textual conventions. Some of these include: M. E. Brown, *Television and Women's Culture: The Politics of the Popular* (London: Sage, 1990); Rosalind Coward, *Female Desire* (London: Granada, 1984); Tania Modleski, *Loving with a Vengeance: Mass Produced Fantasies for Women* (New York: Methuen, 1984); Janice Radway, *Reading the Romance: Feminism and the Representation of Women in Popular Culture* (Chapel Hill: University of North Carolina Press, 1984); and Judith Williamson, *Consuming Passions: The Dynamics of Popular Culture* (London: Marian Boyars, 1986). The classic essay on desire in film is Laura Mulvey's 'Visual Pleasure and Narrative Cinema' (*Screen* 16: 6–18).

More demanding studies of the social functions of narrative are Fredric Jameson's *The Political Unconscious: Narrative as a Socially Symbolic Act* (Ithaca, New York: Cornell University Press, 1981) and M. M. Bakhtin's long essay, 'Discourse in the Novel', in *The Dialogic Imagination: Four Essays* (Austin: University of Texas Press, 1981).

7 Medium and mediation

Signs and texts, then, involve people in social settings, who recognise and use them for different purposes. We now need to consider in more specific detail the various ways in which signs and their intertextual links connect with social and institutional contexts.

Institutions

All forms of sign activity are regulated and conditioned by social organisations and language structures. For instance, any act of speaking takes place within a context which defines certain **protocols**: what can most properly be said, by whom and how. Adults rarely speak frankly to children about a range of topics, such as sex, money, and politics. This is not entirely a matter of personal choice. It has a lot to do with the way in which family roles are structured and played out. The structures and inter-actions of these roles can be examined by considering the family as an **institution**.

An **institution** is a relatively stable set of social arrangements and relationships.

In general terms we can say that institutions provide a structure of roles, relationships and functions for those who inhabit them. The institution of the family consists of a number of social identities, such as mother, father, children, uncle, aunt, etc. The relationships between these figures are played out according to protocols of varying formality. The parent-child relationship is constantly reinforced and revised through the full range of daily routines and interaction: when the child is to go to bed, when homework is to be done, when television can be watched.

But the parent-child relationship is far from merely inter-personal. Some aspects are formally legislated by the state, such as the parent's responsibility for the child's education, health and moral well-being. The state also offers less rigorous guidelines to the parent. These include censorship and the classification of films and television programs, pre-schooling and immunisation programs. Further, there are the many informal but influential protocols of etiquette, dress and demeanour, involving things as disparate as the available styles of children's clothes, magazine advice on child rearing, advertising, and conversations with neighbours and friends. All of these affect that seemingly natural, personal bond between parent and child.

Other bonds within the family institution also work in this way. As Figure 7.1 suggests, an array of codes and protocols may come into play in the link between wife and husband. These come from both inside and outside the relationship.

Thus institutions are not merely self-enclosed systems. They are always open to each other and to the social world in which they exist and to which they respond. Furthermore, every individual relates to others through a network of intersecting institutionalised values and relations. The child who disagrees with her parents about whether she is to do her homework or watch television is negotiating about the intersection of family (the dutiful or recalcitrant daughter), TV (audience member) and education system (conscientious student).

Discourse

Institutions are made up not only of interactions among people but also of *practices of producing texts*. The negotiations between child and parent involve certain kinds of talk which signify their attitudes and feelings about the issues under discussion. Even the noisiest family table-talk is not sheer chaos but a contest for speaking positions, in which family members test and redefine duties, obligations and power relations.

Talk is one of many forms of textuality that are produced institutionally. Government departments are administered through issuing and exchanging many kinds of oral and written texts (directives, memos, etc.) which contain information, requests, commands and so on. The main textual work of media institutions may seem to be newspapers, magazines, radio and television programs for mass audiences. But they also produce a host of other, administrative texts, along with the entire range of routine talk between their workers. All these texts serve various purposes. Some define, limit or reinforce people's positions and courses of action. Others clarify the way in which jobs are to be done. Still others communicate information to the outside world.

Figure 7.1

Institutions, then, are not just groups of people who live, work or interact together. They also include the full range of texts and genres through which interactions take place. An institution takes on different characteristics through the genres it uses. The way a customer speaks to a shop assistant in purchasing a product will be different from the way the same person, as a student, speaks to a teacher. The institution of retailing consists of a different set of speech genres from that of education, even though the same person can participate in both institutions. *Institutions set up addresser and addressee positions.*

The mode of textuality which allows an institution to operate is called a **discourse**. Institutions reproduce themselves through discourse. One of the key effects of this is that discourse produces addressers and addressees as social identities. In discourse, people are placed, and place themselves, in institutionally located roles.

> A **discourse** is a set of textual arrangements which organises and co-ordinates the actions, positions and identities of the people who produce it.

Discourse locates and orientates talkers with respect to one another. It defines *protocols. Discourse structures, in an institutional setting, the genres and texts that people use.*

Take, for example, the drinking ritual of 'shouting', in which each member of a group takes a turn at buying the drinks. Shouting is often part of a particular discourse of masculinity. What are its features? First, it involves a recognition of group identity (mateship) and a competitive mode of friendship (keeping up with the shout). Second, it defines common values and interests. Third, the ritual is one of the ways that the institution of patriarchy is reinforced through everyday routines: it reproduces patriarchal relations through a discourse of male bonding.

These various discursive effects are illuminating because shouting is such an ordinary kind of activity. The accumulation and repetition of everyday talk and practices in various contexts— in the workplace, at the pub, or at home—construct a network of cultural positions and values which are *embodied* in the daily lives of those who take part in them.

Embodiment

The ways in which people interact with one another in everyday life may appear to be instinctive and natural. But this ease is actually the outcome of a process of learning and habituation. One of the key paradoxes of cultural studies is that in many, if not all cases, the 'natural' is repeatedly revealed to be the culturally learnt. Let's try to unravel this paradox in a little detail, beginning with a simple example.

In driving a car, the competent driver does not consciously invoke and weigh up the rules of the road (which side of the road to drive on, who to give way to, which lane to drive in, when to turn lights on or indicate), or the specific techniques of driving (such as clutch and brake manipulation, use of mirrors, cornering). She simply drives. In other words, we can say the driver has **embodied** a discourse: that is, she applies a technique (how to operate a certain machine, the car) and a set of knowledges (about rules of the road and conventions of driving) which allow things to be done in interaction with others. She can get from one place to another through a shared network of roads.

> **Embodiment** is the learning of a set of knowledges and competences which can be habitually reproduced.

Embodiment produces a certain identity or set of multiple, intersecting identities. The driver becomes recognised as a driver by the state when she passes her driving test. There are, then, many possible variants of this identity. The 'good driver' displays the requisite courtesies to others, such as giving way and allowing adequate space between her vehicle and others. (In contrast, the 'bad driver' breaks such institutional routines.) Furthermore, the same person already embodies many other quite different competences (as worker, parent, etc.) All forms of social identity depend upon the embodiment of discourse and its display in public interactions.

The exchanges among the natural, the institutional and the discursive that we see in the process of embodiment occur across all social activities and operations. One of the most significant areas of these kinds of exchange is the mass media. We will now turn to examine their institutional processes and their cultural effects.

Mediation

The compendium of discourses which make up **the media** (print journalism, television, film, radio) involves a huge array of institutional values and embodied practices. An analysis of the entire discourse of the media is beyond the scope of this chapter. We will therefore confine our discussion to one aspect: the practice of **mediation**.

Media discourse comprises the set of all media texts, together with the practices involved in producing them. This discourse also has a special function in that its primary job is to *mediate* between one social domain and another. In general terms, mediation occurs when one party acts between two others, bringing them into a relationship.

For example, in a court case a barrister mediates between her client and the judiciary, bringing them into an officially accepted legal relationship. In nineteenth century Europe, middle class young men and women could not become romantically involved unless chaperoned (mediated) by an older person with certain social credentials. *Mediation implies that the relationship between two parties is organised according to social values.*

Media discourse intervenes between social institutions, their discourses, the events surrounding them, and the audiences who read, view and listen to media texts. For example, news reports about political events are broadcast to an audience via the agency of television and radio news programs and newspaper stories. One institution and its discourses (politics) are thus mediated by another (news broadcasting). This makes certain knowledge and information available to yet another institution, the public.

In general, the public does not have direct access to the daily decision making which goes on in government. Through the intervention of the media, however, the public audience gains some access. Audience members can pick up knowledge about political events and decisions from newspapers and television programs. They can construct ideas about the influence and effects of party politics and governmental decisions on the way society works.

While they are readers or viewers of media news, audience members are also citizens, who are subject to the administration of the state. This second relationship intertwines with the first. Being a citizen is conditioned by the intervention of media discourse, and being part of the media audience is conditioned by being a citizen. Media news provides information which it has selected for newsworthiness, and much of this information will be the basis for ways in which people think of their relationship to the state. Accordingly, the news's mediation has the power to *change* the relationship between audiences and social institutions. This power of media discourse becomes especially apparent when used by political parties in election campaigns to try and influence voters.

Media discourse's ability to alter the way an audience relates to social institutions is not confined to the realms of news and politics. All media texts reproduce social institutions and discourses in ways which may run counter to audiences' everyday life practices. We considered some of these ways in our discussions of genre and narrative. *Narrative closure* is one of the most significant. Its apparently commonsense function in ending a story may conceal the kinds of institutional pressures it is exerting.

For example, despite their widespread use, happy ending devices in a TV sitcom like *The Cosby Show*—with family order restored through the father's authority—need not reflect the audience's family situations and experiences. Rarely are such experiences neatly resolved in half an hour. They often have an element of continuing conflict and repair to them. Thus the habitual viewing of situation comedies and soap operas often involves a contradictory experience. The represented reality quite simply does not match the viewers' situations, even though it looks as if it does.

Disjunction, then, is always possible within the mediating process. The audience may have to try and resolve contradictory values and accommodate the media discourses into those of everyday life. Most viewers watching a lavish show like *Beverly Hills 90210* need to resolve an enormous contrast between the metonyms of seemingly ordinary life in the program, and their own more limited circumstances. Such accommodation will be more or less difficult depending on the social position and background of audience members. Rarely is the mediation process neatly concluded. (We will return to this point when we discuss ideology in the next chapter.)

Mediation and self-effacement

We suggested earlier that mediation involves one party bringing other parties into a relationship with one another. In most cases, this relationship is recognised and accepted by the institution in which it is practised. Further, it occurs across a wide range of social activities, from those generally considered to be morally proper—a priest mediating between lay person and God, a general practitioner between patient and specialist—to those which many might think of as immoral or illegal—a pimp mediating between a sex-worker and client, or a dealer as middle-man between grower and marijuana smoker. Mediation must be appropriate to the kind of institution in which it takes place.

For the institution to continue to operate, the mediator needs to act at least partly on its behalf rather than solely for his or her own benefit and must relegate or efface personal interest in favour of the act of mediation. Thus a real estate agent appointed to sell someone's house acts in their interests, and so hopes to serve her own. The accountant preparing a client's tax return must ensure that deductions will be acceptable, thereby guaranteeing an appropriate relation between client and tax office.

Media discourse is also subject to this kind of **self-effacement**. To gain the co-operation of the parties which they bring together (social and commercial institutions and audiences), the media must offer certain kinds of guarantees that their texts do represent the way things are, and do not simply serve their own interests.

Otherwise they risk losing the respect of both audiences and institutions.

This self-effacing function is one of the central features of media discourse. Media discourse includes an array of techniques and modes of signification that seek to make it acceptable to those to whom it is addressed.

Media self-interest and community

The professional techniques of the media involve various narrative schemes and categories of representation which reproduce certain versions of the world. In this way media discourse seeks to sustain itself. The schemes attempt to make the world look familiar to many of the people who participate in media discourse, from employees to members of audiences, to primary definers and participants in events. All these groups are seen as bound together in a community of like-minded people, who supposedly share the same sets of values and engage in similar lifestyles.

In this manner, the media, as a group of institutions, act to construct a **simulated** world: one full of objects, people, actions and values which comprise a stable, unchanging set of relationships. And the media likewise seem to suggest that the relationships between audiences and the world in which they live are also stable and unchanging. We discuss these kinds of communal effects in Figure 7.2.

The concealed side of the media's myths of community is that media institutions are motivated by self-interest. As commercial enterprises, they must ensure that they have some kind of control over the way they work. The *realpolitik* of media institutions involves survival and profitability in the marketplace. Media success is not defined by an ability to please audience taste or to be united with audience views. Rather, success results from engaging with other institutions in the market economy, which are all tied to the administration of a capitalist social system.

Because of this, Western media institutions find themselves in alliance with other institutions that serve the needs of a society marked by a capital–labour hierarchy. At the same time, media discourse must construct for itself a mass audience whose values it claims to represent. This contradiction means that media discourse must proceed in a complex, ambiguous way. The media rely on their ability to represent the interests of one group (the media in alliance with capital) as the interests of an entire society.

To realise this ambiguous representation, media texts must use certain strategies and devices. In the next sections, we will consider these strategies in more detail.

Figure 7.2

Global Warring

Australian troops are keeping the peace in 10 of the world's trouble spots as we increasingly take on the role of the world's 'policemen'.

Aussie diggers are stationed in Syria, Cyprus Afghanistan, the Persian Gulf, Western Sahara, Cambodia, former Yugo- slavia, Sinai, Iraq and most recently, Somalia, where these pictures were taken.

They show Queensland-based soldiers in action in the UN peacekeeping force in Somalia.

Colonel Bill Mellor commander of the Australian forces there, talks with children orphaned by the nation's four-year civil war and famine.

Above, Cpl Luke Entink of the 3/4 Cavalry based in Townsville, mans his .50 calibre machine gun on an armored patrol in the streets of Baidoa.

(*Sunday Mail*, 14 February 1993)

This text constructs a certain notion of community by endorsing values assumed to be held collectively by its readers. It suggests that the readers ('we') and the troops perform the same action. All Australians, not just the soldiers, are responsible for keeping the peace. By mentioning Australian troops only, and not those from other countries, it isolates the notion of national interest. This appeal to a nation-community of peace-minded Australians also sees Western democracy as an advanced form of civilisation with a duty to defend and protect less advanced social groups. Note how 'action' is portrayed. The top photograph shows a street patrol with armaments prominently displayed, connoting warfare and aggression, while the bottom photograph of an officer speaking with orphaned children connotes the opposite values of peace. The message becomes, '*We* are technologically superior to and morally better than *them*.' At the same time, and rather ironically, 'peace' is regarded as a repressive act, much like the act of eradicating diseased areas ('trouble spots').

Orality and the media

So far we have been considering the institutional structure of the media. We have looked at their internal structure, their relations with other social institutions, and the aims and effects of media discourse. We now want to develop this last aspect. In this and the following sections we will be concerned with the way that media discourse tries to efface itself as a motivated or self-interested practice. The process of *self-effacement* has become the dominant mode through which the media provide audiences with knowledge and images of their society and the world at large. Technology offers some of the key ways of realising self-effacement.

Media discourse is bound up with print and electronic technologies. It depends upon huge investment in equipment which is capable of reproducing type, images and sound over vast social spaces. The means of producing media texts are thus far removed from those used to produce the private discourses of everyday life.

The predominant mode of discourse in everyday life is *speech*. Through conversing with each other we manoeuvre ourselves within the social world. Speech is linked to our presence in the world and anchors our social and cultural identity.

On the other hand, the technologies used by the media deal with speech in a different way. For a start, newspapers convert speech into written words, while television uses videotape and live electronic transmission to replicate it. Hence there is a huge technological and institutional gap between oral forms of communication and their translation into media texts. Media discourse may even seek to reproduce the tones and rhythms of oral conversation in a visual genre. For example, as we saw earlier, news photographs are often used to capture the immediacy of personal interaction.

Newspaper photography does a good job at duplicating certain features of an event. Yet, like all media texts, it is *edited*, a process that comes between the event and its reproduction in the newspaper. Discursive practices such as editing prepare media texts for their audiences. And despite the delay that editing would seem to suggest, one of its main results is the *simulation of spontaneity*—of being there, of witnessing the event as it happens.

As noted earlier, a key effect of media technology is to define the audience as a homogeneous group of people, present to each other and sharing a common identity through speech. This enables the media to efface their own discourse. By passing themselves off as a kind of speech, the media can then lay claim to a common mode of communication with their audience. A phatic effect of *community* seems to be realised. As we can see in Figure 7.3, orality and humour may work together to produce this effect.

Myths of community

The simulation of speech in media discourse invokes a **community** of mutually present people to which the media claim to belong. Media texts address their audiences as if engaged in conversation. Television discourse, for instance, presents programs framed by images and voice-overs exhorting the audience to stay tuned. Much television promotion is about the way TV stations are part of the community, sharing the same values and providing a neighbourly service for their audience.

This appeal to communal values is repeated across a range of TV texts, particularly where television actors such as newsreaders, comperes, games hosts and so forth, are required to look straight at the camera. In this case the audience is being addressed as if it shared a mutual presence with the representatives of the television network.

Television advertisements, slipped in between and during programs, are also orally coded. By interrupting the narrative flow of a program, advertisements remind the audience of its specific location in time and space (in the home). The audience and media

Figure 7.3 Imitating orality

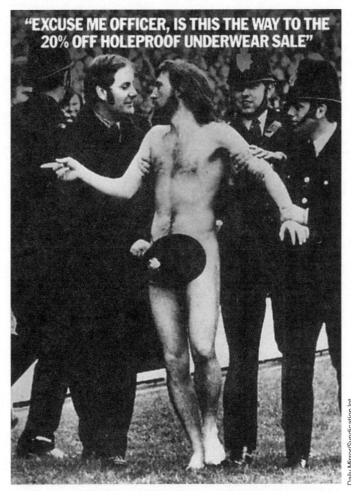

"EXCUSE ME OFFICER, IS THIS THE WAY TO THE 20% OFF HOLEPROOF UNDERWEAR SALE"

Daily Mirror/Syndication Int.

Buy 2 pairs of Underdaks, 2 pairs of All Seasons Briefs or 2 pairs of All Seasons Singlets this week, and we'll give you 20% off the normal price.

Head straight for any one of the participating stores and look for the special packs with the 20% off wrapper. **Holeproof.**

The posture of the man, together with his nakedness, seems similar to traditional Renaissance art images of Jesus. But the text also connotes humour, through the placement of the policeman's cap and the added caption. Through its joking tone, the text seems to echo everyday speech, despite the use of religious and aesthetic codes.

voice then seem to share the experience of watching the program. This effect is heightened by the routine placement among the advertisements of network promotions advertising future programs. Everyone seems to be watching together.

Imagery and photographic technology

These communal and oral effects are also realised in media texts by linking speech to images, thereby simulating the visual experience of presence, of 'being there'. Photographs are used in newspapers to anchor stories in the actual world. They seem to be more real than the printed word.

Visual images in photography, film and television work in a doubled fashion. On the one hand they resemble the objects for which they stand. On the other, they exist as actual traces of these objects: light rays from the object produce an image on silver nitrate paper. Photography thus mimics sight, while at the same time carrying with it something of the object which has been photographed.

This double signification explains why photographs and other such images are commonly regarded as authentic and accurate signs of spatial domains, free from the personal subjectivity associated with sight. Photography becomes *super-sight*, in which the image and thing are one and the same.

The coding of newspaper photographs presupposes that the audience will accept this coincidence as part and parcel of everyday signification. Photographs seem to act as windows on to the world, offering more direct experiences of life than the printed words. The effect of this is to play down the constructedness of newspaper texts and to reinforce their denotative, referential functions. The photographs seem to neutralise any signs of the institutional factors that might peep through the media's production of social and cultural values.

The effects of orality and presence achieved through images are even more pronounced in television. In this case, texts are composed of audio-visual signs in which speech is nearly always linked with an image which acts as its source. Television comperes and newsreaders seem to address the audience directly, like people in conversation.

Like newspaper photographs, however, television imagery is a complex construction. It depends on a number of technological and institutional practices designed to cover its discursive features. One obvious example occurs when television newsreaders read from an autocue. The autocue is normally placed so close to the camera that the newsreader gives the impression of direct eye contact, thereby producing the effect of presence.

But orality—the invocation of a mutually shared presence through speech—can also work in reverse. Some television programs, such as the Australian comedy shows *Live and Sweaty* and *Hey, Hey, It's Saturday*, deliberately expose the conventions of television discourse. The hosts of these shows adopt a casual, intimate relationship with both of their audiences, the one in the studio and the one at home. It is not unusual for camera shots to show other cameras in the process of shooting, exposing the machinery of production to the audience. The hosts often comment on the conduct of the program, while mistakes and mistiming are displayed as part of what is going on rather than hidden or edited out.

Risky as this style first appears, it is in fact a powerful endorsement of presence. It seems to emulate the condition of everyday life in which people often find themselves in the thick of things. Control can always be reasserted by the host who calls the shots: asking for certain cameras or responses from the audience, 'conducting' the background orchestra, playing fast and loose with guests and fellow actors.

Tomfoolery such as this suggests that the host is free from the restraints of television discourse. This freedom is easily transferred to the audience, whose position is constructed as one of equality. The host and audience seem to share a common discourse marked by values such as freedom, individuality and irreverence. For some viewers, these programs may even tap into popular myths about the Australian character as fun-loving and egalitarian.

For all its ability to bring life-like images into our living rooms, television imagery is nevertheless a device for neutralising the discourse of the media. Like news photography, it plays on the myth that technology can reproduce things and processes in an objective and super-visual manner. Its effects seem to surpass sight, yet they maintain the condition of presence necessary to invoke a community shared by both the media and its audiences. The technology seems to efface itself as it is used.

Vernacular language, gossip and personalities

Another way in which the media simulate orality and presence is through the use of vernacular *language styles*. Television sports programs in Australia are often hosted by male presenters with deliberate 'ocker' accents. The effect is of a group of mates sitting around, presenter and viewers together.

Vernacular and colloquial language is also often used in newspapers to counteract the limitations of the printed word in contrast to TV texts.

Figure 7.4

John's in from the cold, but not for long

Yeppoon man John Hoelscher has only been back from Antarctica a week, but already he is planning more trips to cold environs.

Mr Hoelscher has just returned from 16 months at the Australian Antarctic base Mawson, and says he will go back next summer.

He is flying to Minnesota next week to visit some of the husky dogs which were recently removed from the base. He will also visit friends in Canada and Alaska.

The base had 28 huskies, and 22 were taken to Outward Bound School in the United States.

The dogs are being removed as part of the Australian government's involvement in the Madrid protocol on environmental protection of Antarctica.

By April 1994, all wildlife not indigenous to the continent will have been removed.

Mr Hoelscher said he was heavily involved in managing the dogs.

The dogs and machinery were used to get around the area, but

Mr Hoelscher takes some time to enjoy the colourful scenery near his parents' Lammermoor beach home, a stark contrast to the icy surrounds of the past 16 months.

huskies were more useful in some situations, such as over thin ice.

An ABC crew visited the base last year to put together a documentary called 'The Last Husky'.

Yeppoon man John Hoelscher, 29, makes his way across Antarctica with the husky dogs which were soon to leave their life in the snow for good.

The headline of Figure 7.4 seems to echo a spoken comment about the person who is the subject of the story. The use of 'John' suggests friendship. The impression is of someone commenting to another person about a long-lost friend who has suddenly reappeared. The witty phrase 'in from the cold', which is balanced by 'but not for long', as well as the colloquial 'John's, rather than 'John is', also captures more relaxed tones of speech.

There are other ways in which orality can be coded into media texts. Consider the story in Figure 7.5, reporting a bizarre accident. This text aspires to the condition of *gossip*. Gossip is usually about certain kinds of scandals and disgraces, uncommon events which seem to threaten the order of everyday life. Through gossip, people are able to strengthen their social bonds by denouncing or exposing such threats, thus reconfirming values which they mutually hold. Unusual stories such as 'Car kills salon client' replace gossip in newspaper discourse because their subject matter threatens the

Figure 7.5

IN BRIEF

Car kills salon client

ADELAIDE—A 63-year-old woman having her hair done was crushed to death by an out-of-control car which smashed through the front window of a hairdressing salon here yesterday. A witness said a green Mazda 626 careered on to the footpath and through the window at Fringes Hair Salon at Seaford in Adelaide's southern suburbs. Police said initial investigations showed the driver's foot had slipped off the brake on to the accelerator.

---

taken-for-granted values of everyday life. We don't expect danger while having our hair done.

Another common newspaper practice based on gossip is to give priority to stories about the private lives of élite figures. In Figure 7.6, golfer Greg Norman's private life is turned into front-page news. Norman's jetset world and the readers' everyday life seem suddenly to coincide. He is portrayed as an ordinary person who sheds tears and suffers from depression. Yet the story then exceeds the ordinary, since Norman's suffering is made to seem tragic: his 'agonised reaction' to Sam's death 'was seen by millions around the world on TV'. Greg Norman thus takes on the proportions of a tragic hero, who bears the burden of human suffering through his concern for an AIDS-infected youth.

This kind of story constructs a world order governed by the deeds and thoughts of 'great men'. It suggests that the values and actions of everyday life are infused with distant and difficult virtues, fully attainable only by certain figures: sporting heroes, film stars, royalty, TV personalities, politicians. The social distance between audience and élite personality is simultaneously collapsed and maintained. Greg Norman is just like us, but he's also greater and nobler than we are.

Figure 7.6

Greg Norman playing in black yesterday—with Sam's name beside the shark emblem on his hatband

Shark's sorrow

QUEENSLAND'S champion golfer, Greg Norman, has vowed to win today's Australian Masters for the memory of young fan Sam Roberts, who died on Friday.

The secret of the Great White Shark's tears was revealed yesterday when he wore black for his little mate Sam—son of television commentator Sandy Roberts—who died as the result of an AIDS-contaminated blood transfusion.

Norman was plunged into depression for Sam, 15, and broke down in tears during Friday's second round when told of the youngster's death.

The teenager had a fierce admiration for Norman since he was a toddler—and the golfer visited him in Geelong hospital last Thursday as a reward for his bravery.

Norman frequently visited and telephoned Sam, taking him to Melbourne zoo and for rides in his personal helicopter.

When Sam died on Friday morning, the news was flashed to Norman at the Australian Masters at Huntingdale, causing an agonised reaction that was seen by millions around the world on TV.

**Sandy Roberts
— son's death
shocked Greg**

Realism: facts and fictions

Our discussion so far has shown that the relationship between media discourse and the everyday world is a complex one. In fact, when we start to analyse media texts, we find that we are always dealing with highly mediated signs of the real. What media produce in presenting the real is a *discourse* on the real: a discourse of **realism**.

> **Realism** is a mode of representation that claims to reproduce faithfully events that happen in the world.

Newspapers, television, radio and magazines provide their audiences with a vast amount of information about the world. Some of it is generically marked as factual: news stories, current affairs, documentaries. But a lot of it is hypothetical. Narratives in the form of TV sitcoms, soap operas, dramas and movies offer fictional accounts of the way the world operates. Because of the popularity of these types of programs, they may take on a credibility which exceeds their fictionality. They seem to offer models for people's behaviour.

It is therefore important to consider all forms of media text, both fictional and factual, as mediating and legitimising certain kinds of knowledge about the world. The family structure typical of situation comedies may be as effective in persuading audiences to adopt and modify their lifestyles as depictions of 'real life' family situations in documentaries. Some groups of viewers may debate issues arising from soap operas and situation comedies, comparing their own moral and social practices with those depicted in such programs.

These debates may even spill out into the public arena, mobilising popular opinion and polarising community groups. For instance, in the American sitcom *Murphy Brown*, the leading character, a single career woman, decides at one point to have a baby, but not to live with the father. The ensuing debate which occurred in the program was picked up and repeated in television and newspapers, and even became an issue in the 1992 American presidential election.

In 1992 and 1993, in Australia and Britain, *Sylvania Waters* produced a similar response. *Sylvania Waters* was a documentary series depicting several months in the life of a Sydney family. Although it used actual people in actual situations, not actors, in a fictional script, its editing and narrative construction clearly drew on soap opera conventions. The effect was to collapse the distinction between the real and the fictional. The family's everyday life became a television text. Each member played out roles which developed 'real life' consequences and placed pressure on the parents' relationships with each other and with their children.

One of the criticisms levelled at the makers of *Sylvania Waters* came from various members of the family. They claimed that the text was edited to highlight negative aspects of their lives, and to downplay the positive. As noted earlier, the construction of media texts always involves editing processes in which certain values tend to be privileged while others are downplayed or excluded. *Sylvania Waters* was not an exception to these conventions, but exemplified them. The conflict arose because family members believed their lives were still in the discourse of 'real life', not of the media.

It is not only fictional media genres that produce fact–fiction hybrids. Similar effects arise in supposedly factual genres. We considered examples of this when looking at the narrative structure of news. Various media analysts have also studied these effects in institutional terms. In the coverage of industrial disputes between management and unions, media discourse tends to show the opposed parties in different ways. Management is usually represented in indoor settings, in face-to-face interviews, while unionists tend to be shown outdoors, on picket lines, sometimes in violent and confrontational circumstances. The decision to choose a moment of violence out of the entire duration of a picket line is based on certain values related to the institutional notion of what is newsworthy.

In the absence of imagery which might suggest otherwise, the audience is invited to conclude that the violent event is typical of the behaviour of unionists. By excluding other moments on the picket line which could have been chosen, perhaps when unionists and management were negotiating, the media are engaged in constructing and reinforcing stereotypes which have an ideological basis.

The repeated coding of news texts which feature management–union dispute along these lines serves to reproduce a set of cultural values that favour management over unions. It thereby reinforces the media's institutional alliance with capital at the expense of labour. In this case, complex social events are reduced to simple oppositions which the audience is invited to recognise and understand instantly, in stereotypical terms. And while audiences may always respond to texts in diverse ways, media discourse works to position them to accept the apparent truth of these oppositions.

Stereotypes

As we saw in our discussion of narrative, stereotypes are a conventional form of characterisation. They encourage certain kinds of interpretation of a story's characters. In media discourse, stereotypes work in a similar way, but their ideological impacts may be intensified.

The representation of social identity in stereotypical terms is one of the major signifying practices of the media. Women and men are portrayed through oppositions such as indoors/outdoors, domestic/public, worker/boss, passive/active, irrational/rational. This is a form of mediation which translates the complexity of social relations into a set of simple distinctions. Women are often depicted in domestic and family situations, playing nurturing roles, or in seductive scenes, as alluring objects of the male gaze. Men are nearly always seen in terms of work and career, or outdoor activities such as sport. TV soap operas, situation comedies and popular movies may all exhibit this kind of coding.

By excluding other possibilities, media texts endorse a certain set of social values as inevitable and natural, and certain beliefs and myths about social identities and cultural norms. These may become entrenched and take on an authority which eludes the pressure of change. A good example of this is the way in which contemporary images of women, despite current awareness of sexism in the media, persist in portraying women as passive objects of male desire and control (see Figure 7.7).

The repeated structuring of media texts in such terms is an important discursive feature with powerful socialising effects. A media text can be highly **redundant**, consisting of standard codes easily recognised by large numbers of sign users. Through redundancy, media discourse confirms a common world view, and bonds many readers and viewers through the sharing of repeated and accumulated discursive practices.

Redundancy is the repeated structuring of texts
according to a set of readily identifiable social values.

The analysis of social discourse will want to describe the practices of stereotyping, redundancy and exclusion which operate across texts that derive from a particular institution. In other words, it will aim to examine the phatic and metalingual functions of the discourse.

Figure 7.7

Even in women's magazines, images of women are dominated by scenes of flirtation or seduction. To whom is this woman's gaze addressed? Whose is this desire?

The discursive practices which produce orally coded media texts are related to institutional values specific to the media. As we have seen, these values concern the need for media institutions to disown their particular interests in favour of a proposed community of like-minded people. By coding texts as if all who read them share a common set of values and beliefs, and experience the same things, the media are able to bring together the social and commercial institutions, who commission and lend support for the programs and publications, with the audiences who read them. In the next chapter, we will further examine how discursive contradictions reveal conflicts of interests between audiences and media institutions. Through these kinds of conflicts, ideological processes and effects unfold.

Exercises

1 Analyse Figure 7.4 ('John's in from the cold') in terms of the ways in which it produces (a) its effects of realism and (b) certain myths of community.
2 To what extent do stereotypes change or remain constant over time? Compare various examples of advertisements drawing on stereotypes, such as Figures 7.1 ('Are you a good wife?' from the early 1960s) and 7.7 ('Are you a Quartz woman?' from the late 1980s). Do these texts position readers in different ways? What kinds of changes in the institutional discourses of the family do they register?

Sources and further reading

For a basic theoretical working through of the concept of institution, see Peter Berger and Thomas Luckmann, *The Social Construction of Reality: A Treatise on the Sociology of Knowledge* (London: Penguin, 1991, particularly pp 65–109). The concept of discourse, as presented here, is derived from the work of Michel Foucault. You can go to his *The Archeology of Knowledge* (London: Tavistock, 1972) for a detailed discussion. For a condensed version, refer to Alan Sheridan *Michel Foucault: The Will to Truth* (London: Tavistock, 1980).

For definition and summary of the concept of discourse as it is applied to media and cultural studies, see Fiske's *Television Culture*. Also see Tim O'Sullivan *et al., Key Concepts in Communication Studies* (London: Methuen, 1983). John Hartley's *Understanding News* (London: Methuen, 1982) looks at the discourse of print media news. Norman Fairclough, in *Language and Power* (London: Longman, 1989), and Roger Fowler, in *Language in the News* (London: Routledge, 1991), analyse print media discourse from a linguistic perspective. For a seminal study of the media's treatment of crime along the lines of mediation, see Stuart Hall *et al., Policing the Crisis: Mugging, the State, and Law and Order* (London: Macmillan, 1978).

8 Ideology

Deriving from Marxist theories of society based on class conflict, the concept of **ideology** has always been a key analytical tool in cultural studies. In recent times, cultural theorists have redeveloped it in terms of discourse. Throughout this chapter we will deal with ideology as a *product of discourse*, that is, as a particular mode of knowing the world through signs and texts.

Broadly speaking, *ideo*logy is about the 'ideas' held in common by social groups in their everyday lives. It also suggests that these ideas are organised in certain ways. An ideo*logy* is a 'logic' of ideas, indicating that the groups who hold various ideologies perceive and understand the world in a relatively consistent manner.

Ideas, like signs, are organised into signifying systems. Ideology is thus related to all of the semiotic concepts discussed throughout this book, but in particular, to those concepts we looked at in the previous chapter: discourse, institution and mediation. In Chapter 7, we considered texts in terms of larger systems of cultural beliefs and attitudes, especially in terms of myth's *naturalising* of sign structures, as if their meanings and values occurred in a commonsense way, with universal applicability.

Ideology is the process of representing material social relationships, and of attempting to reconcile them in discourse.

In this chapter, we turn to the manner in which the naturalising process making signs seem obvious and universal is part of social structures (groups and institutions) which produce and receive discourse. We will examine how discourse and society intermesh: the ways that texts represent, and are represented in, social contexts of behaviour and values.

Ideology and power

In order to study how this complex mechanism of text and social context operates, let's begin with an example of ideology at work in the print media. Newspapers tend to represent world events in terms of economic crisis or warfare, resolved through the decisions of authorities (business leaders, politicians) or the actions of groups (armies) which are, for the most part, male.

This kind of discourse enacts a *patriarchal* ideology, proposing that social order is derived from the automatic assumption of male authority. To produce texts like this is to have a stake in patriarchal authority, to make a claim that the world is *really* ordered in this manner and no other. Such a claim not only refers to the world 'out there', but also reflects upon the media institution itself, legitimising values and means of text production which are, in practice, strongly based on male control.

From the reader's point of view, to read these kinds of news texts is to be addressed in a specific manner: to be oriented to the world as if it were, by *nature*, a patriarchal order. The reader is thereby tacitly positioned to accept and endorse the discourse of the media institution as if it constituted a legitimate 'voice', speaking on behalf of society in general. The media's phatic function has an ideological effect.

(This would be precisely what we earlier described as a *dominant reading*. Of course, not everyone simply submits to ideology in this manner. Readings may also be *negotiated* or *oppositional*.)

We can sum these points up by saying that through ideology, groups and individuals signify and respond to common sets of values and beliefs. These sets bind them more or less closely into a community. The phatic function of ideology thus allows community members to identify with, and against, each other at the everyday level.

Ideology works both to include and to exclude social groups. It does so by suggesting standard sets of values against which everything can be measured. For instance, businesswomen may often be represented in the media as having sacrificed their family lives. Their success in business is defined by their denial of 'traditional' women's roles, not by their ability to compete with men. Through patriarchal ideology of this kind, men and women are oriented to each other in such a way that one group is placed in a dependent relationship to the other. As we shall see, this sort of hierarchy arises because ideology always serves the *interests* of one group, proposing that its needs, aspirations and desires serve those of other groups as well.

Ideology is more than a system of ideas or values. It entails the relations between textual meaning and the various groups involved in producing and receiving texts. Ideology is thus concerned with *the politics of everyday life*: the power relations, defined by group and class interests, into which individuals enter in their routine dealings with others.

Ideology is a powerful sign-logic of the ways people behave and formulate beliefs. In this case text and reader are not entirely separate; they are both part of a larger process of meaning production in which group and class interests are defined, negotiated and fought over in the politics of the everyday.

This interconnection between text and reader can be considered in terms of the model we introduced in the first chapter of the book. One of the most important points which this model suggests is that there are always *gaps* between actual senders and receivers and the addresser and addressee positions encoded in texts. When we consider ideology, we are concerned with the ways discourse can exert pressure so that the gaps between the various functions appear to dwindle, as if the text were speaking unanimously—to everyone, on behalf of everyone. The major communication functions seem to merge, as if senders and receivers can interact with one another in a social context devoid of conflict and difference. Certain powerful ideologies (for instance, those concerning nationality, gender and race) tend to construct social contexts along these lines.

Ideology and hegemony

One of the problems in developing a model of ideology concerns the kinds of power relations which determine social hierarchies. In contemporary Western societies, power relations between groups and institutions tend wherever possible to represent themselves in terms of *consent* rather than coercion or force. In this process, powerful social groups represent themselves as providing a kind of *cultural leadership*, through which their values and interests may gradually become adopted and embodied in a widespread manner.

In this **hegemonic** model, power operates in a collective, consensual manner. Ideology is offered to, rather than imposed upon, individuals within groups and institutions. The dominant discourses position people to accept ideology. This consensual, positioning process can be extremely powerful, since it may disguise a particular group's need to oppose a dominant discourse.

> **Hegemony** is the social process of consensus in which power relations follow the cultural leadership of a dominant group.

An ideology is hegemonic when its acceptance becomes widespread, providing structures of meaning for many groups and institutions. An historical example may illustrate. As Figure 3.6 suggested, it was common practice in nineteenth century Western societies to consider human character in terms of an essential type. According to this belief, the working class looks and behaves differently from the aristocracy and the middle class, while members of non-European races belong to an entirely separate category of human existence. Commonly-held notions of justice and criminality were, in turn, defined by the way various groups fitted into these class and ethnic stereotypes. These beliefs were partly the result of wider public adoption of arguments circulating in the scientific, legal and medical institutions of the time.

Although these values are no longer held in any official scientific sense, they survive and continue to flourish in other domains. For instance, they motivate many of the stock character and narrative features of media discourse. Consider the long-lived generic cycle of television crime dramas which extends at least from the original 1960s Roger Moore series of *The Saint*, through *Hart to Hart*, *Remington Steele* and *Macmillan and Wife* in the 1970s and 1980s, to more recent manifestations such as *Murder She Wrote*. In them, genteel or well-to-do private investigators work for the wealthy, solving crimes committed by characters whose social traits and behaviour patterns often type them as members of a 'criminal class'.

By coding texts in this manner, television discourse implies that criminality is an issue which can be represented only by dividing society into criminal and non-criminal types, which are closely linked with concepts of class, ethnicity and race. The villains receive their just rewards not so much because they break the law, but because they are entirely distinct from the law-abiding bourgeoisie.

This TV genre thus reproduces a hegemonic ideology about the individual in a class society. As we have said, such an ideology stretches back at least to the nineteenth century. It suggests, first, that the law is in some sense the property of the middle classes, perhaps even their most valuable property. More it suggests that all social classes aspire to the condition and rewards of the bourgeoisie, and that criminality may just be a matter of envy.

Through producing texts like these, media institutions align themselves with a dominant, capital-controlling class which has a vested interest in proposing lawfulness in terms of protecting valuable property. Other social groups (who may make up the bulk of the TV audience) are provided with what seem to be exemplary models of behaviour. These models legitimate as a specific set of attitudes, beliefs and lifestyles, embodied by professional, entrepreneurial and property-owning groups, as if these attitudes belonged to everyone as a natural, pre-ordained, social given.

This kind of textuality promotes particular class and group interests as though they were *universal*. In so doing, it offers audiences these interests as their own. Through lack of access to alternative models and representations of justice, criminality and lifestyle, audiences may become assured that their everyday life is governed by principles of justice geared towards their own needs. Of course, in many ways their needs and desires might be quite different from those of dominant and powerful groups. Yet through media discourse they may be led to aspire towards the 'better life' portrayed in texts with which they are encouraged to identify.

Conflict and contradiction

So far our discussion of ideology presupposes that society is not a single, homogeneous structure, but is made up of different groups and classes of people in unequal power relations. Conflicts occur because the interests of each group do not necessarily coincide. To take an obvious example, it is in the interests of an employer group to keep wages down and working hours up. For an employee group, however, such as a trade union, the reverse is the case: wages need to be kept up, and working hours reduced. The relationship between employee and employer is thus marked by conflict. But it can also become more complicated. Employees may be encouraged to identify with the interests of their employers—for instance, through reward for improved output, leading to higher profitability—in a way that places them *in contradiction* with their own group interests. Such encouragement is hegemony at work.

By universalising knowledge about the world, ideology proposes that all social groups and classes are governed by common principles and commonsense. But ideology is itself the product of institutional discourses which serve the interests of a dominant group. In effect, this means that ideology proposes that the interests of all groups match those of the dominant group. This proposition can mask the contradictions and conflicts which serve to maintain the differences between groups and the power relations within society.

Further analysis of Figure 7.2, 'Australian troops are keeping the peace . . .', can draw out these kinds of masking effects. Readers are invited to identify collectively as 'we', an identity that elides the many different group and individual interests in the large readership of a popular newspaper. With readership set up as a homogeneous community, providing receivers with a single addressee position, other sets of values can be introduced which define how this imagined community of readers might understand itself. In this text, the 'we' slips into an opposition between 'us' and 'them' that is governed by an implied ascendancy of technologically advanced countries, the so-called First World over other, Third World nations.

There is nothing natural or essential about this ascendancy: it is the product of nineteenth and twentieth century colonialism. Technology has never just denoted cultural superiority or advancement. It has always been used exploitatively to build trading empires to service an expanding First World based on commerce and industry.

The ideological coding at work in this text wipes out the traces of this historical residue. It also effaces class and social divisions which have emerged in First World countries during the process of industrialisation. The text realises such effects by situating technology as a provider of security that is offered by a benign nation (Australia), itself marked by homogeneous community and unified national character. The interests of dominant military and government groups are reproduced as if they were the interests of all members of Australian (and by implication, First World) society. The actual relations between readers and social institutions are disguised by a single, unified set of values.

Through the process of hegemony, ideology becomes closely connected with what seems to be the *commonsense* world of everyday life. It indicates that our everyday experience is informed by the kinds of discursive practices—producing and reading texts—in which we engage in our ordinary dealings with others. It also indicates that the taken-for-granted values which seem to make routine life understandable and credible are the product of alignments between social groups with different, and often conflicting, interests.

Textuality and polysemy

In previous chapters we considered that a text is not a homogeneous structure containing a single meaning, but is made up of disparate codes producing multiple meanings. To read a text is to engage in a series of strategic placements through which meanings often compete for dominance. This *dialogical* process may result in one set of meanings taking precedence over others, through various strategies of containment and domination. Textual analysis can enable us to map out these strategies.

Figure 7.1, 'Are you a good wife?', presents us with a specific kind of argument about social identity. The question 'Are you a good wife?' immediately raises the issue of the role of women in the institution of the family. The text's signifiers foreground certain positive connotations for women (such as squeaky cleanness and 'saintliness'). Yet these connotations are at odds with other implications raised by posing the question in the first place. The ideal identity of women is placed in jeopardy because even asking the question suggests that the role of being a wife needs to be carefully evaluated.

Women readers are placed in a subordinate position to an authority that can ask such questions and monitor responses. This authority gains its credibility by appealing to what passes as a set of self-evident, commonsense values shared by all readers: the text's list of things that a good wife should be and do. These values are generalised in the phrase '1960s standards', which implies objectivity and disinterestedness. Yet the standards are defined by male needs. An ideology is operating here in which the general 'voice' that asks the question links itself to a single dominant group and subordinates the group which answers.

Our analysis of this text reveals that ideology limits and contains its polysemic structure by using such stereotypes and myths as good, obedient wives and patriarchal authority. The possibility of a positive understanding of women's social identity has to be read through a male-defined position, disguised in universal terms.

The textual analysis of ideological coding is concerned with discursive practices which turn specific group interests into universals, so that a text seems to speak on behalf of an entire society. At stake here is the phatic authority of the text to command the attention and respect of its readers, to speak the truth of the world as if it were a matter of commonsense. As analysts, our task is to *denaturalise* the text, demonstrating that its commonsense meanings are not givens, but the product of ideological coding.

Transformation

Throughout this chapter we have seen that ideology is not a set of false beliefs held by a particular group or individual. Rather it is a semiotic process which brings individuals and groups into certain power relations and provides social identity and knowledge about the world. One way in which it may do this is through the power of texts to **transform** one thing into another, their ability to represent something, or state of affairs, as something else.

Transformation can initially be understood in terms of grammar. For instance, the sentence 'He is working the machine' transforms one thing, 'he', into something else, someone who is doing something. The event itself (involving human and machine interaction) is transformed into a grammatical sequence. A number of aspects of the event are singled out and placed together in a syntagm. The context and complexity of machine operation are reduced to a simple statement. The sentence places one agent in charge of another, and in so doing suggests an ideology related to technology which proposes the world is 'naturally' ordered when humans control the machines they operate.

There are other ways in which this event could have been signified. The statement 'The machine is working him' reverses the power relations between the agents involved. Such reversals are uncommon in mass media discourse because they suggest a world order which runs counter to commonsense based on myths of human control. When these kinds of reversals do occur, it is usually to define deviant behaviour or states of affairs, thereby re-affirming the supposed normality of everyday life.

In Figure 7.5, 'Car kills salon client,' the machine is placed in the active, 'doing' role usually reserved for people, even though it is defined by being 'out-of-control'. The context of the accident, a women's hair salon, may serve to explain the reversal of human-machine power and control. Routines of female grooming and beauty are often marginalised activities, the butt of male jokes. That a reversal of human-machine control is located in such a setting seems to suggest that norms of control are being implicitly defined as masculine.

Media discourse consistently uses such simple grammatical transformations to define and explain complex social relationships between people, events and things. It produces texts which many readers recognise and understand in terms of collective, commonsense values, assumed to be operating throughout the social domain. Grammatical categories and transformations may mask both different readings of socially significant events and the strategies and motives at work in representing them in different ways.

Consider Figure 8.1, 'The $725 mil drought'. This headline for a front-page story in the Brisbane *Courier Mail* is reporting on a recent drought in Queensland. In this case a *natural* event, the prolonged absence of rain, is transformed through a series of grammatical conversions into a particular *cultural* form, a costly problem.

Figure 8.1

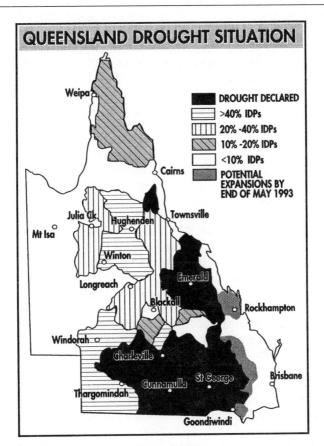

The $725 mil drought
Canberra considers state's cry for help

By WALLACE BROWN, national affairs editor, in Canberra

THE Federal Government is examining an urgent Queensland request for $6 million in special drought aid—and more is likely to be needed.

The impact of the drought could be as high as $725 million in lost revenue in Queensland and could equate to the loss of 15,500 potential full-time jobs.

The State Government says the damage would include the wool industry losing $200 million revenue this year, the beef industry $150 million, the wheat and sorghum industries $130 million, and the cotton industry $11 million.

If rain does not fall in the next two months in the 35 percent of Queensland which is drought-declared, the Commonwealth and State governments will be asked for more help for the affected industries.

A background document obtained by *The Courier-Mail* on the effects of the state's latest severe drought reinforces the plea by Premier Wayne Goss to Prime Minister Paul Keating this week for concerted help from the federal coffers.

Mr Goss told Mr Keating this week that the drought was a natural disaster.

A total of 8539 Queensland properties are drought-declared.

The labelling of this event as 'drought' fixes its meaning within in a paradigm of signs related to nature (natural disasters like flood, fire, cyclone, etc.) and sets it in *opposition* to culture. Nature seems unpredictable, inevitable and uncontrollable, while culture seems predictable, controllable and made by people. However, the words 'The $725 mil' shift 'drought' from the category of nature to that of culture. Assigned a monetary value, the drought is immediately framed as a cultural event: it takes on the characteristics of an expensive human undertaking, such as the construction of a shopping centre, large building or tourist complex.

The headline also has intertextual connotations. 'The $725 mil drought' echoes other phrases circulating in our culture, such as 'the Six-Million Dollar Man' or 'the $64,000 question', both of which transform seemingly non-monetary issues—the human body, a challenging problem—into cash terms. The concept of drought is likewise changed from the category of natural disaster to that of a culturally defined problem or undertaking. This shift also suggests the possibility of a certain type of solution: one that can be 'bought' with the right amount of capital.

The sub-head, 'Canberra considers state's cry for help', provides a potential solution to the problem, now proposed in specifically human terms. 'Canberra' functions as a metonym which substitutes the name of the place, the capital of Australia and the location of Parliament, for the administrative institution of government. By reducing a complex system to a simple name, the headline suggests that a solution can be defined by the decisions of a single entity, perhaps a person or a committee.

There is a similar metonymic transformation at work in the phrase 'state's cry for help'. The administrative, commercial and agricultural structure of Queensland, together with its population, is characterised in terms of one person's emotional act—just as someone who is injured might cry for help. The complex relations among state and federal governments, farmers and social authorities, are reduced to a single interaction between a provider and a recipient. The whole issue is now characterised by a humanitarian concern for the individual.

Each of these statements—the headline and sub-head—belongs to a different discourse. 'The $725 mil drought' is the kind of statement associated with an economic view of the world, in which all things are determined by their cost function. The statement 'Canberra considers state's cry for help' belongs to a humanist view of the world in which society is understood in terms of a collection of individuals, each with their own needs and wants.

At the level of discourse, then, these two statements are in contradiction. Yet other factors suggest that the economic discourse dominates the humanist. Such dominance is signalled by positional and typographical codes: one statement comes before and appears larger than the other. Contradiction is resolved, however, when the second statement is read as a supplement to the first, converting the hard economic reality into human terms. In this case, the transformation moves back from culture to nature: 'Canberra', signifying governmental and financial values, is humanised by the phrase 'state's cry for help', which seems to signify a *natural* expression of human emotions.

As an ideology, economic rationalism is aligned with governmental, commercial and propertied groups whose interests are served through a hardline adoption of fiscal accountability. In the public sphere of the everyday world, however, economic rationalism is less dominant. It is frequently seen as conflicting with a more traditional ideology of humanism comprising such values as respect for individual rights, fair play and class equality.

Presumably because they have embodied these values in everyday life, many readers of the *Courier Mail* may be socially and historically oriented to accept humanist ideology as the natural view. But the allegiance of the newspaper is more complicated. On one hand its publicly avowed policy, often expressed in editorial statements by terms such as 'free speech' and 'freedom of the press', is aligned with the humanist tradition of individual freedom. On the other, its business commitments suggest otherwise: that it is as much concerned as any other corporate institution with maximising profits and, by extension, with economic ideology.

This contradiction is resolved by transforming the threat of economic disaster into a human crisis. A grammatical move translates one set of ideological values into another, providing readers with a secure position from which to understand a potentially conflictual situation. Even though the main body of the story is made up of a series of factual statements, completely devoid of humanist values (there is no mention of those who are suffering from the drought), readers are invited to interpret it through the frame of a humanist ideology, even though this is compromised by its subordination to economic rationalism.

The text motivates readers to consent to a certain way of thinking about the world. Yet it also enables them to believe they are thinking about things in traditional and accepted terms. Here we can see the phatic flexibility of hegemonic discourse, and the power of ideology to contain divergent viewpoints.

An ideological analysis of *Top Gun*

The commercially successful film of the late 1980s, *Top Gun*, is an excellent example of the way ideology often operates in a complex and contradictory manner. In basic terms, it is about the training of American naval fighter pilots in combat manoeuvres. It also, however, reproduces long-standing myths of male superiority and an ideology of individualism.

The film starts on an aircraft carrier in the Indian Ocean. 'Maverick' Mitchell, a hot-headed navy pilot, and his partner 'Goose' are engaged in a reconnaissance mission. During the flight, contact is made with a suspicious aircraft. Maverick manoeuvres close to the suspicious plane, showing great skill and daring, but breaking the rules of flying. He later nurses one of his fellow pilots, whose nerve has broken, back to the carrier. Although reprimanded for reckless flying, Maverick and Goose are selected to attend an élite training school for up-and-coming fighter pilots. As we will see, this opening sequence works as a metonym for the rest of the narrative.

The school operates by pitting the trainees against one another in a competition to establish who will be 'top gun'—the best fighter pilot in the navy. We are told that Maverick's deceased father, Duke Mitchell (an old War-time buddy of the school commander), had developed a bad reputation, which has led to his son's exclusion from officer school. At one stage, after Maverick buzzes the control tower, resulting in a dressing-down from the commander, Goose says: 'I know it's tough for you. They wouldn't let you into the academy because you're Duke Mitchell's kid. You have to live with that reputation. It's like every time we go up there you're flying against a ghost. It makes me nervous.'

On their nights off, the male trainees go to a local night club, looking for women. Maverick meets and attempts to seduce a beautiful woman, Charley, who at this point, playfully resists his advances. Unbeknown to Maverick, she is a highly-qualified instructor at the school and holds a PhD in air combat. The following day, Maverick is surprised to meet Charley again, this time in her role as instructor for the group of trainees.

Because of her background and qualifications, Charley's instructions are based on a textbook understanding of air combat. Her ideas immediately come into conflict with Maverick's intuitive style of flying. In practice runs, Maverick repeatedly out-manoeuvres the older, more experienced instructor pilots by breaking heavily when tailed, thereby slipping behind the pursuing plane to gain an advantage. Even though it goes against the textbook, this move gains grudging admiration from the instructors.

Charley and Maverick continue their 'cat and mouse' relation-ship. It seems to mirror the competition between Maverick and his fellow trainees. In particular, it parallels Maverick's rivalry with the Ice Man, who sets the pace in the competition, and eventually be-comes 'top gun'. Despite her resistance, Charley finally 'surrenders' and declares her love for Maverick.

In one training incident, Maverick's plane (co-piloted by Goose) goes into an uncontrollable spin. Maverick and Goose are forced to eject, and the jump causes Goose's death. Shaken by the loss of his best friend, Maverick is unable to finish the course. He surrenders the race for top gun to the Ice Man. At the same time, Charley leaves for a job in Washington.

Later, Maverick returns to normal duty in the Indian Ocean, but a number of his fellow pilots now have doubts about his nerve for combat. Maverick and another pilot are sent out to investigate suspicious radar sightings. Their planes are ambushed by a superior force which threatens to destroy them. Maverick panics and turns to leave, but recalling the death of Goose, he summons up his courage and enters battle, shooting down many of the enemy planes. He returns to a hero's welcome. Finally, having accepted a position as instructor in the top gun school—a reward for his bravery—he is reunited with Charley, who has given up her Washington job to be with him.

The narrative of *Top Gun* sets up a series of oppositions between group and individual, male and female, youth and ma-turity, outsider and insider. At the ideological level, these oppo-sitions work through a series of contradictions which are resolved in favour of a particular masculinist version of the world.

Maverick represents the outsider, an individual whose skills and self-understanding are based upon an intuitive grasp of his place in the world. The outsider doesn't think too much about things; he needs only to act. But Maverick is also part of a unit, the fighter pilots, whose group well-being depends upon recognising shared interests for the common good. This opposition between self and group cannot be easily reconciled. It even pressures the bond between Maverick and Goose. After Maverick has buzzed the control tower, Goose expresses concern that this display of individual bravado will jeopardise his own place on the course: 'I've got a family to consider,' he reminds his partner.

In many ways, *Top Gun* is about Maverick learning that indi-vidual action has to be integrated into group behaviour. The film works as a *rite of passage* narrative, showing the trial and ordeal of a young male's induction into full manhood. But the film also en-dorses the values and attitudes associated with the male hero *before* he becomes an adult who can accept authority and group responsibility. For instance, in dropping out of the top gun course, Maverick symbolically fails to move into a fully adult state. This failure is not total. The way is left open for a second chance, but under conditions which are entirely different from those of the course. In shooting down the enemy planes, Maverick confirms his independence as an intuitive outsider. He successfully uses the 'illegal' breaking manoeuvre to outsmart the enemy. His triumphant return is a victory for the individual over the group, and in this way confirms, rather than transforms, his character as initially depicted in the film.

This kind of narrative structure, showing male individuals in contradiction with larger social groups, is common to Hollywood films. It suggests an ideology of masculine authority which can work in tandem with group interests as long as it coincides with the goals of the male individual.

This structure works through constantly occurring conflict. The individual, often the hero, perceives his interests to be at odds with those of the group. This sets in train a series of challenges and resolutions which ultimately allow the group to redefine itself in terms of a new order, with (though sometimes without) the hero.

In *Top Gun*, the hero re-enters the group on his own terms. This move suggests a rejection of the authority of textbook rules in favour of the individualistic values of manly intuition and youthful exuberance. But Maverick's re-entry is also an endorsement of the authority of the group. When he is told that as a reward for his brave deeds, he can have any posting he desires, he *chooses* to become a top gun instructor. Maverick projects his resolute individuality back to the group. He is both outsider and insider, youth and adult, individual and group member. Maverick signifies an ideal hero for a culture whose ideologies are based upon notions of individual freedom, but whose social realities are determined by group and class interests.

Male authority is also signified in the film through mythic conflict between father and son. As in many *rite of passage* narratives, Maverick's journey to full maturity is defined in terms of handing down proper male identity from father to son. It's as if these males can perpetuate and procreate themselves with no women involved in the process. All the trainee pilots are known by nicknames given to them by other men. This naming process denies a mother's role in their family origins, and naturalises their identity as part of a totally male-defined group.

Masculinity is celebrated and desired throughout the film. There are numerous homoerotic images and references: planes gradually extend across the frame of a shot, seeming to imitate a male erection; when watching a training film in which a missile destroys a target, one pilot says to another, 'This gives me a hard on,' while the other replies, 'Don't tease me.' These characters live in a world where women are almost entirely excluded. Masculine identity seems to engender itself in a never-ending cycle of heroic action.

All of this takes place in displaced form, through the sibling rivalry between the trainee pilots for the honour of being top gun, itself a symbol of phallic power. The structure of masculine authority is never really in threat because each pilot-son seeks only to replicate the father. This authority figure can be challenged and replaced by different men, but the position and system of authority he signifies can never be removed. (He is signified in the film by such characters as Duke, Maverick's father, and the commander-pilot whose flying skills always surpass those of the trainees.) Indeed, the 'sons' don't really want to get rid of the father, but to become him.

The structure of father-son rivalry makes it difficult for Maverick to become a fully fledged member of the group. He has inherited his father's skills and prowess at flying, which will eventually enable him to defeat rivals and become top gun. Yet he has also inherited his father's negative reputation, which blocks his passage to full male maturity. The father is an ambiguous figure, whom Maverick must both imitate and supersede. It is Goose's death which paradoxically grants him the opportunity to follow both paths. For in refusing to finish the course, Maverick defers to the authority of the group and is eventually able to throw off the weight of his father's reputation and pass through to full male adulthood.

The single prominent woman in the film is Charley. She, too, is an ambiguous figure. She seems partly masculinised—through her name, but also as a member of the crew—and hence is both a rival and an admirer of Maverick. Maverick's relationship with her thus reflects the homoerotic links between him and the other trainees. At the same time, through his romance with Charley he is able to confirm his straight masculinity and group membership, and to break out of individual isolation.

The heterosexual romance also works to naturalise the homoerotic implications of the narrative. Charley provides a pretext and model for how members of the audience, male and female, may admire Maverick. If she accepts him, we all can. The role of the woman character is thus to legitimate a myth of male supremacy, enabling Maverick to take his place as hero-leader of the group.

We can sum up the ideological workings of a film like *Top Gun* in the following terms. Male authority is confirmed as the natural result of innate skills and youthful exuberance, which are tied to the concept of winning. It is textually and generically framed through a mythic narrative form which represents male authority as the perpetuation of traditional virtues. These include a reverence for things which went before (the ways of the father); the assumption of an essential heroism, which determines everything; and the proposal of a world whose order is entirely dependent upon the fulfilment of male destiny. *Top Gun* is thus a deeply conservative film. It leaves little room for the development of cultural values, social identities and reading positions other than those defined by a dominant ideology of male supremacy.

Reading ideology

As our analysis of *Top Gun* suggests, ideology works by orienting people in social contexts towards accepting certain values about the world as natural, obvious and self-evident. Social identity is reinforced through the continual recycling of particular ideological codes. Readers and audiences of mass media texts may adopt these codes as their own, even if their interests and those of the media do not always coincide.

Textual analysis reveals the ways that discourses and texts position readers to *embody* ideology. In this process of embodiment, people resolve contradictions and accommodate values which do not necessarily equate with their own day-to-day life. The values become built into their understandings of their own desires, identities and expectations of future situations.

Of course, there are many ways in which different audience groups would respond to a text like *Top Gun* other than the one we have outlined. Each of these alternative responses would involve phatic processes of ideological address, positioning and resistance.

The reading of mass media texts is not a passive exercise in which readers are duped into accepting dominant ideological values without question. In reading media texts, they may be able to construct, reinforce, modify and even reject the social identities offered them. They work to define, modify or contest their place in the world as it is determined by group and class interests. The analysis of ideological coding reveals the *constructedness* of the social contexts in which readers and texts interact. Thus ideological analysis suggests possibilities for changing these contexts.

Exercises

1 What ideologies seem to be at work in Figure 7.3? Consider the relation between the photographic image and supplementary written commentary. Can you see any intertextual associations?

2 Consider Figure 7.4 ('John's in from the cold'). How does the text work in terms of transformation? What contradictions do you see? How are they resolved?

3 Tape an episode of a television situation comedy, soap opera or other narrative text. Spend some time in class or at home analysing the text in terms of ideology. Construct an alternative narrative which uses the same situation and characters but leads to different ideological conclusions.

Sources and further reading

Two Continental theorists whose ideas underlie much of the contemporary discussion of ideology in cultural studies are Antonio Gramsci, *A Gramsci Reader: Selected Writings 1916–34* (London: Lawrence and Wishart, 1988) and Louis Althusser, 'Ideology and Ideological State Apparatuses (Notes, towards an Investigation)', *Lenin and Philosophy and Other Essays* (London: NLB, 1977). For a general discussion of media, discourse, power and ideology, the set of essays in *Culture, Media, Language: Working Papers in Cultural Studies, 1972–79*, edited by Stuart Hall *et al.* (London: Unwin Hyman, 1980) is an excellent introduction. In *Channels of Discourse: Television and Contemporary Criticism*, edited by Robert C. Allen (London: Routledge, 1987), there is also a useful essay on ideology by Mimi White. Eve Kosofsky Sedgwick's *Between Men: English Literature and Male Homosocial Desire* (New York: Columbia University Press, 1985) is an important and interesting study of the effects of masculinist ideologies in literature and culture.

For a detailed discussion of ideology from a linguistic and social semiotic point of view, refer to Robert Hodge and Gunther Kress, *Social Semiotics* (Cambridge: Polity Press, 1988). The concept of transformation presented in this chapter derives partly from their work. Ideology is also discussed at some length in Norman Fairclough, *Language and Power* (London: Longman, 1989), and Roger Fowler, *Language in the News: Discourse and Ideology in the Press* (London: Routledge, 1991). A recent overview of different theories of ideology is provided in Terry Eagleton's *Ideology: An Introduction* (London: Verso, 1991).

9 Systems and strategies

One of the major attractions Saussurean semiotics held for us was the way in which it insists that meaning is not primarily a quality contained within, or possessed by, an individual sign, but something which exists outside the sign, in the various sorts of relationships in which it exists, and into which it enters.

We have examined some of the implications of this in earlier chapters. In Chapters 2 and 3, we looked at some ways in which meaning results from relationships which are internal to a sign system—that is, from relationships among signs themselves. Chapters 5 and 6 were concerned largely with ways in which this sort of systematic structuring could be generalised to some of the larger unities signs display, such as genre and narrative structures.

We have also tried to emphasise, however, that even though there might be distinct regularities in the ways signs are used, they are never just the mechanical product of rules. Signs are never produced in a vacuum, but in specific contexts, and with certain concrete (if not entirely foreseeable) effects. In Chapter 4, we developed some ideas of textuality as a series of social practices, and kept these ideas in mind when discussing genre and narrative. Genre's interest and enormous flexibility, after all, comes from the fact that meaning can come from transgressing, combining and playing freely with conventions, rather than blindly following them. It is now time to examine in a bit more detail just what these relationships might be between the rules and the practices of signs.

Contexts and citation

According to Saussure, the system (*langue*) can account for the almost infinitely large number of possible utterances. All of them are intelligible because they are constructed according to the rules of a certain 'grammar'. Knowledge of the rules of the system allows one to construct, and make sense out of, utterances one might never have come across before. Saussurean semiotics thus takes this governing sign *system* as its object of study.

When Saussure relates signs to what is outside them, he is primarily interested in their relationships to other signs within the system as a whole, and not to things which aren't signs. He's not denying that signs really do have relationships with other things outside the sign system; he just brackets these off, and says that they're not really the concern of the linguist or semiotician, but of the sociologist or anthropologist or historian. Saussurean semiotics shows signs taking their meaning from *other signs in the same system.*

We have seen in our first chapter that contextual functions are, however, unavoidable. *Deictic* features of language ('pointing' words such as *here, now, this, I, you*) rely to some extent on a knowledge of the context in which the utterance is used. Signs are never emitted into a void: they always occur in specific situations, where they aim to do things, to have effects, to do work, to elicit responses. And this broader context may include a lot of things which aren't signs, or at least which can't easily be included in Saussure's idea of the sign system.

We will examine this further, because it implies a very important qualification of the Saussurean system. It points out the extent to which Saussurean semiotics has simplified what happens in sign use. Now let's complicate matters.

You'll recall this example from Chapter 2:

Figure 9.1

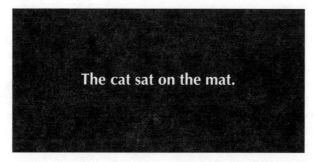

There, we treated this sign as an utterance produced by the application of rules. We divided it up into paradigm sets, and showed how it has a clearly discernible syntagmatic structure. In doing this, we focused on certain features of the sign, the individual units (words) and their order, while ignoring others. We had nothing to say, for example, about the fact that this might be a sentence written in chalk on a blackboard, or that it might be a facsimile, in a textbook, of words in chalk on a blackboard. What we did, in fact, was examine this sign in complete isolation from any particular context.

We didn't ask any questions about who would be likely to use such a sentence, why, under what circumstances, in what situations, to whom, or with what possible effects. All we wanted was to get an idea of the internal structure of the utterance, the way it drew on and used a certain system of regular rules.

But is context really so negligible? Every utterance occurs in a situation. This one did, although we didn't say much about it then. It's a context so obvious it's easy to overlook: the book you're holding, this textbook on social semiotics and cultural studies. The utterance is being used within that as an example of the type of sign-process we want to model. What's more, it's a *cited* utterance, one which has been drawn from other contexts and transplanted here. You doubtless recognised it as a schoolroom sentence: the simple words, the repetition of sounds and letters. Neither of these contexts is negligible, and each leads to a somewhat different meaning: as a schoolroom sentence, the utterance is naïve, but as a sentence in a semiotics textbook it is part of a more sophisticated argument. The utterance would be different again if it were given other contexts, such as, say, an answer to a question from the cat's owner, or a crossword clue. We could even go so far as to say that two radically different utterances can be verbally identical but differ only in context.

Every utterance has some sort of context, even though none is completely tied to a single context. Utterances may be cited in contexts and situations conceivably very distant from the original, but they are never *without* context. Every utterance is a reaction to a situation, a response to another utterance, even if this utterance is a silence. Every utterance invites another in response. Silence may be just as much a response as words. For a start, it has a very strong phatic function: it says things like, 'I'm closing down all communications with you; this conversation isn't worth continuing; you're wasting my time; go away.' All of these may be read as meaningful utterances.

Consider the use which can be made of silence in a television interview. If the interviewer asks a question to which the interviewee merely responds with a 'Yes' or 'No', the interviewer may rephrase the question and try again, hoping for a more satisfactory response. More subtly, though, the interviewer may just keep silent. Eventually, in order to fill in the silence, the interviewee offers more information. With any luck, this may even include information the interviewee hadn't originally been intending to say, so strong is the import of the silence.

Even silence and withdrawal from an exchange, then, are responses. If for Saussure the basic *object* of semiotic study is the system of *langue*, and the basic *unit* of meaning is the *syntagm*, we must now augment that: the basic *situation* of meaning is the

exchange. Exchange is not, of course, something new to the Saussurean system: with the idea of value, it is already one of the key features of his theory of signs, though it is exclusively limited to relations among signs. Here, we will draw other consequences from the idea of exchange. Saussurean semiotics works very economically and elegantly to describe what it characterises as the internal relations within a system. These do not, however, by any means exhaust the relations a sentence can enter into in the real world, or all the contextual forces which have formed it.

Citability provides the potential for signs to be and do new things. Figures 9.2 and 9.3 are two such occasions. How would we reconsider Saussure to think through such potentials in signs? It may help to take as an example a process which clearly takes on its meaning in the sort of exchange we've just been suggesting, and have a close look at what is happening in it.

Figure 9.2

In Australia in the 1980s, Sheridan ran a famous series of billboards showing a male model asleep in their sheets. In their choice of a good-looking and well-muscled young man, the advertisers were clearly aiming at women, who are by far the biggest buyers of manchester goods. What the advertisers didn't seem initially to have foreseen was that the billboards would become gay icons. More than one gay pub in Sydney displayed its own copy of the poster behind the bar.

Figure 9.3 The Mod revival

The late 1970s saw the rise of Punk and the revival of 1960s Mod among working class British youth. It is easy to suggest contributing social causes for this: obvious ones would include the high and rising rate of unemployment (particularly in urban areas and particularly among youth), made more irksome by the ostentation of that year's celebrations of the Queen's Silver Jubilee. The Mod revival embraced the clothing, music and lifestyle of the original 1960s movement: a sharp and immediately recognisable sartorial sense; a taste for the music of the original bands associated with 1960s Mod (such as The Who); and lovingly restored Vespa motor scooters. Much of the Mod revival focused on music: Mod not only had its own bands, but also its own venues and independent record labels.

British cultural studies, of course, found all this intensely interesting. Its classic text on the topic is Dick Hebdige's *Subculture: The Meaning of Style* (London: Methuen, 1979). It reads Punk and Mod as forms of 'revolt into style', symbolic gestures of social resistance. For Hebdige, Mod fashions work by quotation: that is, they repeat in new contexts and for new purposes signs which have their origin elsewhere. The Mod revival is not just a copying of the fashions and tastes of a decade-and-a-half ago, but a knowing, witty and socially critical citation of them in a contemporary framework and for contemporary purposes. The music of bands such as The Jam, for instance, took a polemical and broadly Left stance against many of the features of 1970s British society. What's more, one could say exactly the same thing about the 'original' Mod. In their fastidious neatness, relative costliness and immediately distinctive lines, for example, the original Mod clothing fashions are themselves re-workings and re-citations of mainstream styles, which are simultaneously playing with and against various ideas of class and respectability.

Since popular music is a highly saleable and increasingly internationalised commodity, by the end of the 1970s much of the music associated with the urban British Mod revival had made its way to other parts of the world, and taken on a life quite removed from the conditions under which it had arisen. The Mod revival itself became the object of quotation and re-citation at yet another remove. For a few years in the early 1980s in Sydney, for example, there was a thriving Mod culture, complete with bands and venues marked out as its own, and, yes, lovingly salvaged and detailed Vespas. Sydney Mods, like the originals, tended to be working class youth, in their mid-teens to early twenties, but unlike the originals, they were taking up and reworking signs from a culture half a world, and nearly a generation, away. One of the frequently circulated books of Sydney Mod was Hebdige's *Subculture*, circulated and read not as sociology or a study of social semiotics, but, in a final demonstration of Hebdige's point of the unforeseeable citability of the sign, as style guide.

The gift

Whatever else it might be, a gift is very clearly a sign. It means something. It says something about the giver's relationship to the receiver, or at least about what the giver imagines this relationship to be—that is, it has very important phatic, conative and expressive functions.

Sometimes the bare act of giving is a sign, regardless of what the gift itself might actually be. Consider the peculiar practice of giving cards. Cards are a sort of Clayton's gift, something you give when you're not actually giving a present. Giving a card, you are offering something with very little actual use value at all: at best a joke or witticism or attractive picture that sits on a shelf for a week or so and then goes out with the vegetable peelings. In the obvious absence of any other use, the important thing with a card is simply the act of giving it. With a card, you say, 'I gave you something, even though it's something which has no other use whatever than to say "I gave you something".'

This is not so much an indicator of the vapidity of greeting cards as of the significance of the act of giving. It might be more accurate to say in a case like this that it isn't so much the card as the ritualised act which is the sign. The card itself is a sort of receipt, the minimal something that has to change hands just so there can be that act. Giving a card reduces the act of giving to almost nothing *but* a sign, one which is almost pure formal function.

There is, however, a certain skill involved in gift giving. You have to judge all sorts of things, including the interests, likes and dislikes of the person you're giving to. You don't usually give an expensive wine to a non-drinker, or to the person who runs the shop you bought it from. You have to judge your relationship with the recipient. How close is it? Too expensive or too cheap a present may be embarrassing, for both parties. A present which a receiver feels is too expensive may be seen as a way of insisting on a closeness which the receiver doesn't want; one which is too cheap may speak of a distance, and may well produce it even if there wasn't one there before.

Very importantly, you have also to consider that a gift places a symbolic indebtedness on the receiver. If you get a gift, you have to reply. If you don't send a gift in your turn on the next corresponding occasion, that very silence and absence will itself be seen as a response ('I sent something to X for his birthday, but he didn't send me anything for mine: guess he's not interested any more.'). There is the same sort of skill in responding to a present. Give too large a present, and you may escalate things. And so on.

Some of us are doubtless better at handling these situations and exchanges than others. Such skills aren't simply the result of applying rules. There's no simple ready reckoner which will tell you reassuringly that if someone of a certain degree X of closeness to you, with interests A, B and C and positive dislikes P, Q and R, has given you gift Y, worth $Z, on occasion W, then the absolutely correct thing to give them for Christmas is a vinyl wallet worth $12.95. If there were a system of *langue* behind all this, there would be a single correct response. But in gift giving there obviously isn't. What you do depends both on a whole host of factors too numerous and unstable even to try to systematise (such as what you actually want to do with the relationship, and on factors which are perhaps quite unforeseeable, such as what the other party might want to do with the relationship).

There's certainly a skill involved, however. Indeed, you could argue that it's precisely because there isn't a system that skill comes into it. What's more, it's a skill you can get better at. While the phatic, conative and expressive functions are tremendously important in the gift-as-sign, the metalingual function (the one which suggests which system of rules to decode this by) is relatively unimportant. Although systems might to some extent exist (there are such things as books of etiquette), they don't cover much of the intricacy of what's happening. What is important, though, and governs a lot of the subtlety of the exchange, is the contextual function. In gift giving, you monitor the situation, and decide accordingly. You play things by ear.

System may be a very important set of considerations if we consider the sign shorn of any context. But once we start trying to take context into account, it is no longer possible to treat sign usage simply as a matter of correct application of rules. Rather than see signs as the result of the application of a system of rules, we must now try to think of them in terms of *strategies of behaviour.*

This means we will have to rethink the status of the language system. It doesn't mean we are now having doubts about the existence of the various regularities which we have been bringing to light, but just that we should not think of these internal relations as the sole determinant of meaning. On the one hand, there is a system of rules. On the other, there are questions of what you do with those rules, what strategies you employ. In other words, it is beginning to look as if the relationship that system has to signs doesn't so much resemble the relationship between a set of instructions and their results, as that between the rules of a game and an actual match played according to them.

Games of strategy

Let's follow the analogy, by considering a game like chess or tennis.

Both are highly codified. Each has quite definite sets of rules (*langue*) which govern play (*parole*). In chess, each piece can move in certain ways and not in others; in tennis, a legal shot is one which lands in certain parts of the court and not in others, and so on. In each case, there is a relatively small number of rules, but a virtually infinite number of moves which can be made on their basis. They are quite independent of the players. In this case, they are even objectively codified: if there's any dispute over them, the rules can be consulted and a definitive ruling can be made.

To this extent, a game works much like a semiotic system. But there's a lot more to games than this limited comparison might imply. Knowing the rules does not account for the vast variety of ways in which the rules can be used, and the effects of such uses. Though both may be equally familiar with the rules, there's a big difference between Martina Navratilova and a Sunday player. Far from being the enabling source of sign usage, the system of rules may be just one feature the user can implement—not necessarily the determining one. As with gift giving, there may well be certain non-systematised (and even non-systematisible) strategic aspects involved.

Let us suggest, then, that sign processes do behave with the sorts of systemic regularity Saussure describes, but also that this system is not enough to describe everything involved in sign processes. From the point of view of the one who uses the signs, we could say that a knowledge of the relevant systems is a *necessary* but never a *sufficient* condition of competent use. The difference is between knowing the rules and playing the game. I can know the rules of tennis without ever having played it—or quite conceivably without ever even having *seen* it played. A copy of the LTA rules will tell me the size and shape of the court, what constitutes a foul, and what scores points. But compare that codified knowledge of the game to an actual situation in play. You are standing on the court, racquet in hand, with a ball coming at you at high speed. You have a fraction of a second in which to react. In that time, you not only have to interpose your racquet, but do it in such a way as to send the ball back over the net into your opponent's court. The best shot will be the one which lands the ball in that part of the court which your opponent finds most difficult to get to in time. A fraction of a second's hesitation, or a slight miscalculation in the placement of your body or reach, may mean the difference between your scoring or your opponent's. And at every shot, though you are playing all the time within the same set of rules, the ball comes at you in a way that's never the same twice, and you hit it back in a way that's never the same twice, never perfectly replicable.

So some aspects of the game, perhaps the most important ones, can't easily be formalised. Though they refer to and involve the formal regularities of system, they are extremely fluid, and depend on things that are in principle unpredictable from the system. This is not in any way to suggest that they're in some way mysterious or ineffable. On the contrary, they're often highly teachable and transmissible skills. That's why there are sports coaches. These skills are just relatively uncodified, an area of free play. You have to learn them on the court, rather than from a book. They're a matter of training bodies, muscles, reflexes.

As an antidote to the formalising and decontextualising tendencies in Saussure, then, it's useful to think of sign use in terms of a game of strategy, a **sign-game**. We have already considered actual language use as an exchange. Now think of it in particular as a tennis game, tossing the ball of response back and forth. There may be relaxed games of tennis, where no-one cares much who wins, and there may be intense, fast, fierce ones. Something similar holds for conversations. There may be situations where there's little at stake except the immediate pleasure of playing (phatic bonding), and the game continues just because both parties enjoy it; or there may be a lot at stake, and the exchange continues even in the face of difficulties for one or some or all of the participants (cross examination, justification, argument, persuasion, etc.). There are situations where you live on your nerves and must reply on the instant, since hesitation will be fatal; where you can't even stop to consider what you're saying. What we could call the skill or strategy rather than the system of language use is largely unaccounted for in Saussure. Again, we must emphasise that this is not to say that Saussure is simply wrong, but just that we have to revise our view of the relationship which system has to sign processes.

There may be loose rules for dialogue, just as there are for gift giving. The forms of behaviour known as *etiquette* are cases in point. Etiquette demands that one doesn't interrupt a speaker, for example. In fact, of course, interruption is something we all do frequently. Interruption is a way of asserting domination: one interrupts those one dominates more than one interrupts those one is dominated by. On the whole, men interrupt women more frequently than women interrupt men. This 'rule' about non-interruption, then, must have a somewhat different status from the rules of a Saussurean system. It is not a directive which must be followed; nor is it a condition for the utterance to make sense. It is more like a set of available options with well-codified consequences, rather than a set of prescriptions about how things have to be done. Even in a literal game, where the rules are stricter, the skill in playing is often to use the rules with the utmost flexibility, right at the very limits of legality. This is the way John MacEnroe and Pat Cash used to play tennis, for example. It's also the way Bobby Fisher played chess in the 1970s: completely within the legal rules of the game, but employing all sorts of dirty tactics to unnerve and disturb the concentration of his opponents.

Improvisation and negotiation

The examples we've been looking at (dialogue, gift, game) suggest that systematicity is simply one of the aspects available to a flexible and only partially codified *situational* play of strategies. Of necessity, these are largely improvised, according to changes in the situation, and with whatever comes to hand, whether or not it was originally intended to serve that purpose. Such improvisation is often known as **bricolage**, a term first used in structural anthropology.

The textures of day-to-day life are full of—indeed, almost characterised by—this sort of improvisation, which takes social givens and deflects them towards other ends, investing them with other meanings. These may be spur-of-the-moment reactions to a temporary situation: an office marker temporarily disguises a run in black tights, an egg seals a leaking radiator until the next garage, a paperclip fastens the earpiece back onto a pair of glasses. Other improvisations may become part of the semi-permanent practices of some groups, first of all on the fringes of received practice, and then either becoming absorbed into, or forcing a rupture with, the official version. Trodden pathways between buildings show where their inhabitants and users habitually decline to take designated footpaths; walls become unofficial supports for advertising, or personal messages or graffiti; after school and at weekends, shopping centre carparks become skateboard ramps.

The feel for the game

These concepts of strategy and improvisation emphasise that semiotic events are in no way automatic products of the application of a system: you can be perfectly fluent in the rules of grammar and still be tongue-tied when called on to give a speech or begin a letter. In all systems, there is a more or less wide margin of indeterminacy. The system will give you the rules, but will not tell you everything about how these rules can be used.

On the other hand, it is important to emphasise that strategy is not simply a matter of individual choice, as though all possible options were available to the user, who has only to choose freely among them. We have argued from the outset that sign processes are primarily social, and that a sign's various functions of address (conative, expressive and phatic) show some of the ways in which individuals are positioned and produced within social processes. Not all possibilities may present themselves equally to all individuals. In general, the options available in a given case are strongly linked to individuals' positions within a complex social structure, according to factors such as class, race, ethnicity, gender, sexuality, age and language.

Take the case of applying for a job. Most jobs will require a formal written application, such as the one in Figure 1.1. First, before we examine the complex and sophisticated role strategy plays in such a letter, let us consider the main code system required by a written application. In nearly every case, it is understood that a job application is to be written in Standard English. The applicant's competence in using this form of English may assume immense importance, since it will very often be treated as an index to many other things: skills in language and communication in general, or even powers of reasoning, intellectual abilities or social skills. Obviously, in such a case an applicant who is unfamiliar with the code of Standard English—its syntax and grammar—is at a disadvantage, no matter what his skills might be in other non-standard forms of English, or in abstract reasoning, management or financial affairs.

In practice, the situation is likely to be a lot more complex than a simple distinction between those who have access to a code and those who do not. Standard English is after all, in one form or another, the English taught in schools throughout the English-speaking world. What is going to be crucial in a job application is not just a knowledge of grammar, but something else which often gets referred to in terms like *fluency of expression, stylishness* or (though it may appear to be a contradiction) *naturalness*, all of which, as we have just suggested, may well be attributed metonymically to the addresser as much as to the letter. This 'something else' is considerably less easily codified than grammar and syntax, but may nevertheless provide a vital touchstone in judging both letter and addresser. It corresponds to what we earlier referred to as 'a feel for the game', and is a matter not just of access to a code but of the way in which one *inhabits* the forms of behaviour the code involves.

Consider the functions of address (the expressive, conative and phatic), and the subtle juggling act they require. As applicant, you may have to paint yourself as knowledgeable, but certainly not as a know-all; as respectful but not deferential; as forceful, but not pushy; as independent and individual, but also as a team worker rather than a lone wolf—and so on, and so on. Optimally, you have to demonstrate that the qualities demanded by the position are not only yours, but yours by nature: unlearned and unstrained natural expressions; in short, everything covered by the concept of *talent*. That is, what you have to show is that the qualities which are

Figure 9.4 On the fridge

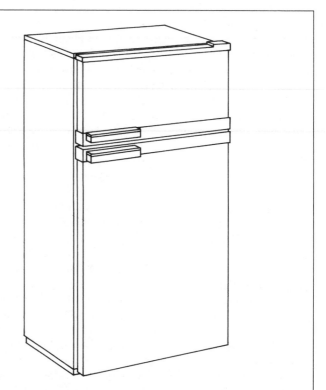

The primary purpose of the domestic refrigerator is, of course, to keep food and other perishables cold. Advertisements for fridges rarely mention any other use for them. But cooling is far from their only function, as a glance at one in use readily shows. The refrigerator is a focal point of the kitchen and the household.

The top of a refrigerator nearly always comes to serve as a shelf. For reasons of efficient management, hygiene or safety, most kitchens will have well-designated storage areas. Utensils will be put in one set of cupboard shelves, foodstuffs in others, and cleaning goods in another. But because the area on top of the fridge is 'not really' a storage area as such, it can serve as a miscellaneous catchment area for things which don't have any other easily assignable place, either in the kitchen or elsewhere. This surface is often a metre and a half or more above the ground, so it also serves as the ideal place for items which need to be kept out of the reach of children, or household pets or insects.

But it's the white enamelled vertical surfaces of the refrigerator which most clearly show improvisation at work. Like a caddis-fly larva, a fridge gradually covers most of its visible surface with bits and pieces gathered from its environment: notes, magnets, advertising, information, decoration. The refrigerator becomes a clearing-centre for household information, both transient (shopping lists, notes from one household member to another) and durable (emergency telephone numbers and procedures). It is a place for filtering information which comes from outside the household: local businesses, tradespeople, power utilities and political parties all offer magnetic fridge advertising, but not all of it ends up on the fridge. It is a sort of semi-public scrapbook of personal bric-à-brac, open to and even inviting the visitor's gaze. Because of its non-designated status, visitors who would see scrutinising a host's noticeboard as intrusive will happily pore over their fridge door. Refrigerators may display personal or family mementoes: cards, photographs, concert or theatre tickets, school photos, children's drawings (that the refrigerator is such an open display may make it a symbolic reward for the child). Brightly coloured magnets even mean that the refrigerator door can be a temporary child-minder under the supervision of a parent preparing food—not to mention a walking aid for the very young. And, of course, the fridge is always one of the focal points at parties.

On top:

Radio; ½ loaf of sliced bread; odd-shaped bottle (empty); part of fridge door handle (broken);

Ice-cream container with small number of sweets inside;

Ice-cream container with a candlestick, a jar of thumbtacks, a plastic bag of magnetic letters and numbers, and the handle to a broken saucepan lid (not yet claimed on the guarantee);

Ice-cream container holding three containers of Play-Doh;

Plastic tray containing: a plastic bag of party goods (cake candles and decorations, party blowers, toothpicks); 2 packets of sparklers; Blu-Tack; jar with cake candles; 2 children's whistles, on cords; bottle-opener; 8 household candles; flower seeds; bulldog clips; lighter; 4 children's paintbrushes; more cake candles (numerals and sparkling tapers); herb slicer; picnic salt and pepper shakers; pie crust support; pastry stamp; aspirin; kitchen knife (believed lost); 5 plastic cordial bottle tops; 2 crayons; toy bottle-brush; reusable plastic iceblock sticks; mixer attachment; whistle from disused kitchen kettle; marble; 4 sweets; 2 plastic coffee measures; clothespeg; string; 2 plastic drinking straws; 2 egg rings.

Left-hand side:
Magnetic cards from local phar-
macist, milk vendor, 2 plumbers,
bank, ice-cream vendor, hamburger
chain;
Takeaway menus from local pizza
and seafood places;
Memo board with black felt pen
on string;
Two school photographs;
Eight non-advertising magnets
(letters, numerals, animals, etc.).

Front:
Magnetic cards from gas utility,
ice-cream vendor (again), hamburger
chain (again) and local seafood take-
away;
Magnetic calendar from local
Lebanese takeaway;
Magnetic frame with photograph
of children in bath;
Three pictures by children;
Price list for school tuckshop;
Sticker from cereal packet (non-
removable);
Sixteen non-advertising magnets.

phatically those of the group you wish to enter are already yours, not by learning but by endowment. The form the letter requires is not *I can do it*, but *I have a gift for it.*

Now because these qualities tend to be represented metony-mically by your 'feel for' formal Standard English, you will tend to be at an advantage the closer your habitual English use—the one in which you were brought up—is to Standard English. And as Standard English is an educated middle class use, this then trans-lates into a tendency for the procedures of the written application to favour members of the middle classes: they are the ones who tend to be the most *at home* in Standard English, for the simple reason that their English defines the standard. Written applications are nearly always required for jobs which lead to a career trajectory (promotion, salary increases, etc.), and hence to a possible upward social or class trajectory. What this amounts to is a sort of *gate-keeping*: the very procedures by which one can get a job which will define one as middle class favour those who are already there.

It is important to remember that these links are not rigid, but matters of tendencies and probabilities. The point is not that *only* people from the middle classes get middle class jobs; this would obviously be untrue. Individual counter-examples are easy to find. Indeed, they are often freely offered as 'proof' that Western capitalist societies are genuinely free and without class. What we are talking about here is not the possibility of an individual experience so much as a distinct tendency across a group, a pattern which may show up clearly only through statistical analysis of a large number of individual cases. Neither are these links necessarily the results of conscious decisions to include or exclude. Deliberate decisions may of course be involved, but all that's really necessary in the case of a job application is a desire to find 'the best for the job', the applicant who has the best 'feel for the game'.

Habitus and disposition

The French sociologist Pierre Bourdieu uses the term **habitus** to describe the ways in which this feel for the game comes about in its various forms. The term suggests *habit*: habitus refers to the everyday, the situations, actions, procedures, demands, practices which go along with a certain kind of life, and the ways in which an individual is positioned within the social world (gender, class, race, etc.). The habitus in which you go about your daily affairs means that you acquire a certain set of **dispositions**. You tend to do some things rather than others—and, what's more, to do these things in certain ways rather than in others.

On the one hand, these dispositions are not so much consciously learned as acquired through practice; they're the ways of doing things which your social environment presents to you as natural or obvious, ready at hand, commonsensical. But then, on the other hand, neither are dispositions unconscious systems of rules. They're much looser, altogether less binding and more flexible than rules. Rather than proscribe what can or can't be done, they actively offer goals and means.

> A **habitus** is a lived network of objective social relationships and situations. Its effect is to produce agents with *dispositions* to certain practices rather than others.
>
> **Dispositions** are the 'second nature' one gains through *habitus*.

In terms of our previous tennis analogy, habitus is like a regime of regular play, training and practice. The dispositions this inculcates are the trained speed and strategic abilities which have become the second nature of the expert player.

Individuals make choices according to their habitus, but do not choose it. It is the product of their individual history, and depends on factors such as the place, society, class or cultural group they are born into, their education, work, socio-economic status, and social trajectory. Individuals belonging to the same group will largely share the same habitus, but there will always be all sorts of secondary differences among them: it is hardly possible, after all, for all members of even the most closely-knit group to have identical histories.

Habitus *disposes* individuals to make certain choices. Rather than choose practices (as free individuals) or get impelled into them (as determined), agents *fall into* practices which present themselves as obvious and reasonable choices offered by their environment. Habitus can certainly be overridden by other considerations such as rational calculation. An individual may well realise that the way in which he is disposed to act in a certain situation may not be the best response to it. Habitus may even conceivably inculcate conflicting dispositions. In any case, what it produces is a tendency rather than a necessity: the likelihood that, *over all*, individuals sharing a habitus will react in similar ways to the same situation.

What habitus inculcates as disposition is experienced as a *sense of place*, both one's own and others'. Habitus is at work in *judgements*: 'That's not for me,' 'I suppose that's the way some people choose to live,' 'Give me a good honest feed any day,' 'It's a real yuppie pub,' 'A nice outfit, but not my style,' 'You feel at home right away in this neighbourhood,' 'The shop assistants seem to check you out to decide whether they're going to serve you.' Habitus is one of the main social mechanisms of the *phatic*: it makes distinctions which are all the time negotiating who is, and isn't, part of a given group, between who is, and isn't, being addressed. And as we shall see shortly, one of the most significant social arenas for this phatic contestation is *taste*.

In summary, the concept of habitus has four benefits for our investigations:

1 It lets us think not only of some of the ways in which the individual is positioned within the social, but also of the ways in which the social is already present in the individual.
2 It lets us think of these relationships between individual and social in terms other than those of *ideology*. Ideology invokes notions of conceptual structures and systems of belief, which tends to beg the question of the very thing it seeks to explain, the human subject. Habitus, on the other hand, explains in terms of behaviours, actions, processes, and available options. One acts the way one does not because one holds certain beliefs, but because one's habitus makes available certain ways of doing things, which thus appear obvious, second nature.
3 Habitus does not postulate individuals as totally free makers of their own fates who are independent of the social world in which they exist. It acknowledges the important constitutive

effects of the social on the individual. On the other hand, it does not see individuals as wholly determined by the social, the product of forces which are forever beyond them. Thus it gets round that classic dilemma of free will versus determinism.

4 Habitus is inherently under-determining. It requires us to think of social relations as dynamic processes which are always necessarily somewhat open-ended; they are never simply resolved once and for all, but always have to be renegotiated, actively sustained, reconsidered. It also requires us to think of the individuals who act out these relations as social agents within a social world they are potentially capable of changing.

Forms of capital

In its economic sense, capital refers to what circulates in the process of economic production. Capital is that part of the product which will be ploughed back into the cycle to ensure further production. A factory is a form of capital: it is something which is made, and which in turn is used to make other things. The raw materials it uses are another form of capital, as is the money which maintains this stock, though both of these tend to have a much shorter cycle of turnover than the factory which uses them. Capital comes from production and goes towards feeding more production: in short, *capital reproduces production.*[1]

> **Capital** is a social product used in social production.

Bourdieu extends this idea of capital to a number of other aspects of the social. All of them can be seen as social products which are put in circulation and are themselves used to produce further capital. As well as the familiar **economic capital** we have just been describing, there are several other types. For the moment, we shall consider only three: *educational capital, cultural capital* and *symbolic capital.*

One gains **educational capital** through schooling. The amount depends on factors such as the length of one's stay in the education system, the course of study, the qualifications one receives, and the prestige of the institutions one attends. Educational capital gets exchanged for other forms of capital, particularly economic: well-paid jobs often require quite specific educational capital.

Where economic capital is concerned mainly with products of the economy (that is, goods and money), **cultural capital** involves the circulation of cultural products and the consequent reproduction of cultural relations. It lies to varying degrees in activities such as concert or museum or movie-going; in a knowledge of television or movies or, even more so for film directors; in collecting (from Meissen china to Ninja Turtles); in a taste for wines (or beers, plural); in house decoration; in choice of reading matter, or style of coffee. Cultural capital may come from the possession of certain cultural artefacts, such as paintings, *objets d'art* or books. Actual physical possession, however, is not really the point. More importantly, cultural capital comes from *having access to the codes* of such artefacts: knowing how they work, what they do, what to say about them, how to appreciate, value and evaluate them: in short, how to consume them as cultural signs. To grow up in a habitus which inculcates these abilities and practical knowledges may clearly be a considerable advantage; in effect, cultural capital can be accumulated and passed on from generation to generation, just as economic capital may be.

Cultural capital is a type of **symbolic capital**, which is a *capital of signs*. All forms of social behaviour have the potential to operate as signs of their addresser's position in social space. To wear a Rolex watch signifies 'large income'. To prefer beer to wine is a sign saying 'working class'. To prefer a small Thai restaurant to the local Pizza Hut may be read as 'yuppie'.

Signs like the Rolex or different kinds of coffee do not necessarily provide anything like an accurate representation of social position. This is not their main function. As we know, signs are capable of producing a variety of meanings in a variety of contexts and codes, and this mobility means that symbolic capital can even be largely independent of other forms. A Rolex is a very expensive piece of equipment, and I may buy one to signify my wealth. On the other hand, though, a Rolex will still signify 'wealth' whether I'm wealthy or not. If I'm not wealthy, I may even be able to achieve some of the effects of wealth in my dealings with others if I wear a Rolex (or better still, a Rolex clone): the sign may have very real effects. Far from being simply an obedient (or even misleading) representation of social position, the symbolic capital of the sign is a strategy for *negotiating* position.

That signs should function as a type of capital is hardly surprising. For Saussure, after all, the system of *langue* is basically an economic model: meaning is not so much a property of the individual sign as something which arises in the exchanges among signs. Bourdieu argues that economic capital is only one among many possible types: not even the most basic type (anthropology shows that there are societies where other forms of exchange,

Figure 9.5 Coffees of distinction

BEANS
Brazil Royal
Supremo Blend
Pure Nicaraguan
Pure Guatemalan
Kenya Mocha Blend
Arabia Mocha
Golden Royal
Santos Blend
Light Turkish Blend
Dark Turkish Blend

DRINKS
Cappuccino
Flat White
Caffe Latte
Macchiato
(long/short)
Gourmet Flavoured
Coffee
Vienna Coffee
Espresso

There are two main ways in which coffee comes ready to prepare: beans (or grounds), and instant. Instant is the less distinguished one of the pair: quick, functional and without ceremony, it's what you make at home or work when you need a fix of caffeine, or just a break. Ground bean coffee is the one around which elaborate processes of distinction arise. First there are all the various types of bean available (often distinguished by the name of their country of origin), the various types of roast to which they've been subjected, and even the additives (such as hazelnut). Then there are the methods of use, each of which requires its own regime of assembly, preparation and cleaning: pot, bag, infusor, percolator, filter, cafetière plunger, and most highly valued of all, espresso. After that, there are the ways of presenting the finished product, each with their own conventions: short black, in a small cup; long black, in a large cup; caffe latte, made on milk and served in a glass; and of course, cappuccino, coffee with steam-frothed milk, lightly sprinkled with chocolate or cocoa and served in a wide shallow cup. The ability to negotiate such distinctions determines in part the status a coffee bar can claim; indeed, when the most prestigious coffee bars may offer the customer some twenty or so choices, status is clearly tied to an ability to *produce* distinctions.

These distinctions may be small or large, but they must in principle be clear and discernible (even if the ability to discern does require apprenticeship). On the one hand, there is the ostentation of the classic commercial espresso machine, elaborate, expensive and functioning as a very public sign of the establishment's own distinction. The espresso machine foregoes the modesty of most catering equipment, which is designed to be used unseen and unheard by the customer. It sits where it can hardly be missed, on the bar between customer and proprietor, often close to the entrance and in clear view from the street, visible (and audible) from most of the establishment, a bulky conglomerate of fairing, tubes and duco, dreaming of a 1950s Plymouth. On the other hand, there are the smaller distinctions which mark out the *cognoscenti.* The *macchiato* is a black coffee 'stained' (as the name implies) with the merest hint of milk. This 'staining' can serve as a figure for the distinctions which practices of taste introduce: the practice which best lends itself to distinction is the small, subtle, crucial variation.

such as honour or the gift, are of paramount importance), but certainly the one that dominates in industrial Western societies. In some ways, Bourdieu's conclusion is the opposite to Saussure's: where Saussure suggests that semiotics is based on an economic model, Bourdieu sees symbolic capital as the grounds of possibility of all economies.

There is something quite arbitrary about symbolic capital: about *what* can be accumulated, the *type* of symbolic capital it is to function as, and its relative *value* as capital. It is far from obvious that it is intrinsically, naturally or logically more worthy or praiseworthy to have a taste for late Beethoven quartets over Country and Western music, wine over beer, live theatre over movie going, or Ermenegildo Zegna over K-Mart. Nevertheless, all of us have quite definite opinions and preferences on such matters; no doubt most of us have, at one time or another, even got quite heated about some of them. What is valuable cultural capital in one group is not necessarily worth much in another, once those practices are removed from the habitus which gives them value. Various forms of cultural capital compete to assert their own value, and thus the positions of those who hold them. The forms which tend to be most effective in this struggle are those which belong to the most powerful groups. These present themselves not as arbitrary capital, but as *legitimate culture*, then define all others in their terms (which is to say that they generally find all others lacking). To the extent that capital is arbitrary, it is defined in terms of the values of dominant groups, who thus impose both the constitution and legitimacy of capital.

Like economic capital, all of these various types of capital stand to be ploughed back into circulation to produce further capital, either of another or the same kind. The Rolex watch is not just an expenditure, but an investment in another sort of capital. Economic capital is invested in symbolic capital in order to gain social or cultural capital, such as prestige. Under certain conditions this too may in turn be exchanged back into economic capital, with interest. My Rolex helps me impress a client as being a corporate high-flier, with the result that I clinch a large deal for the company and get a promotion (which more than pays for the Rolex). In choosing to take up an opportunity to go to university, you forego several years' accumulation of economic capital in favour of a variable mixture of educational and cultural capital, according to the course of study; gaining entry to one of the professions on graduation, you exchange educational for economic and social capital.

Some of these effective exchange rates among forms of capital are relatively fixed. To become a medical doctor, for example, requires a certain amount of educational capital (a medical degree from an accredited institution), and there are even legal and professional restrictions and bodies to police the consistency of this exchange. Many exchange rates, though, are much more fluid: there's nothing like a standard rate of exchange between the symbolic capital of a Rolex and the economic capital of salary and promotions. Exchanges may be open to group or individual negotiations: one of the functions of unions is, after all, to negotiate between certain forms of capital.

Social space

This concept of capital lets us envisage the ways in which individuals and groups are distributed throughout what we can call *social space*. We can picture their positions in this social space as being characterised not only by the overall amount of capital they possess, but by the way that capital breaks down into various types. Individuals may possess more of one type of capital than another.

An unemployed university graduate has a high educational capital she is at present unable to exchange at favourable rates for economic capital. A writer may earn as much as a tradesperson, let's say, but may have a considerably higher cultural capital, depending on the type of writing. Writers like Stephen King and Barbara Taylor Bradford are financially highly successful and immensely popular, but write mainly in genres with low cultural capital (the horror story, the romantic family saga). (This is not to judge Bradford nor King 'inferior' authors, nor to champion them because of their democratic popularity. Rather we are taking a received dominant cultural evaluation in order to ask what follows from it, trying to see something of how it works.)

This social space, then, comprises a series of *positions* according to volumes and types of capital. It is not hard to see that each of these positions corresponds to a habitus, each producing various *dispositions*. Positions which are close together in this social space will tend to share a habitus, the more so the closer they are. As we suggested earlier, these positions are in constant struggle and negotiation with each other, both for capital and for the relative values of the types of capital each possesses: that is, this social space is also made up of a dynamic, unstable and ever-changing series of *oppositions*.

Strategies of taste

As you might expect, in industrialised Western societies and those to which their political influence extends, the dominant form of capital tends to be economic. High stocks of economic capital are generally worth more than high stocks of any other sort; economic capital can be more readily exchanged for other sorts than they can for it, and at more favourable rates. In short, in Western societies *power* is generally more closely bound to economic capital than any other sort.

Nevertheless, other types of capital can and do contest this dominance. Cultural capital in particular is the occasion for a number of highly visible and significant strategies, focusing on issues of *taste*. These work by and as *distinction*, in both main senses of the word: they *make* distinctions among things and practices, and they *endow* those who practise them with distinction.

Making distinctions, of course, is precisely what the sign does. For Saussure, a sign functions as a sign first of all because it can distinguish itself from all the other signs and things around it. We also added that, as a parallel condition of its existence as a sign, it produces a phatic group of addresser and addressee. Now because the sign is relatively independent of its referent, symbolic capital may be a way of contesting economic capital. This opens up the possibility of *symbolic struggles over representation,* where a group attempts to impose its representations and concepts of legitimacy. Again, because of the relative autonomy of the symbolic, this is a very real power of producing phatic groups, or imposing social divisions, altering the objective structure of a society. Not surprisingly, Bourdieu calls this symbolic power 'the political power *par excellence*'.

Symbolic power can work in many ways, towards all sorts of ends, from jockeying for prestige through taste, to the assertion of the rights of an oppressed group. It is both one of the mechanisms of social consumption and something which under the right circumstances may disrupt certain social relations. Advertising, of course, uses symbolic distinctions of taste as an indispensable strategy, producing distinctions which may be almost purely symbolic. Products sold under designer labels, for instance, are rarely produced under the direct control of the designer whose signature they bear, and in many cases are not even designed by that person. Almost tautologically, the designer's signature may merely indicate that the designer has given legal approval for the product to be marketed under that name. There may be multiple variations on the same label, each with its own relative status: the Italian designer Giorgio Armani markets a variety of Armani labels, each with its own distinctive retail outlets and clientele.

Advertising is far from the only arena of symbolic distinction, though it is, of course, an immensely important one. Elaborate distinctions are often made in the set of practices surrounding one single product: wine is an obvious example, as is coffee (Figure 9.5).

Cultural capital tends to require a certain minimum of economic capital. Although you don't actually have to own Van Gogh's *Sunflowers* to make cultural capital out of it, you do need a certain freedom from economic necessity, in the form of the leisure time in which to study art, read books on it, or visit galleries. Cultural capital is an investment of the economic capital left after you've paid the bills, and it also functions as a sign of economic freedom. Not surprisingly, accumulating it is for the most part a pursuit of those classes and class fractions which have a relatively large overall volume of capital. Nevertheless, because cultural capital is symbolic, it is partly autonomous of economic capital (remember the Rolex watch), and may thus lend itself to strategies for contesting the power and legitimacy of the more dominant economic capital.

Cultural capital tends to be used most effectively not by the most powerful groups, but by those just below them, the dominated

Figure 9.6 Shibboleths

> In the village churchyard she lies,
> Dust is in her beautiful eyes,
>> No more she breathes, nor feels, nor stirs,
> At her feet and at her head
> Lies a slave to attend the dead,
>> But their dust is as white as hers.
>
> Was she a lady of high degree,
> So much in love with the vanity
>> And foolish pomp of this world of ours;
> Or was it Christian charity,
> And lowliness and humility,
>> The richest and rarest of all dowers?
>
> Who shall tell us? No one speaks;
> No colour shoots into those cheeks,
>> Either of anger or of pride,
> At the rude question we have asked;
> Nor will the mystery be unmasked
>> By those who are sleeping at her side.
>
> Hereafter?—And do you think to look
> On the terrible pages of that Book
>> To find her failings, faults and errors?
> Ah, you will then have other cares,
> In your own shortcomings and despairs,
>> In your own secret sins and terrors!

In 1924, the Cambridge academic and literary critic I. A. Richards published under the title *Practical Criticism* the results of some experiments he had been performing with the members of his literature classes. He had presented his students with a sheet of paper bearing the text of a poem to which the student was asked to respond briefly in writing—a response Richards called a 'protocol'. The poem was left unidentified: no title, no poet's name, no period, and, perhaps most important of all, no indication of what Richards expected his students to feel about it. *Practical Criticism* summarises and analyses some of these protocols.

This poem is one of those Richards used. Try it yourself, as an unseen text on which you have to comment. What is the exercise asking you to display?

(At the end of the chapter, you will find the poem identified, along with some of Richards' comments on what his students wrote.)

fraction of the dominant class. **High culture** in its various forms is the cultural capital this fraction defines and seeks to impose as legitimate culture. In turn, a mastery of cultural capital distinguishes its practitioners from those with smaller overall volume of capital, who have neither the economic freedom nor the disposition to practice culture in this way. Their cultural practices, **popular culture**, will be seen by the practitioners of high culture in terms of a *lack* of taste.

Taste, then, attributes the effects of a set of social dispositions to personal, individual abilities. It provides powerful passwords, or **shibboleths**,[2] for determining who is and is not part of a given social group. These criteria may present themselves as tests of the individual's innate ability to appreciate something universal ('quality'), but in fact the responses they evoke are products of social habitus.

Representation and interest

Habitus disposes individuals towards certain practices. As we have seen in the case of matters of taste, it also disposes them towards what we can call certain **representations** of these practices: perceptions, evaluations, appreciations and *knowledges* of them, particularly as they concern their own positions and those of others. These representations in turn tend to make the very features of the habitus appear as natural and commonsensical. The process is circular, and emphasises that representations are not only themselves practices, but practices which are essential to the *reproduction* of habitus.

Habitus is not coercion. As we have argued, it *offers* certain practices as self-evident and the obvious thing to do in a given situation, but it does not *force* these on the individual agents. There is always the possibility of taking up other options which are objectively present. We can say the same thing for the representations generated by habitus: representations may be contested. In fact, since representations play such a significant part in the reproduction of habitus, to contest a set of representations may be a way of altering that habitus and the objective social structures of which it is part.

In the past two decades, for example, and particularly since the 1988 Bicentenary of European arrival, many indigenous Australians have increasingly abandoned the term 'Aborigine' to identify themselves. The Latin term ('original inhabitants') registers only the basic phatic distinction between conquerors and conquered. It imposes the conquerors' representations of the indigenous peoples as undifferentiated, ignoring their sheer cultural plurality (we can

get an idea of this by considering that at the time of the conquest,
there may well have been over 500 indigenous languages, in some
28 linguistic families). Aboriginal people have been represented as
little more than the phatic outside of a European world: without
social organisation, without culture, without claims. Today, while
government organisations favour terms such as 'Aboriginal
Australians', with its assurance of a single nation to which various
cultures all contribute, indigenous peoples now often describe themselves by a number of specific names from their own traditions:
Murri in Queensland and northern New South Wales, Koori in
New South Wales and Victoria, Nyungah in the south-west of
Western Australia, etc. The names assert a counter-representation
of a culture which is refusing the silence and invisibility assigned
to them by dominant representations. To claim a name enacts on a
symbolic level other claims for traditional ownership and traditional
law.

   Habitus disposes its agents towards certain representations,
and these in turn tend to reproduce the habitus which gave rise to
them, by making it appear self-evident. In other words, representation is always **interested**, to the extent that it is a product
or a contestation of habitus. Again, we should take this *interest* as a
matter of disposing agents and actions in a certain direction, not of
compelling them. Interest is what makes the reproduction of the
original habitus somewhat more likely, the easiest path for events
to fall into in the usual course of things. There may often be several
conflicting interests at work in a single representation or practice.
Here, one need only think of the changes the word 'black' has
undergone over the last few decades as a term applied to race.
From a derogatory term (replaced in liberal American usage for a
long time by the more genteel 'Negro'), since the Civil Rights movements of the 1960s it has become a popular affirmation (James
Brown's 'Say it loud, I'm black and I'm proud').

   To say that a given representation is interested is not to say
that it is untrue or a matter of false consciousness; neither is it to
say that it or its agents are consciously hypocritical or unconsciously
complicit. In itself, the fact of a representation's interest says nothing
about whether it is true or false. All representations, after all, are
interested in the sense we have just discussed. Interest is not an
option a discourse has, or something it slips into through a lack of
vigilance; it is a necessary consequence of its positioning and the
sorts of functions of address it is able to gather. Truth, then, is not
so much what is opposed to interest as something which is found
across a variety of interests. We might imagine truth as what is
independent of all interests, but this is to abstract from the actual

situations in which we find it, which are always interested ones. The most objectively true of discourses have their own interests, without which they could scarcely exist; the sciences' guarantee of an objective truth is, after all, dependent upon a set of institutional, professional, financial and often political interests, which make possible its strict regimes of laboratory experimentation. *Interest, we may say, is the mode in which a discourse exists as practice.* It is also an index of the point we made very early in this book, and have been unfolding in its complexity ever since: **meaning is always contextual.**

Figure 9.7 The interest of knowledge

Internal and External Elements of a Language
(from Chapter V of Ferdinand de Saussure, *Course in General Linguistics* (London: Duckworth, 1983)

Our definition of a language assumes that we disregard everything which does not belong to its structure as a system; in short everything that is designated by the term 'external linguistics'. External linguistics is none the less concerned with important matters, and these demand attention when one approaches the study of languages.

First of all, there are all the respects in which linguistics links up with ethnology. There are all the relations which may exist between the history of a language and the history of a race or a civilisation. The two histories intermingle and are related one to another... A nation's way of life has an effect upon its language. At the same time, it is in great part the language which makes the nation.

Secondly, mention must be made of the relations between languages and political history. Major historical events such as the Roman Conquest are of incalculable linguistic importance in all kinds of ways. Colonisation, which is simply one form of conquest, transports a language into new environments, and this brings changes in the language...Advanced stages of civilisation favour the development of certain special languages (legal language, scientific terminology, etc.).

This brings us to a third point. A language has connexions with institutions of every sort: church, school, etc...

Finally, everything which relates to the geographical extension of languages and to their fragmentation into dialects concerns external linguistics...

It is sometimes claimed that it is absolutely impossible to separate all these questions from the study of language itself... In our opinion, the study of external linguistic phenomena can teach linguists a great deal. But it is not true to say that without taking such phenomena into account we cannot come to terms with the internal structure of the language itself... In the case of certain languages, such as Zend and Old Slavonic, we do not even know exactly which peoples spoke them. But our ignorance in no way prevents us from studying their internal structure, or from understanding the developments they underwent. In any case, a separation of internal and external viewpoints is essential. The more rigorously it is observed, the better...

...In the case of chess, it is relatively easy to distinguish between what is external and what is internal. The fact that chess came from Persia to Europe is an external fact, whereas everything which concerns the system and its rules is internal. If pieces made of ivory are substituted for pieces made of wood, the change makes no difference to the system. But if the number of pieces is diminished or increased, that is a change which profoundly affects the 'grammar' of the game. Care must none the less be taken when drawing distinctions of this kind. In each case, the question to be asked concerns the nature of the phenomenon. The question must be answered in accordance with the following rule. Everything is internal which alters the system in any degree whatsoever.

One of the things Saussure is doing here is launching a justification of a new discipline of study. He argues that there are aspects of language which have been ignored by all other disciplines, and which can be treated adequately only by the type of investigation he's advocating. Given that such investigations are usually done by highly trained professionals in specialised institutions—generally academics in universities— his argument is inescapably and at least in part an interested argument about careers and university budgets. What's more, it is one which does not provide any terms for talking about its own interests, as it has started by excluding social, historical and institutional factors from its object of study: though it happily admits their importance, they are the objects for *other* forms of study, not for linguistics. We cannot talk in Saussurean terms about the interests of the Saussurean system. Disinterest necessarily hides interests.

Notes

1 At least, this is so for classical economics. The definition might be difficult to sustain when capital seems to come from the apparent thin air of speculation rather than production, as seen in the massive stock market and currency fluctuations of the 1980s–90s.

2 The word *shibboleth,* according to *Brewer's Dictionary of Phrase and Fable,* is a Hebrew word meaning 'ear of wheat', 'stream' or 'flood'. Judges xii, 1–6, tells how Jephthah and the Gileadites uncovered the Ephraimites in their midst by their enemies' inability to pronounce the word's *sh*-sound.

Exercises

1 Newspapers comment on grammar, spelling, punctuation and language usage frequently, and in many ways. Columnists will often discuss it as a topic; many newspapers even have a regular column devoted to it; educational columns debate the quality of language education children receive today; and language is always a popular topic for letters to the editor.

Gather some examples of these. What is being asserted in these cases, and by what means? Do some of these texts use a rhetoric of crisis? If so, how, and what does it do? Do these conflicts work across class and class-fractional lines of division? If so, which?

2 Discuss the application letter in Chapter 1 (Figure 1.1) in terms of habitus. What dispositions is it attempting to show, and in what fashion? How can those functions of address, and in particular the phatic, now be reworked in terms of habitus and disposition? Are there any advantages in this new conceptual apparatus? That is, does it reveal something more than the earlier model did? If so, what?

3 In what senses could we talk about *knowledge* as a form of capital? Given the boom in information technologies over the last two decades, to what extent is it possible to talk about *information* as a form of capital? Do they differ? If so, how? What relationships would both of these proposed forms of capital have with other forms of capital? What relationships would both of them have with educational capital in particular? Keeping our arguments about habitus and the inculcation of dispositions in mind, is educational capital simply a variety of the capital of knowledge? What other qualities or processes might it be useful to think of in terms of capital, and why?

4 Try I. A. Richards' 'protocol' exercise from Figure 9.6. Compare your comments with those Richards cites, a selection of which you'll find in Figure 9.8. (This is an exercise which works well in class. Do you find that on the whole the responses of your class differ from those of Richards' groups? If so, how? What does this imply, in terms of habitus? What aspects of habitus are being highlighted in Richards' comments?)

Figure 9.8

Richards' students' comments on his unseen poem, and his own comments on these

As has been remarked before, a very wary eye is needed with any poetry that tends to implicate our stock responses. And this for two opposite reasons. If the easiest way to popularity is to exploit some stock response, some poem already existent, fully prepared, in the reader's mind, an appeal to such stock responses, should the reader happen to have discarded them, is a very certain way of courting failure. So that a poet who writes on what appears to be a familiar theme, in a way which, superficially, is only slightly unusual, runs a double risk. On the one hand, very many readers will not really read him at all. They will respond with the poem they suppose him to have written and then, if emancipated, recoil in horror to heap abuse on the poet's head. On the other hand, less emancipated readers, itching to release their own stock responses, may be pulled up by something in the poem which prevents them. The result will be more abuse for the hapless author.

Now to illustrate and justify these reflections. Here is a writer who finds only a stock experience in the poem. He is only mildly disappointed however:

13.1. This one seems to me a successful communication of an experience whose value is dubious, or which at most is valuable only on a small scale. Plainly, I think, the communication succeeds by reason of its medium; simple, straightforward, almost bald language, making no demand on any peculiar individual characteristic which might be a bar to general appreciation, as in the poetry of Blake, for instance. The reasons for my judgement of the experience–value are harder to formulate. I think one may be that *the experience does not go very much further than it would in the case of an 'ordinary man'* who was not a poet, so that its very *raison d'être* is a questionable quantity. It does, in fact, seem to me rather trite.

... It was very generally assumed that since the subject of the poem is solemn the treatment must be solemn too, and many readers made it as solemn as they could. Not unnaturally their results often displeased them.

13.8. *If the poem tends to check the reader from making speculations on other people's lives then it has some value.* The poem however does not seem to do this, but *rather stimulates than quiets a man's interest in the private deeds of other people.* ... This form of stimulation to the mind *can do it no good and may do it harm.* The poem is therefore bad.

This seems perfectly to express a possible way of reading the poem. A reading whose solemnity fully merits all the adjectives that other readers found to fling against it. Sanctimoniouis, didactic, pompous, portentous, priggish, seem, indeed, if the poem is looked at in this light, hardly too strong. Only one reader attempted to state the issue between this view of the poem and another view by which it would escape these charges. And he so over-states his case that he discredits it.

13.9 I am in two moods as to the intention of this poem. If the mood in which it is written is serious, *if we are meant to take the situation in profound meditation closing in self-abasing remorse,* then the whole thing is clearly vicious and preposterous. The idea of an eternity spent in turning up the files of other people's sins or crouching to cry *peccavi* for our own is *either amusing or disgusting or both.* But if the last three lines are a sudden impish whirl on the complacent moral speculation of the first three stanzas the whole is *a very delightful little whimsy...*

... If this interpretation of the poem is right, 'rude' ('the rude question we have asked', stanza 4) is simply an acknowledgement of the social convention, not in the least a rebuke... The word belongs to the texture of the poet's meditation and is not aimed at anyone, not even at the poet himself. It is the admission of a fact, not an attack upon anyone, or anything.

On this theory...the last verse would be in the same tone. Not a grim warning, or an exhortation, but a cheerful realisation of the situation, not in the least evangelical, not at all like a conventional sermon, but on the contrary extremely urbane, rather witty, and *slightly* whimsical... (In this reading), the poem becomes a very unusual kind of thing that it would be a pity to miss. That so few read it in this way is not surprising, for if there is any character in poetry that modern readers...are unprepared to encounter, it is this social, urbane, highly cultivated, self-confident, temperate and easy kind of humour.

The unseen poem is 'In the Churchyard at Cambridge', by Henry Wadsworth Longfellow (1807–82), who is best known for 'The Song of Hiawatha'. It was by far the least popular of the poems Richards presented, disliked by over 90 percent of his students.

As these extracts show, while Richards phrases his project in terms of psychology and the abilities of more or less finely tuned individual minds, what he is discerning here can also accurately be described in terms of habitus: a dispositional, class response to poetry in particular and high culture in general. Richards' investigations helped provide a way of *testing* the student's response to literature; in showing that a student's reaction to literature could be assessed, they helped establish 'English' as the central subject of the humanities curriculum.

5 The very enterprise of knowledge, even of the most objective sort, has its own interests, which are minimally those of the groups who produce the knowledge. This is clearly so in the sciences and technologies, with their reliance on access to equipment, laboratories, funding, etc., but it is also no less the case in the humanities. Figure 9.6 gives a sample of a text we have mentioned since the early chapters of this book, Saussure's *Course in General Linguistics*. How does it include within it a discourse on its own interests? What about this book, *Tools for Cultural Studies?*

Sources and further reading

The concepts of *capital*, *disposition* and *habitus* all come from the work of the sociologist Pierre Bourdieu. Bourdieu's work is voluminous and wide-ranging; he has written on areas such as North African and French marriage practices, taste, the French education system, literary biography, philosophy, museum-going, universities, popular culture and photography. Much of his work engages in a running polemic with structuralism and academic philosophy. Bourdieu offers some initial difficulties for the beginner: in an attempt to mirror the complexities of relationships in the material he is examining, his writing is often syntactically elaborate, demanding but not obscurantist. One of the best introductions to his work is the essays and interviews collected in *In Other Words: Essays Rowards a Reflexive Sociology* (Cambridge: Polity, 1990). The interview 'From rules to strategies' and the essay on 'Codification' are of particular interest to the discussion in this chapter. On the strategies of taste, the massive *Distinction: A Social Critique of the Judgement of Taste* is almost a standard work. For an overview of Bourdieu's work, see Richard Harker, Cheleen Mahar and Chris Wilkes (eds), *An Introduction to the Work of Pierre Bourdieu: The Practice of Theory* (London: Macmillan, 1990).

Deyan Sudjic's *Cult Heroes: How to be Famous for More Than Fifteen Minutes* (New York: Norton, 1990) is mostly anecdotal rather than analytic, and it's about the designer signature and its effects rather than cult heroes, but it does contain some fascinating material.

On ways in which daily practices are improvisatory negotiations of an environment, see Michel de Certeau's *The Practice of Everyday Life* (Berkeley: University of California Press, 1984), and Henri Lefebvre's *Everyday Life in the Modern World* (London: Allen Lane, 1971).

The term *bricolage* comes from Claude Lévi-Strauss, in *The Savage Mind* (London: Weidenfeld and Nicholson, 1966).

The tennis melaphor owes a lot to Anne Freadman's discussions of genre (see her 'Untitled: (On Genre)', *Cultural Studies* 2 (1) 1988) and Freadman and Amanda Macdonald's *What is This Thing Called 'Genre'?* (Mt Nebo, Queensland: Boombana, 1992).

10   Other directions

We suggested in the Introduction that the semiotic approach with which we began was far from the only approach to cultural studies. In fact, since that point we have moved a considerable distance from semiotics, as we came across issues which demanded other considerations, other types of investigation. In this final chapter, we will briefly survey some further ways of doing cultural studies.

Audience studies

As we have seen in Chapter 9, semiotic analysis may unravel the ways in which texts construct addresser and addressee positions, but it has little to say about what actual receivers do with these.

One of the ways cultural studies has reacted to this has been to switch attention from analysis of texts to a study of the way actual audiences behave when they watch or read media texts. Focusing mainly on television, this research has adopted an ethnographic approach, borrowed from anthropology. **Ethnography** is a form of field research in which the researcher attempts to understand a culture by becoming part of it. Ethnographers classically try to live the lives of the subjects they study, taking extensive notes (written or tape recorded) at the same time.

Audience studies are somewhat more limited in their procedures than this. David Morley and a team of researchers in Britain spent some weeks living in a number of households, watching television with family members. His book *Family Television* contains the results of this research.

Morley's work demonstrates that there is a vast difference between the ideal reader proposed in structuralist models, and the way actual audience members behave in everyday life. He was able to show that audiences are not simply passive subjects, duped by television discourse into responding in a predictable manner. Rather, audiences use television texts for a range of purposes within domestic and other everyday contexts. For instance, the patriarchal organisation of family life means that husbands and fathers tend to override female members of the family audience when it comes to program choice. Morley's work indicates that males and females give markedly different accounts of their viewing experience, suggesting that audiences are not homogeneous groups, but are made up of different kinds of subjectivities, based on gender and other culturally defined values.

Ethnographic work in audience studies is not without its problems. The idea that researchers can become one with the audiences under study raises methodological and theoretical issues concerning speaking positions. Precisely who speaks for whom in ethnography? Does audience research really speak on behalf of the subjects it analyses, or does it reproduce its own values which it sees reflected in the context of research?

This problem is overcome to a degree with a shift from ethnography to **ethnomethodology**. In audience studies based on ethnomethodology, the focus is on explanations constructed by the participants themselves. Ethnomethodological field work on audiences tends to be more modest in its requirements: group discussions, rather than extensive 'live in' researcher/subject interactions, are generally sufficient to display the participants' own theories and methods of audienceship (ethnomethods).

The research task is to show how this self-analysis by group participants can be read as a text involving strategies of, and against, power and domination, much like cultural studies' own analyses of the discourses and institutions of the media and other cultural forms. This work can be combined with data concerning educational, occupational and other social factors which determine many of the values which come into play when members account for their audienceship to each other.

This qualitative research, in both its ethnographic and ethnomethodological modes, leads to a different notion of audience from the one which has prevailed in more traditional social science and communication disciplines. It's worth discussing this traditional strand of **empiricist** audience study in some detail, because of its enormous influence over media and academic research in the past.

In these studies, mainly based on empirical data collection (surveys, interviews), audiences have been understood in terms of a massed group of individuals (hence the terms *mass media, mass communication,* etc.). The aim of this work has been to locate consistent values and trends which can then determine the character of a *typical* audience member.

This research has been used extensively in the media industry itself in an attempt to define, and hence gain control over, its audiences. In *Desperately Seeking the Audience*, Ien Ang has shown how the institutional practices of television audience measurement are not neutral and objective, but motivated by industry interests. The methodology of data collection for ratings measurement is based on an ideal notion of audience which anticipates and pre-determines audience response.

Quantitative research takes place under strictly controlled circumstances, guided by scientific objectives. Subjects are selected for study with a view to making general claims about social and cultural values. As a result, selection cannot be on a purely volun-tary basis, because there is no guarantee that a group of volunteers will be representative of the society as a whole. Much care is needed to ensure that this kind of research is *repeatable*, as this is the prime confirmation of its objectivity. Another way of ensuring objectivity is through *triangulation*: different methods of data collection (e.g. surveys, interviews, discussions) are used in order to confirm results.

In cultural studies, quantitative audience research of this sort is not widely used. Though the two may seem a long way apart, this research has at least one crucial point in common with struc-turalism: both of them posit an abstract, ideal reader, and thus tend to overlook the sheer diversity of actual audience behaviours.

Cultural studies' work on audiences attempts to focus on this situated actuality of audience behaviour. Post-structuralist notions of intertextuality, discourse, strategy and power are used to show how the 'reading' of television and other media texts is always contextual, framed by many other cultural values and institutional structures. The audience member is seen as an active participant in the reading process, able to adapt and exploit media discourse for socially defined purposes. The move here is away from the notion of audience as 'mass', with its implications of a homo-geneous identity and uniform response, towards audience as part of a group or network, not necessarily defined by the social space in which the reading of media texts takes place.

Policy studies

What audiences do with television is one aspect of the wider questions of the politics of everyday life, on which we touched in Chapter 9. Through the strategic use of signs, people define, main-tain and transform their cultural identities within social contexts. Research and analysis based on a critique of the politics of every-day life expose the various signifying practices which maintain and resist structures of domination and subordination, making them available for scrutiny and possible change.

Nevertheless, this kind of critique has been questioned by

many from within the ranks of cultural studies. The problem lies in whether critique on its own has the power to change the social structures which contribute to the formation of cultural identity. Critique, it has been argued, is purely an academic pursuit, isolated from the rest of society. It overlooks the importance of governmental and corporate policy in providing the social conditions necessary for cultural identity to exist in the first place.

Accordingly, a school of research, policy studies, has emerged which looks for a direct connection between academic work and the policy making procedures of government and corporate bodies. Drawing on the theoretical work of Michel Foucault, Norbert Elias and others, policy studies shows how the possibility of individual behaviour is always conditioned by the discourses in, and through which, individuals live their everyday life. Desire and pleasure, the hallmarks of individual self-expression, are always framed by a set of administrative procedures (either in a public sense or as a form of self monitoring), governed by institutional and social contexts.

As a consequence, policy studies works towards the development of an *ethics of citizenship*, in which the subjective, interior life of individuals is subordinate to, and conditioned by, the public arena in which individuals relate to one another as community members. This subject-as-citizen approach puts a new complexion on the study of cultural practices, because it indicates that they are subject to change in the administrative policies of the state and its corporate institutions. Academic research and argument can help bring about changes in cultural identity, through direct input into policy formation at the governmental and corporate level. In this way, policy research becomes instrumentally related to the culture it seeks to define and transform.

In particular, policy studies have been active in the area of the media, becoming politically engaged with the policy forming bodies which determine the institutional practices of media discourse. Issues such as television violence, Australian content in television programming, and the introduction of pay television (cable, satellite), for instance, have become topics of focused research, analysis and argument. From the perspective of policy studies, these issues need to be understood in terms of the complex interrelations between media institutions, governmental bodies and the public. Other areas to receive attention include the film industry, education, museums and local government planning.

This form of direct intervention by the academy in outside bodies is motivated by a pragmatic desire to have a hand in the way social structures operate, leading to empowerment to change them. It argues that orthodox methods of critique, such as semiotic text analysis, are of limited use in altering the dominant ways in which cultural identity is formed.

There are, of course, risks involved in this approach. It has been argued that by surrendering critique, policy studies could very well become a compliant armature of government and corporate policy, supporting and entrenching the very practices it wishes to change. Furthermore, it has been objected that the social model promoted by policy studies privileges a bureaucratic concept in which cultural identity is entirely a matter of strict, 'top-down' institutional definition. From this point of view, policy studies seems to assume that people in everyday life accept the programs of cultural practice instigated through policy implementation, which is to deny audiences and readers an active role in the reception of media discourse. By rejecting textual analysis, policy studies runs the danger of overlooking the ideological coding inscribed in media texts, thus neglecting the media institutions' discursive orientation to the larger socio-political contexts of which they are a part.

These objections suggest that policy studies has limits, and does not supplant work in other areas of cultural studies. In fact, policy-minded academics are increasingly striking a rapport with their counterparts in textual and critical analysis. Current work in cultural studies is moving towards integrated research projects, drawing upon policy, textual analysis and audience studies, aiming to develop a thorough account of cultural meaning and identity as socio-politically defined phenomena.

The postmodern

If work on audiences and policy has an air of empirical pragmatism, it is easy for the very idea of **the postmodern** to sound like science fiction, with its suggestions that the day after tomorrow is somehow already here today. The term is somewhat difficult to pin down, and there is considerable argument about whether it's a useful or misleading term in cultural analysis. At the very least, however, it encompasses a number of divergent and even opposed arguments, the complexities of whose interrelations we certainly haven't the space to go into here. What we'll do instead is focus on a limited cluster of ways in which the term is used, in each case as a figure of difference from a concept of the **modern**.

One way of taking the terms modern and post-modern is as **successive stages of capitalism**. For the Marxist geographer David Harvey, the inaugural moment of capitalist modernity is Henry Ford's development of the production line for his car assembly plant in 1913. Fordism had its boom years in the prosperity following World War II. But do its conditions still hold today? Harvey argues that the mode of capitalism has changed considerably since then, enough to result in a very different set of social relations.

Consider some of the events since the end of World War II. As the economies of Japan and Western Europe recovered, they began to lose their dependence on American exports and increase the volume of goods they themselves exported. As a result, the United States not only lost much of a significant market, but found itself facing new competition. From the 1960s on, the Western labour market was gradually to be restructured, as the impacts of movements such as feminism and, in the United States, civil rights made themselves felt. The rise of cheaper manufacturing industries in the Third World led to many multinational corporations establishing more profitable off-shore operations to take advantage of a cheaper, non-unionised labour force. By the 1970s, OPEC decisions and the Arab-Israeli War had forced up energy costs for the Western nations. In 1973, a stock market slump heralded the biggest recession since War World II, and the end of post-War buoyancy.

This spiral of increasing crisis, Harvey argues, requires far more flexible means of accumulation and circulation of capital than Fordism could supply. An ever-increasing need for innovation now becomes paramount: new markets, products, financial services and technologies. New industries arise, particularly those connected with electronics, since an enormous expansion in information technologies has led to a situation where information itself can take on the status of a commodity. This in turn produces enormous changes in the ways in which knowledge is produced and circulated. There is a tendency towards a single world money market, a massive growth in private service sectors, and a corresponding diminution of the power of the state. Financial speculation is possible on a previously unheard-of scale; fortunes can be made independently of the cycle of production and consumption. Mergers and take-overs in all areas, coupled with pressures for deregulation (in media, labour relations, etc.) lead to situations such as the present extraordinary concentrations of media ownership. With high levels of structural unemployment, labour relations change; there are crises for union movements, such as the moves towards labour contracts rather than awards.

The cultural effects of all this are, or course, immense. The need for innovation requires an induction of needs through an acceleration of obsolescence and turnover time, and in principle this is capable of affecting virtually all cultural commodities, from music to clothing, from film to cars, from novels to tastes in food.

Out of this comes what Harvey calls the 'postmodernist aesthetic that celebrates difference, ephemerality, spectacle, fashion, and the commodification of cultural forms' (*The Condition of Postmodernity*, p. 156).

Not everyone agrees with this analysis. Harvey and the economic regulationists on which he draws readily admit that if there is indeed a qualitative break from the modern to the postmodern, then the transition is little understood and poses many problems. To begin with, it is not always easy to isolate which apparent shifts in attitudes and cultural practices are due to this particular aspect of change in the economic base, and to trace their detailed mechanisms. Furthermore, if it exists, such a break can hardly be universal and complete: many aspects of Fordist modernity would seem to survive happily and healthily into this postmodernity. Here, Harvey's schema can look just a bit too neatly dichotomous: he loves drawing up ledgers of the characteristic features of Fordist modernity versus those of flexible postmodernity.

In *The Postmodern Condition*, the philosopher Jean-François Lyotard sees modernity as a Western cultural phenomenon whose conceptual foundation is the Enlightenment faith in reason. Modernity is marked by a series of *metanarratives* or 'grand narratives', sweeping stories about history's progressive liberation, by reason, of human potential, labour and science and technology. What these narratives have in common, he argues, is a function of **legitimation**: they endorse the present by promising liberation, though it is inevitably a liberation in a future which is perpetually deferred.

For Lyotard, the postmodern is the collapse of these grand narratives and their functions of legitimation, under the pressures of precisely the features of late capitalism Harvey describes: the acceleration of the new and the rise of information technologies. All exchanges and social relations are atomised to a matter of information. What results is a thoroughgoing *de*legitimation: the only goals this new techno-regime needs are the functional and managerial ones of success and efficiency, allowing it to appear as value-neutral. Against a writer such as Jürgen Habermas, who sees modernism as the incomplete project of Enlightenment (and one whose urgent task of completion falls to Marxism), Lyotard argues that modernism bears its own incompleteness within itself, and thus collapses under its own weight.

This is not to say that Lyotard likes what the postmodern leaves us. On the contrary, the apparent ethical neutrality of the postmodern demand for nothing but efficient performance is profoundly and insidiously despotic in its overriding of all other criteria. In its place, Lyotard suggests a respect for the multiplicity and irreducibility of what he calls, after Wittgenstein, *language games*. Here he approaches the subject of our next section: a politics of identify and difference.

Harvey and Lyotard hardly agree in their diagnoses, or even in the ways in which they use the term postmodern. Nevertheless, for all their differences, one of the issues they both raise is the question of the *break* itself. That necessarily takes us back to the idea of the modern, against which the post-modern must inevitably define itself.

The most banal use of the term modern is simply as a synonym for contemporary: modernity is just where one is now. A somewhat more interesting way of using it is as a description of any period which overtly separates itself from what went before— or at least from what is seen as having gone before, constructed for polemical purposes as precursor. Modernity in this version would be a matter of *progress* and *overcoming*. More than to a particular period, it refers to a *general historical figure of rupture*.

This has some rather interesting consequences. If modernity is defined as a break, how can one break from modernity itself? The very act of trying to make this break is the situation of modernity *par excellence*. If it is characterised as progress and overcoming, how do you overcome it or progress beyond it? You're never more a part of the modern than when you're declaring your intention to break with it.

The paradox may be, then, that *no simple break is possible from modernity*. This all too easily sounds apocalyptic, as though it's positing a final tyranny—or an inertia—against which all resistance is useless. Indeed, it has often been read this way, and responded to with heated polemic. Nevertheless, this version of the postmodern suggests a range of problems which may be of considerable importance for the ways in which cultural studies goes about its business. Various forms of social contestation may see themselves as seeking to introduce radical breaks from existing practices. What if such opposition is already in some ways accommodated (even comfortably) within the mechanisms of social power? The urgent question in such a case would not be one of giving up all idea of contestation, but of rethinking the concept of its possibilities in the new and strange topologies of post-modernity. What we find here, translated to a general conceptual level, are some of the issues raised by policy studies. For example: If there are no positions which are radically external to this (post)modern regime, what strategies will allow one to unsettle it from within? Where does one operate from, how, and with what tools?

In a very different way, the postmodern is also related to, though not identical with, some of the questions of the politics of identity and difference we shall now discuss: what does it mean to be marginalised, as against simply excluded?

Cultural identity

The investigation of cultural identities is one of the main areas in which cultural studies has been developing.

As we have noted throughout, one of the key aims of cultural studies is to explore processes of cultural meaning. To do so effectively and in detail entails not making generalisations about these meanings, and what people make of them. The increasing focus on the variety and range of cultural identities and viewpoints, and their interactions, is one way in which such generalisations can be avoided. This has received the attention of many people working in the area.

As we have tried to suggest, a central step in opening out the study of cultural meanings has been to question the *methods* that theorists and students use. The key point here is that every approach to cultural phenomena always begins from a certain perspective or *position*. Ethnography, for example, can show just how complicated audience groupings and responses to texts can be. In a sense, someone who is studying an aspect of culture is also an audience member, observing the display of activities in front of them.

The position of the student of culture, then, is not a given. Nor is it fixed and objective. Writers on culture, like audiences, are always influenced by a complex range of social factors which affect the way they understand their subject matter. *There is no neutral perspective from which culture can be studied.* The position of the student is going to be crucial to the ideas that are developed.

The concept of position raises a number of questions about the kind of study being performed:

1 What is the student's relationship to the cultural event or activity?
2 In what ways does the student's perspective differ from that of people involved in the activity?
3 Has the student been influenced by one group's experiences of the activity more than by those of other groups? If so, what are the effects of this influence?

These are all difficult questions to answer. And the point of asking them is not simply to end up being able to identify a biased or slack account of things. Rather, the aim is to go on to supplement the initial study's attitude with either a more comprehensive, or an alternative, viewpoint. Invariably, this kind of revisionary perspective operates by referring to, and incorporating, the outlooks of a different cultural group, one that is fully involved in the activities being analysed.

When we stop to think about it, cultural identity is a very complex idea. In Chapter 1, we met a letter writer, Sam West (see Figures 1.1 and 1.2). He seemed like an ordinary sort of guy, perhaps similar in some ways to many of us: he was going to university, was concerned about getting a job, had a lover, and so on. Sam's identity was neither singular nor fixed. He played different roles depending on the situation he found himself in: an earnest would-be banker, a somewhat impatient, lovesick boy-friend. Outside these texts, Sam would play many other roles as well.

There also seemed to be a range of other attributes implied about Sam. What do you think we glean about his age, from these two texts? His social class? His ethnic background and sexuality? (If you try to answer these questions, ask yourself why you come up with the answers you do. What is your position, as a cultural analyst, on the small social phenomenon of 'Sam West'?)

This example suggests that the identity of any figure is a social composite. It comprises attributes that will combine in different ratios according to the demands and pressures of the situation. Social selfhood involves *role playing*, fulfilling varying addresser and addressee positions.

Further, a person may not be in charge of the roles he or she plays. They may be irresistibly imposed by the context. Identity is also structured by prevailing social discourses. (How much choice, for example, does Sam have in writing his job application letter?) Questions of address (Chapter 1), genre (Chapter 5), discourse (Chapter 7), and strategy (Chapter 9) are all involved in the social construction of selfhood.

A number of factors come into play in determining cultural identities. Some of these may have come up as we pondered who 'Sam West' is: race, class, gender, ethnicity, age, sexuality. When studying an individual in social action it may appear possible to check these factors off and note which ones are dominant in different settings. But it is the *interaction* of the factors that it is most important to consider. The factors of cultural identity may work together in contradictory ways.

For example, gender and class can work to produce identities that many people find difficult to handle. Men may be unsure how to treat women from a higher class, or who are professionally successful. Think of the controversy which surrounded Hillary Rodham Clinton's arrival, with her husband, in the White House. Identity is never a neat total of factors.

If cultural identity and position are complicated in individual cases, the interactions and layers get much more involved when we turn to group situations. It is when studying the interactions of groups that issues of cultural identity have been raised in most detail. In turn, these issues affect many of the important ideas in cultural studies that we have considered in previous chapters.

Once variations of identity are acknowledged, any theory of the audience becomes much more complicated. Whom does an audience for any mass media or popular text consist of? It must comprise a wide array of groups and sub-groups. Their different cultural identities will see them produce more or less varied readings and interpretations of texts.

Cultural identity is a crucial question in considering the production of social meaning, and a key motive in the dialogism among social texts. Attention to questions of identity can alert us to a much broader range of social texts and textual producers. As we have discussed in the chapters in the second half of the book—those on genre, narrative, medium and ideology—the power of authoring texts and representing the real is a formidable social power. It is not a coincidental or natural state of affairs that prevailing historical accounts of the settlement and growth of countries like Australia and the United States are told from white male social perspectives.

By raising the notion of authors' cultural (and not simply their personal) identities and positions, we can start to see the ideological impacts of these accounts. In the first place, we may perceive the erasure of the viewpoints of other racial and ethnic groups, or the orientation of these histories around masculine values and actions.

Second, we can also start to become aware that marginalised groups, including white women and men and women of colour, have their own histories and narratives to tell. Their texts challenge and subvert the dominant images of both the past and the present.

These kinds of challenges take place across the whole range of contemporary social activities—for instance, investigating how female subcultures differ from male ones, and historical traditions, such as examining the resistance of native peoples to European colonists in the eighteenth and nineteenth centuries.

In studying all such activities and traditions, questions of cultural identity in terms of race, class and gender open up the *ideological stakes* of representation.

This line of thinking in cultural studies reveals the **politics of identity**. (It is only an apparent paradox that this is also and at the same time a politics of *difference*.) It makes us aware that one of the key ways in which power operates in societies is by setting up groups and versions of the **other**—figures who can be both excluded from the opportunities of support and well-being that society may offer and scapegoated as the cause of social problems.

At the same time, theories of cultural identity are also crucial in preventing the concept of the other being reduced to that of a victim. In studying the complexities of identity, the independent actions and strengths of marginalised groups emerge in their own right.

For practitioners of cultural studies, the most important lesson to be learned from analysing issues of identity and position is to try to avoid reproducing the effects of discriminatory power in one's thought and work. In this way, the notion of cultural identity foregrounds what may well be the overriding revelation of cultural studies: the complex interweavings of culture with the negotiations and contestations of social power.

Sources and further reading

Audience studies

For a comprehensive coverage of contemporary research in television audiences, see *Remote Control: Television, Audiences and Cultural Power*, edited by Ellen Seiter *et al.* David Morley's *Family Television: Cultural Power and Domestic Leisure* (London: Comedia, 1986) presents a detailed ethnographic analysis of audience in a domestic context. His earlier *The 'Nationwide' Audience: Structure and Decoding* (London: British Film Institute, 1980) is also useful. Other studies of television audience include Greg Philo's *Seeing is Believing: The Influence of Television* (London: Routledge, 1990); James Lull's *Inside Family Viewing: Ethnographic Research on Television's Audiences* (London: Comedia, 1990); and Tony Wilson's *Watching Television: Hermeneutics, Reception and Popular Culture* (Cambridge: Polity, 1993). Ien Ang's *Desperately Seeking the Audience* (London: Routledge, 1991) provides an account of the institutional values of the media with respect to audience. For a study of the reading of popular literature, see Janice Radway's seminal work, *Reading the Romance: Women, Patriarchy, and Popular Literature* (Chapel Hill: University of North Carolina Press, 1984). Denis McQuail's *Mass Communication Theory: An Introduction* (London: Sage, 1987) contains a useful account of empirical research methods and theory. For a good introductory book on qualitative methodology, see Klaus Bruhn Jensen and Nicholas W. Jankowski (eds) *A Handbook of Qualitative Methodologies for Mass Communication Research* (London: Routledge, 1991).

Policy studies

For an introduction to the policy debate within cultural studies, see various essays by Morris, Frow, Bennett and Johnson in *Beyond the Disciplines: The New Humanities*, edited by K. K. Ruthven (Canberra: Highland Press, 1992). This debate is continued by Hunter, Meredyth, Frow, O'Regan, Cunningham, Morris and Levy, in *Meanjin* 51(3), 1992. For a thorough account of the policy position and its relation to the humanities, see Ian Hunter *et al.*, *Accounting for the Humanities: The Language of Culture and the Logic of Government* (Brisbane: Institute for Cultural Policy Studies, 1991); see also Stuart Cunningham's *Framing Culture: Criticism and Policy in Australia* (Sydney: Allen and Unwin, 1992). For an integration of critique and policy, see Stuart Cunningham and Graeme Turner (eds) *The Media in Australia: Industries, Texts, Audiences* (Sydney: Allen and Unwin, 1993). And once more, Grossberg, Nelson and Treichler's collection, *Cultural Studies* (New York: Routledge, 1992) contains essays from standpoints of both cultural critique and cultural policy.

The postmodern

John Frow's *What was Postmodernism?* (Sydney: Local Consumption, 1991) offers a judicious survey of the literature and the polemics. David Harvey's *The Condition of Postmodernity: An Enquiry into the Origins of Cultural Change* (Oxford: Blackwell, 1989) argues that postmodernity is primarily due to a change in the mode of accumulation of late capitalism, though Harvey sometimes has a dismaying fondness for summing up complex phenomena in rather simple oppositions.

A brief statement of Habermas's position on modernity can be found in his 'Modernity—An Incomplete Project', in Hal Foster's anthology, *Postmodern Culture* (London: Pluto, 1985). Max Horkheimer and Theodor Adorno's *The Dialectic of Enlightenment* (London: Allen Lane, 1973) stands as the pessimistic obverse of Habermas' argument. Jean-François Lyotard's *The Postmodern Condition* (Minneapolis: University of Minnesota Press, 1984) is his best-known statement on the matter, though the shorter pieces in *The Postmodern Explained to Children* (Sydney, Power Publications, 1992) are also important; *The Differend* (Minneapolis: University of Minnesota Press, 1988) is Lyotard's most thorough statement yet of the implications of this for philosophy. Gianni

Vattimo's *The End of Modernity: Nihilism and Hermeneutics in Post-modern Culture* (Cambridge: Polity, 1988) and *The Transparent Society* (Cambridge: Polity, 1992) elaborate postmodernity in terms drawn from Nietzsche and Heidegger; the essays of these two books are generally concerned with philosophical rather than socio-cultural discourse, though they have important implications for cultural studies.

Cultural identity

A wide range of issues involving the politics of cultural identity is raised in *Cultural Studies*, edited by Grossberg, Nelson and Treichler (New York: Routledge, 1992). Specific studies that take up some of the issues mentioned above include Erving Goffman's *The Presentation of Self in Everyday Life* (Garden City, New York: Doubleday, 1959), on social role-playing; Annabel Patterson, *Shakespeare and the Popular Voice* (Cambridge: Basil Blackwell, 1989), and Patrick Brantlinger, *Crusoe's Footprints: Cultural Studies in Britain and America* (New York: Routledge, 1990), on historical representations of popular culture and different racial and ethnic groups. Angela McRobbie's *Feminism and Youth Culture: From 'Jackie' to 'Just Seventeen'* (Basingstoke: Macmillan, 1991) examines differences between male and female teenage sub-cultures. *The Empire Writes Back: Theory and Practice in Postcolonial Literatures* (New York: Routledge, 1989) by Bill Ashcroft, Gareth Griffith and Helen Tiffin, is a clear introduction to theories and practices of post-colonial cultural representation. Jonathan Dollimore's *Sexual Dissidence: Augustine to Wilde, Freud to Foucault* (Oxford: Clarendon, 1991) looks at the complex ways in which homosexuality has been both central to and marginalised by Western cultures since the Renaissance. Lastly, *Yearning: Race, Gender, and Cultural Politics* (Boston: South End Press, 1990) by bell hooks studies the politics of identity in relation to gender and race.

Bibliography

Allen, Robert C. (ed.) (1987) *Channels of Discourse: Television and Contemporary Criticism*. London: Routledge

Althusser, Louis (1977) 'Ideology and Ideological State Apparatuses (Notes towards an Investigation', Translator, Ben Brewster. In *Lenin and Philosophy and other Essays*. London: NLB

Ang, Ien (1991) *Desperately Seeking the Audience*. London: Routledge

Ashcroft, Bill, Gareth Griffiths, and Helen Tiffin (1989) *The Empire Writes Back: Theory and Practice in Post-colonial Literatures*. New York: Routledge

Bakhtin, M. M. (1981) 'Discourse in the Novel'. In *The Dialogic Imagination: Four Essays*. Editor, Michael Holquist, translators, Caryl Emerson and Michael Holquist. Austin: University of Texas Press

_____ (1986) 'Speech Genres'. In '*Speech Genres and Other Late Essays*. Translator, Vern W. McGee, editors, Caryl Emerson and Michael Holquist. Austin: University of Texas Press

Roland Barthes (1967) *Elements of Semiology*. Translators, Annette Lavers and Colin Smith. London: Cape

_____ (1977a) 'Change the object itself' from *Image–Music–Text*. Editor and translator, Stephen Heath, Fontana: London

_____ (1977b) 'Introduction to the structural analysis of narratives'. *Image–Music–Text*. Editor and translator, Stephen Heath. Fontana: London

_____ (1983) *The Fashion System*. Translators, Matthew Ward and Richard Howard. New York: Hill and Wang

_____ (1987) *Mythologies*. Translator, Annette Lavers. New York: Hill and Wang

Bennett, Tony and Janet Woollacott (1987) *Bond and Beyond: The Political Career of a Popular Hero*. London: Macmillan

Berger, Peter L. and Thomas Luckmann (1991) *The Social Construction of Reality: A Treatise on the Sociology of Knowledge*. London: Penguin

Blonsky, Marshall (ed.) (1985) *On Signs: A Semiotics Reader*. Oxford: Basil Blackwell

Bourdieu, Pierre (1984) *Distinction: A Social Critique of the Judgement of Taste*. Translator, Richard Nice. Cambridge, Massachusetts: Harvard University Press

_____ (1990) *In Other Words: Essays Towards a Reflexive Sociology*. Translator, Matthew Adamson. Cambridge: Polity

Brantlinger, Patrick (1990) *Crusoe's Footprints: Cultural Studies in Britain and America*. New York: Routledge

Brewer's Dictionary of Phrase and Fable (1970) London: Cassell

Brown, M. E. (ed.) (1990) *Television and Women's Culture: The Politics of the Popular*. London: Sage

Certeau, Michel de (1984) *The Practice of Everyday Life*. Translator, Steven Rendall. Berkeley: University of California Press

Chatman, Seymour (1978) *Story and Discourse: Narrative Structure in Fiction and Film*. Ithaca: Cornell University Press

Cohan, Steven and Linda M. Shires (1988) *Telling Stories: A Theoretical Analysis of Narrative*. New York: Routledge

Cohen, Stan and Jock Young (eds.) (1973) *The Manufacture of News: Social Problems, Deviance and the Mass Media*. London: Constable

Coward, Rosalind (1984) *Female Desire*. London: Granada

_____ and John Ellis (1977) *Language and Materialism: Developments in Semiology and the Theory of the Subject*. London: Routledge

Culler, Jonathan (1986) *Saussure*. New York: Cornell University Press

_____ (1981) 'Story and discourse in the analysis of narrative'. In *The Pursuit of Signs: Semiotics, Literature, Deconstruction*. London: Routledge

Cunningham, Stuart (1992) *Framing Culture: Criticism and Policy in Australia*. Sydney: Allen and Unwin

_____ and Graeme Turner (eds) *The Media in Australia: Industries, Texts, Audiences*. Sydney: Allen and Unwin

Dollimore, Jonathan (1991) *Sexual Dissidence: Augustine to Wilde, Freud to Foucault*. Oxford: Clarendon

Dubrow, Heather (1982) *Genre*. London: Methuen

Eagleton, Terry (1985) 'Capitalism, Modernism and Postmodernism', *New Left Review* 152: 60–73

_____ (1991) *Ideology: An Introduction*. London: Verso

Ellis, John (1982) *Visible Fictions*. London: Routledge

Fairclough, Norman (1989) *Language and Power*. London: Longman

Fiske, John (1982) *Introduction to Communication Studies*. London: Methuen

_____ (1987) *Television Culture*. New York: Methuen

_____ (1989) *Understanding Popular Culture*. Boston: Unwin Hyman

Fiske, John, Graeme Turner, and Bob Hodge (1987) *Myths of Oz:*

Readings in Australian Popular Culture. Sydney: Allen and Unwin

Foster, Hal (ed.) (1985) *Postmodern Culture*. London: Pluto

Foucault, Michel (1972) *The Archaeology of Knowledge*. Translator, A. M. Sheridan Smith. London: Tavistock

Fowler, Roger (1991) *Language in the News: Discourse and Ideology in the Press*. London: Routledge

Freadman, Anne (1988) 'Untitled: (on Genre)' *Cultural Studies* 2 (1)

_____ and Amanda Macdonald (1992) *What is this Thing Called 'Genre'? Four Essays in the Semiotics of Genre*. Mt Nebo, Queensland: Boombana

Frow, John (1991) *What was Postmodernism?* Occasional Paper No 11. Sydney: Local Consumption

Geertz, Clifford (1983) 'Blurred Genres: The Refiguration of Social Thought'. In *Local Knowledge: Further Essays in Interpretive Anthropology*. New York: Basic Books

Genette, Gerard (1980) *Narrative Discourse: An Essay in Method*. Translator, Jane E. Lewin. Ithaca: Cornell University Press

Gilman, Sander L. (1985) *Difference and Pathology: Stereotypes of Sexuality, Race and Madness*. Ithaca, New York: Cornell University Press

Goffman, Erving (1959) *The Presentation of Self in Everyday Life*. Garden City, New York: Doubleday

Goodwin, Andrew and Garry Whannel (eds) (1990) *Understanding Television*. London: Routledge

Gould, Stephen Jay (1981) *The Mismeasure of Man*. New York: Norton

Gramsci, Antonio (1971) *Selections from the Prison Notebooks of Antonio Gramsci*. Translators and editors, Quintin Hoare and Geoffrey Nowell-Smith. New York: International Publishers

_____ (1988) *A Gramsci Reader: Selected Writings 1916–35*. Editor, David Forgacs. London: Lawrence and Wishart

Grossberg, Lawrence, Gary Nelson and Paula Treichler (eds) (1992) *Cultural Studies*. New York: Routledge

Habermas, Jurgen (1985) 'Modernity—An Incomplete Project', Translator, Seyla Ben-Habib. In *Postmodern Culture*. Editor, Hal Foster. London: Pluto

_____ (1987) *The Philosophical Discourse of Modernity*. Translator, Frederick Lawrence. Cambridge: Polity

Hall, Stuart (1980) 'Encoding/Decoding'. In *Culture, Media, Language: Working Papers in Cultural Studies, 1972–79*. Editor, Stuart Hall *et al*. London: Unwin Hyman

_____ Crichter, T. Jefferson J. Clark and B. Roberts (1978) *Policing the Crisis: Mugging, the State, and Law and Order*. London: Macmillan

Harker, Richard, Cheleen Mahar and Chris Wilkes (eds) (1990)

An Introduction to the Work of Pierre Bourdieu: The Practice of Theory. London: Macmillan

Harris, Roy (1987) *Reading Saussure: A Critical Commentary on the Cours de linguistique générale*. London: Duckworth

Hartley, John (1982) *Understanding News*. London: Methuen

_____ (1992) *Tele-ology: Studies in Television*. New York: Routledge

Harvey, David (1989) *The Condition of Post-modernity: An Enquiry into the Origins of Cultural Change*. Oxford: Blackwell

Hassan, Ihab (1971) 'POSTmodernISM'. *New Literary History* 3 (1)

_____ (1985) 'The culture of postmodernism'. *Theory, Culture and Society* 2 (3)

Hawkes, Terence (1977) *Structuralism and Semiotics*. London: Methuen

Hebdige, Dick (1979) *Subculture: The Meaning of Style*. London: Methuen

_____ (1988) *Hiding in the Light: On Images and Things*. New York: Routledge

Hjelmslev, Louis (1969) *Prolegomena to a Theory of Language*. Translator, Francis J. Whitfield. Madison, Wisconsin: Wisconsin University Press

Hodge, Robert and Gunther Kress (1988) *Social Semiotics*. Cambridge: Polity

_____ and Vijay Mishra (1991) *Dark Side of the Dream: Australian Literature and the Postcolonial Mind*. Sydney: Allen and Unwin

hooks, bell (1990) *Yearning: Race, Gender, and Cultural Politics*. Boston: South End Press

Horkheimer, Max, and Theodor Adorno (1973) *The Dialectic of Enlightenment*. Translator, John Cumming. London: Allen Lane

Hunter, Ian, Denise Meredyth, Bruce Smith and Geoff Stokes (1991) *Accounting for the Humanities: The Language of Culture and the Logic of Government*. Brisbane: Institute for Cultural Policy Studies

Hutcheon, Linda (1989) *The Politics of Postmodernism*. London: Routledge

Hymes, Dell (1974) *Foundations in Sociolinguistics: An Ethnographic Approach*. Philadelphia: University of Pennsylvania Press

Innis, Robert E. (ed.) (1985) *Semiotics: An Introductory Anthology*. Bloomington: Indiana University Press

Jakobson, Roman (1988) 'Linguistics and Poetics'. In *Modern Criticism and Theory: A Reader*. Editor, David Lodge. London: Longman

Jameson, Fredric (1981) *The Political Unconscious: Narrative as a Socially Symbolic Act*. Ithaca, New York: Cornell University Press

____ (1984) 'Postmodernism, or the cultural logic of late capitalism', *New Left Review* 146: 53–92

____ (1991) *Postmodernism, or the Cultural Logic of Late Capitalism.* Durham: Duke University Press.

Jensen, Klaus Bruhn, and Nicholas W. Jankowski (eds) (1991) *A Handbook of Qualitative Methodologies for Mass Communication Research.* London: Routledge

Lefebvre, Henri (1971) *Everyday Life in the Modern World.* Translator, Sacha Rabinovitch. London: Allen Lane

Lévi-Strauss, Claude (1966) *The Savage Mind.* London: Weidenfeld and Nicholson

____ (1969) *Totemism.* Translator, Rodney Needham. Harmondsworth: Penguin

Lull, James (1990) *Inside Family Viewing: Ethnographic Research on Television's Audiences.* London: Comedia

Lyotard, Jean-François (1984) *The Postmodern Condition: A Report on Knowledge.* Translators, Geoff Bennington and Brian Massumi. Minneapolis: University of Minnesota Press

____ (1988) *The Differend: Phrases in Dispute.* Translator, Georges Van Den Abbeele. Minneapolis: University of Minnesota Press

____ (1992) *The Postmodern Explained to Children: Correspondence 1982–85.* Translations edited by Julian Pefanis and Morgan Thomas. Sydney: Power Publications

MacCannell, Dean, and Juliet Flower MacCannell (1982) *The Time of the Sign: A Semiotic Interpretation of Modern Culture.* Bloomington: Indiana University Press

McQuail, Denis (1987) *Mass Communication Theory: An Introduction.* London: Sage

McRobbie, Angela (1991) *Feminism and Youth Culture: From 'Jackie' to 'Just Seventeen'.* Basingstoke: Macmillan

Meanjin 51(3) (1992) *Cultural Policy and Beyond*

Modleski, Tania (1984) *Loving with a Vengeance: Mass Produced Fantasies for Women.* New York: Methuen

Morley, David (1980) *The 'Nationwide' Audience: Structure and Decoding.* London: British Film Institute

____ (1986) *Family Television: Cultural Power and Domestic Leisure.* London: Comedia

Mulvey, Laura (1975) 'Visual Pleasure and Narrative Cinema', *Screen* 16: 6–18

Nealey Steve (1980) *Genre* London: British Film Institute

____ and Frank Krutnick (1990) *Popular Film and Television Comedy.* London: Routledge

O'Sullivan, Tim *et al.* (1983) *Key Concepts in Communication Studies.* London: Methuen

Patterson, Annabel (1989) *Shakespeare and the Popular Voice.* Cambridge: Basil Blackwell

Philo, Greg (1990) *Seeing is Believing: The Influence of Television.* London: Routledge

Pierce, John R. (1980) *An Introduction to Information Theory: Symbols, Signals and White Noise.* New York: Dover

Prince, Gerald (1989) *A Dictionary of Narratology.* Lincoln: University of Nebraska Press

Punter, David (ed.) (1986) *Introduction to Contemporary Cultural Studies.* London: Longman

Radway, Janice (1984) *Reading the Romance: Feminism and the Representation of Women in Popular Culture.* Chapel Hill: University of North Carolina Press

Richards, I. A. (1964) *Practical Criticism: A Study of Literary Judgement.* London: Routledge

Rimmon-Kenan, Shlomith (1983) *Narrative Fiction: Contemporary Poetics.* London: Methuen

Robey, David (ed.) (1973) *Structuralism: An Introduction.* Oxford: Clarendon

Ross, Andrew (1989) *No Respect: Intellectuals and Popular Culture.* New York: Routledge

Ruthven, K. K. (ed.) (1992) *Beyond the Disciplines: The New Humanities.* Occasional Paper 13, Australian Academy of the Humanities. Canberra: Highland Press

Saussure, Ferdinand de (1983) *Course in General Linguistics.* Translator, Roy Harris. London: Duckworth

Sedgwick, Eve Kosofsky (1985) *Between Men: English Literature and Male Homosocial Desire.* New York: Columbia University Press

Seiter, Ellen *et al.* (eds) (1989) *Remote Control: Television, Audiences and Cultural Power.* London: Routledge

Sheridan, Alan (1980) *Michel Foucault: The Will to Truth.* London: Tavistock

Sturrock, John (ed.) (1979) *Structuralism and Since: From Lévi-Strauss to Derrida.* Oxford: Oxford University Press

Sudjic, Deyan (1990) *Cult Heroes: How to be Famous for More Than Fifteen Minutes.* New York

Toolan, Michael J. (1988) *Narrative: A Critical Linguistic Introduction.* London: Routledge

Tulloch, John, and Graeme Turner (eds) (1989) *Australian Television: Programs, Pleasures and Politics.* Sydney: Allen and Unwin

Turner, Graeme (1988) *Film as Social Practice.* London: Routledge. 1988

_____ (1990) *British Cultural Studies: An Introduction.* Boston: Unwin Hyman

Vattimo, Gianni (1988) *The End of Modernity: Nihilism and Hermeneutics in Postmodern Culture.* Translator, Jon R. Snyder. Cambridge: Polity

_____ *The Transparent Society.* Translator, David Webb. Cambridge: Polity

Williams, Raymond (1976) *Keywords: A Vocabulary of Culture and Society.* London: Fontana

Williamson, Judith (1978) *Decoding Advertisements: Ideology and Meaning in Advertising.* London: Marion Boyars

_____ (1986) *Consuming Passions: The Dynamics of Popular Culture.* London: Marion Boyars

Wilson, Tony (1993) *Watching Television: Hermeneutics, Reception and Popular Culture.* Cambridge: Polity

Index

Entries in **bold** indicate a boxed definition in the text. Where a range of pages on a topic includes a boxed definition, the page on which the definition occurs is also specified, in bold. For example, '140–**143**–146' indicates that the topic is dealt with on pages 140–6, with a boxed definition on page 143.